Rachel Cusk

Contemporary Critical Perspectives

Series Editors: Jeannette Baxter, Peter Childs, Sebastian Groes and Kaye Mitchell

Guides in the *Contemporary Critical Perspectives* series provide companions to reading and studying major contemporary authors. They include new critical essays combining textual readings, cultural analysis and discussion of key critical and theoretical issues in a clear, accessible style. Each guide also includes a preface by a major contemporary writer, a new interview with the author, discussion of film and TV adaptation and guidance on further reading.

Titles in the series include:

J. G. Ballard edited by Jeannette Baxter
Ian McEwan edited by Sebastian Groes
Kazuo Ishiguro edited by Sean Matthews and Sebastian Groes
Julian Barnes edited by Sebastian Groes and Peter Childs
Sarah Waters edited by Kaye Mitchell
Salman Rushdie edited by Robert Eaglestone and Martin McQuillan
Andrea Levy edited by Jeannette Baxter and David James
Ali Smith edited by Monica Germanà and Emily Horton
Hanif Kureishi edited by Susan Alice Fischer
Don DeLillo edited by Katherine Da Cunha Lewin and Kiron Ward
Hilary Mantel edited by Eileen Pollard and Ginette Carpenter
John Burnside edited by Ben Davies
David Mitchell edited by Wendy Knepper and Courtney Hopf
Maggie O'Farrell edited by Elaine Canning

Rachel Cusk

Contemporary Critical Perspectives

Edited by
Roberta Garrett and Liam Harrison

BLOOMSBURY ACADEMIC
LONDON • NEW YORK • OXFORD • NEW DELHI • SYDNEY

BLOOMSBURY ACADEMIC
Bloomsbury Publishing Plc, 50 Bedford Square, London, WC1B 3DP, UK
Bloomsbury Publishing Inc, 1359 Broadway, New York, NY 10018, USA
Bloomsbury Publishing Ireland, 29 Earlsfort Terrace, Dublin 2, D02 AY28, Ireland

BLOOMSBURY, BLOOMSBURY ACADEMIC and the Diana logo are trademarks of
Bloomsbury Publishing Plc

First published in Great Britain 2024
Paperback edition published 2026

Copyright © Roberta Garrett, Liam Harrison, and Contributors, 2024

Roberta Garrett, Liam Harrison, and Contributors have asserted their rights under the
Copyright, Designs and Patents Act, 1988, to be identified as Authors of this work.

Cover design: Eleanor Rose
Cover image © Unsplash

All rights reserved. No part of this publication may be: i) reproduced or transmitted in any form, electronic or mechanical, including photocopying, recording or by means of any information storage or retrieval system without prior permission in writing from the publishers; or ii) used or reproduced in any way for the training, development or operation of artificial intelligence (AI) technologies, including generative AI technologies. The rights holders expressly reserve this publication from the text and data mining exception as per Article 4(3) of the Digital Single Market Directive (EU) 2019/790.

Bloomsbury Publishing Plc does not have any control over, or responsibility for, any third-party websites referred to or in this book. All internet addresses given in this book were correct at the time of going to press. The author and publisher regret any inconvenience caused if addresses have changed or sites have ceased to exist, but can accept no responsibility for any such changes.

A catalogue record for this book is available from the British Library.

A catalog record for this book is available from the Library of Congress.

ISBN: HB: 978-1-3503-7098-2
PB: 978-1-3503-7102-6
ePDF: 978-1-3503-7099-9
eBook: 978-1-3503-7100-2

Series: Contemporary Critical Perspectives

Typeset by RefineCatch Limited, Bungay, Suffolk

For product safety related questions contact productsafety@bloomsbury.com

To find out more about our authors and books visit www.bloomsbury.com
and sign up for our newsletters.

Contents

Acknowledgements	vi
Series Editors' Preface	vii
List of Contributors	viii
Foreword *Clare Hanson*	xi
Introduction *Roberta Garrett* and *Liam Harrison*	1
1 Life Style: Rachel Cusk and the Critique of Minimalism *Pieter Vermeulen*	19
2 Mother Courage and Mother Shaming: Rachel Cusk's Contribution to Maternal Feminism *Roberta Garrett*	37
3 Serial Metaphors: Revising and Rewriting in Rachel Cusk's Life Narratives *Ricarda Menn*	57
4 Perceptions of Failure in Rachel Cusk's *Saving Agnes* and *Second Place* *Sonja Pyykkö*	75
5 'Some things are artificial and some are authentic': Rachel Cusk's Depth Perception *Daniel Lea*	93
6 Autofictional Experiments and Serial Aesthetics in Rachel Cusk's *Outline* Trilogy *Melissa Schuh*	109
7 Being Sent to Coventry: Silence, Cruelty and Rachel Cusk's Discrepant Style *Liam Harrison*	129
Afterword: Second Text: Biography, Intertextuality, and Art in *Second Place* *Peter Childs*	149
An Interview with Rachel Cusk *Merve Emre*	159
Index	171

Acknowledgements

We would like to offer our thanks to the series editors, Jeanette Baxter, Peter Childs, Sebastian Groes and Kaye Mitchell for sharing our enthusiasm for Rachel Cusk's work and supporting the project from the outset, along with our colleagues and students at The University of East London and The University of the West of England. Thanks and gratitude are also due to the contributors of this volume for providing such original, rigorous and insightful work.

Roberta would also like to thank Bob Bunting for offering his proof-reading and indexing skills, and on a more personal note, to thank him and her daughters, Matty and Esme Hadfield, for their comments, contributions and love and support. Liam would also like to thank Chloé Duane for her kindness, support, patience and love.

Series Editors' Preface

The readership for contemporary fiction has never been greater. The explosion of reading groups and literary blogs, of university courses and school curricula, and even the apparent rude health of the literary marketplace indicate an evergrowing appetite for new work, for writing which responds to the complex, changing and challenging times in which we live. At the same time, readers seem ever more eager to engage in conversations about their reading, to devour the review pages, to pack the sessions at literary festivals and author events. Reading is an increasingly social activity, as we seek to share and refine our experience of the book, to clarify and extend our understanding. It is this tremendous enthusiasm for contemporary fiction to which the Contemporary Critical Perspectives series responds. Our ambition is to offer readers of current fiction a comprehensive critical account of each author's work, presenting original, specially commissioned analyses of all aspects of their career, from a variety of different angles and approaches, as well as directions towards further reading and research. Our brief to the contributors is to be scholarly, to draw on the latest thinking about narrative, or philosophy, or psychology, indeed whatever seemed to them most significant in drawing out the meanings and force of the texts in question, but also to focus closely on the words on the page, the stories and scenarios and forms which all of us meet first when we open a book. We insisted that these essays be accessible to that mythical beast, the Common Reader, who might just as readily be spotted at the Lowdham Book Festival as in a college seminar. In this way, we hope to have presented critical assessments of our writers in such a way as to contribute something to both of those environments, and also to have done something to bring together the most important qualities of each of them.

    Jeannette Baxter, Peter Childs, Sebastian Groes and Kaye Mitchell.

Contributors

Peter Childs is Professor of Modern and Contemporary English Literature at Birmingham Newman University, UK. The author or editor of over twenty books, he specializes in the study of contemporary British literature and culture as well as post-colonial and twentieth-century writing. He has published widely on literature post-1900. His books include *Modernism and the Post-Colonial* (2007), *Contemporary Novelists: British Fiction Since 1970* (2nd edition 2012) and *Modernism: The New Critical Idiom* (3rd edition 2016).

Merve Emre is the Shapiro-Silverberg Professor of Creative Writing and Criticism at Wesleyan University, USA, and the Director of the Shapiro Center for Creative Writing and Criticism. She is the author of *Paraliterary: The Making of Bad Readers in Postwar America* (2017), *The Ferrante Letters* (2019) and *The Personality Brokers* (2018). She is the editor of *Once and Future Feminist* (2018), *The Annotated Mrs. Dalloway* (2021) and *The Norton Modern Library Mrs. Dalloway* (2021). She is finishing a book titled *Post-Discipline: Two Futures for Literary Study* and writing a book called *Love and Other Useless Pursuits*. She is also a contributing writer at *The New Yorker*. Her essays and criticism have appeared in publications ranging from *The New York Review of Books*, *Harper's*, *The New York Times Magazine*, *The Atlantic* and the *London Review of Books* to *American Literature*, *American Literary History*, *PMLA* and *Modernism/modernity*.

Roberta Garrett is a senior lecturer on the Creative Writing and Media programmes in the Department of Arts and Cultural Industries at the University of East London, UK. She has published widely on representations of gender, class and race in popular literature and film. She is the author of *Postmodern Chick-flicks: The Return of the Woman's Film* (2008), co-editor of *We Need to Talk About Family: Essays on Neoliberalism, the Family and Popular Culture* (2016) and author of *Writing the Modern Family: Contemporary Literature, Motherhood and Neoliberal Culture* (2021). She has published numerous book chapters and articles in journals such as *Clues*, *Studies in the Maternal*, *The Journal of Screenwriting* and *Feminist Media Studies*. These include pieces on the work of

Hollywood screenwriter, Nora Ephron and on *Game of Thrones*, maternal memoirs, the figure of the 'mumpreneur' in popular culture and, more recently, domestic noir novels and screen adaptations. She has forthcoming chapters and articles on Hulu's adaptation of *The Handmaid's Tale*, the role of older women in domestic noir and the politicization of vulnerability and failure in young women's auto-fictional writing.

Clare Hanson is Emeritus Professor of English at the University of Southampton, UK. She is the author and editor of eleven books, most recently *Genetics and the Literary Imagination* (2020). She is a former editor of the journal *Contemporary Women's Writing* and has published widely on gender in twentieth- and twenty-first-century fiction. She is currently working on multispecies relations in contemporary literature.

Liam Harrison is a lecturer in Creative Writing at the University of the West of England, UK, where he teaches and researches contemporary publishing culture. He completed a PhD researching late style and modernist legacies in twenty-first-century British and Irish fiction at the University of Birmingham. He is a founding editor of the non-fiction literary journal *Tolka*. He is also the co-founder of the Contemporary Irish Literature Research Network, and an elected Ordinary Member of the British Association for Contemporary Literary Studies. He has written research articles on contemporary Irish literature, modernist legacies in twenty-first century fiction, and Irish women's writing and work.

Daniel Lea is Professor of Contemporary Literature at Oxford Brookes University, UK, where he teaches and researches writing of the late-twentieth and twenty-first centuries. He is a specialist on contemporary British prose and has published widely in the field. His books include *Graham Swift* (2005) and *Twenty-first Century Fiction: Contemporary British Voices* (2016) and he is currently writing a book entitled *Liquid Modernity and the Literature of Authenticity*. He is the general editor of Manchester University Press' 'Contemporary British Novelists' series of monographs.

Ricarda Menn completed her PhD in English Literature with a thesis on Serial Life Writing in Contemporary Anglophone Literature. She works as a research manager at the Institute for Advanced Study in the Humanities in Essen.

Sonja Pyykkö is a final-year doctoral candidate at the Graduate School of North American Studies, Freie Universität Berlin, Germany, where she is writing a dissertation on the poetics of confession in the postmodern novel. Her recently published articles include 'Longing to Belong: Disease, Nostalgia, and Exile in Ling Ma's Severance' (*AmLit—American Literatures*, 2020) and 'Confession', a literary-philosophical essay in the German-language companion *Stichwörter für die kritische Praxis* (2023, eds Michel Chaouli et al.). Her article 'Disclosing Structures: Scenes of Confession in Pale Fire' is forthcoming in *Nabokov Studies*.

Melissa Schuh completed her PhD titled 'The (Un-)Making of the Novelist's Identity' in the English department at Queen Mary University of London in 2019 and is a lecturer in English Literature at Kiel University, Germany. She is deputy editor for *C21 Literature: Journal of 21st Century Writings*. Her research interests include English and German contemporary fiction, autobiography and life writing, Brexit in literature as well as seriality and Modernism. Recent publications include a book chapter, co-authored with Ricarda Menn, on 'The Autofictional in Serial, Literary Works' in *The Autofictional* (2022), edited by Alexandra Effe and Hannie Lawlor (2022) and a book chapter on 'Fictionalisation of Testimony', co-authored with Carmen-Francesca Banciu and Alexandra Effe, in *The Palgrave Handbook of Testimony and Culture* (2023), edited by Sara Jones and Roger Woods.

Pieter Vermeulen is an associate professor of American and Comparative Literature at the University of Leuven, Netherlands. He is the author of *Romanticism After the Holocaust* (2010), *Contemporary Literature and the End of the Novel: Creature, Affect, Form* (2015), and *Literature and the Anthropocene* (2020), and a co-editor of, most recently, *Institutions of World Literature: Writing, Translation, Markets* (2015), *Memory Unbound: Tracing the Dynamics of Memory Studies* (2017) and a double special issue of *LIT: Literature Interpretation Theory* on contemporary literature and/as archive (2020). His current writing project studies contemporary world literary circulation from the perspective of valuation studies.

Foreword

Clare Hanson

The publication of this volume is timely, as Rachel Cusk's status as one of the most innovative and significant contemporary writers is now widely recognized and students are increasingly keen to study her work. The chapters that follow trace with insight and acuity the formal and stylistic shifts in Cusk's writing, which are deftly related to the far-reaching socio-cultural and philosophical transitions of the last thirty years. The contributors are alert to the tight interplay between substance and form in Cusk's work and indeed, it can be argued that one of its most striking features is a sense of the mutual imbrication of life and writing. This aspect of her work can be illuminated with reference to Patricia Waugh's contention that fiction operates as a 'work out' for the mind because it mirrors the ways in which our identities and life-stories are forged intersubjectively, in dialogue with others and the wider cultural narratives which both connect and divide us. Through reading and writing we engage with the recursive self-fashioning of others and are prompted to review 'our own expectations and wider assumptions, our own interpretive stance' (Waugh 2015: 37). Cusk's experiments in fiction, memoir and autofiction (a term she dislikes) are centrally concerned with narrative as a constitutive element of life and with the fictional dimensions of the self. Cusk takes up the question of what she calls 'the relational basis of human reality' in an essay where she reflects on the practice of ostracizing someone by refusing to speak to them (known in Britain as 'sending them to Coventry') and notes that 'if other people pretend you're not there, you can lose your belief in your own existence' (Cusk 2019: 24). Such a loss of belief is a key theme in her first novel, *Saving Agnes*, where the protagonist dates her feelings of unreality back to a period in adolescence when a gap opens between herself and her parents, who no longer reflect her identity back to her. At this point her mind disengages from the external world, while at the same time she loses her sense of her own 'there-ness'. When she speaks, her voice sounds distant, as if she were listening to another person: in effect, she has become dissociated from herself – establishing a literary and philosophical concern that reverberates throughout Cusk's writing life. Indeed, the fragile nature of identity is also at the core of the memoir *A Life's Work*, which caused controversy precisely because of its exploration of the challenge motherhood poses to the sense of self. Looking back on the first months of her daughter's life, Cusk sees her relationship with her as one-sided, as 'love for an object, love in the mind, at once everything and nothing' (Cusk 2001: 92). Building on the ideas of the paediatrician D. W. Winnicott, she argues that because the infant has not yet formed a personality and has no independent existence, maternal feeling can only be turned back onto the self: 'what is there to love, what to hate but yourself?' (77). By definition, this is not an intersubjective relationship; rather, it is one in which the mother's identity is undone through her confrontation with a pre-subjective realm of which she has no conscious memory. In caring for her daughter, Cusk re-visits the formation of her own identity, re-enacts her own vulnerability in the world of 'milk and shadows and nothingness' and becomes aware of the adjacency of love and 'the power to destroy' (84–5). The experience is destabilizing but also generative in that it prompts her to contest the external and internal power relations that structure the nuclear family, vowing to risk maternal failure and inadequacy and 'tolerate my daughter until I am negated' (207).

In *Aftermath*, Cusk turns to the wider cultural narratives which underpin and perpetuate the norms of Western family life. She focuses particularly on the role of Christianity and the image of the holy family, arguing that when 'feeble Joseph agreed to marry pregnant Mary' a sentimental cult was established of 'child-worship, of sainted, unambivalent motherhood, of gutless masculinity and fatherly impotence' (Cusk 2012: 100). The roles of devoted mother and dutiful father, dedicated to the child's welfare, constitute 'our deepest sense of family reality' but they are not real: their function is to control 'our visceral knowledge and desires'. The ideal of the holy family thus has a political salience as it mediates between our unruly desires and their repression in the interests of social stability. To counter this conformist ethos, Cusk turns to ancient Greek drama, where the question of what might constitute authority is perpetually at stake. In the context of her discussion of the Holy Family, the Greek world would be considered pre-familial but it might also yield clues to the form that a post-familial household could take. Invoking the figure of Antigone, Cusk develops a perspective which resonates with Judith Butler's reading of her challenge to the authority of the family and state. For Butler, its significance derives from the fact that she is at once inside and outside the kinship relations that are 'a precondition of the human', and Cusk suggests that there may be a parallel between Antigone's situation and her own (Butler 2000: 82). If the concepts of family and marriage are undermined in Antigone's 'perverse' family, they are also put under pressure in Cusk's, which entails a radical, even violent, reversal of traditional gender roles. After the breakdown of her marriage, Cusk and her children inhabit a dimension of formlessness and chaos which is not absence but the prelude to creativity and, potentially, the emergence of novel social forms.

The *Outline* trilogy continues to put critical pressure on the relationship between authority and narrative voice, in self-reflexive texts in which the narrator, Faye, listens to and interprets the autobiographical narratives of others, thereby mirroring the activity of the reader of fiction. Each of the characters is bent on establishing the validity of their own story, which Faye and the reader critically assess. In *Outline* itself the focus is on narratives of marriage and divorce, which lead Faye to the conclusion that marriage is itself 'a system of belief, a story' which requires the suspension of disbelief. The point is amplified by one of her interlocutors who compares the happiness of his first marriage to being absorbed in life 'as you can be absorbed in a book, believing in its events and living entirely through and with its characters' (Cusk 2014: 16). In his view, it was a failure of belief that caused the breakdown of the relationship and the mutual recognition which underwrote the identity of each of the 'characters'. However, as the narratives of others continue to swirl around her, Faye becomes increasingly sceptical about their meaning and value. In conversation with her cousin, she argues for the importance of scrutinizing 'the things that happened, to study their truth', a truth which is often obscured by the 'narrative of progress' that underpins individual and social life (Cusk 2016: 243). Deviating from this narrative is risky for a female artist, whose exploration of alternatives is easily mistaken for nihilism, an issue Cusk takes up through a discussion of the painter Joan Eardley, who is represented as an instance of 'the tragedy of female authority' (Cusk 2018: 195–6). The speaker, a journalist who has trained in art history, describes a painting by Eardley which reverses the traditional dynamic of male painter and female nude and was seen as shocking because in it a female artist depicts the naked male body in a state of dereliction, lacking 'promise or possibility'. Eardley's aesthetic power is undercut by her gender, which leads to her illusionness vision being perceived as 'disturbing and strange' rather than legitimate. Her work is still not well-known, leading the speaker to conclude that it is impossible for a woman to live without illusion, as 'the world will simply snuff her out'.

Cusk's recent novel, *Second Place*, explores the connections between gender and creativity in dialogue with D. H. Lawrence, a writer whom she admires for his ability to 'demystify us to ourselves' (Cusk 2019: 208). The novel is loosely based on Mabel Dodge Luhan's *Lorenzo in Taos*, an account of her relationship with Lawrence during his stay with her in New Mexico. The main protagonists are the narrator, M, who writes 'little books', and a painter, L, who comes to stay in her annexe or 'second place', Cusk drawing here on Luhan's credentials as a memoirist and the fact that Lawrence was a painter as well as a writer. M is initially drawn to L's work because of its 'aura of absolute freedom' and although it is also 'elementally and unrepentantly male' it speaks to her directly, jolting her out of her immersion in 'the story of my own life' (Cusk 2021:12–13). For her, his paintings represent something 'that shares and is inextricable from the moment of being' and convey a powerful sense of human meaning as the only reality to which we have access. The glancing reference here to Woolf's 'moments of being' invokes Cusk's modernist heritage but the novel also speaks to the contemporary moment by invoking a scientific perspective on human meaning, specifically that of evolutionary biology. L broaches this issue in an anecdote about an uncle and aunt with whom he was sent to stay as a child. He remembers them as negligent and crude, caught up in their own adversarial games, but this prompts him to speculate that the 'concept of character' they exemplify might no longer exist because it is 'an animal quality that humans had become distanced from in the modern age' (70–1). Similarly, his paintings suggest to M that humans have moved beyond narrative and that 'there is no story to life, no personal meaning beyond the meaning of any given moment' (134). Elaborating on this point, she explains that she has come to see narrative as an expression of the will and the need to impose on others a version of events which casts the narrator in a favourable light. The implication is that both character and plot – the building blocks of the novel – are formations which belong to an earlier stage of evolution.

In M's view, L's work moves further away from character and plot (in painterly terms, realist representation) after an illness which frees him from his personal identity and history 'so violently and thoroughly that he had been able at least to really see. And what he had seen was not death, but unreality': this is the subject of his famous 'night paintings' (201). An alternative term for unreality might be irreality, as defined by the American philosopher Nelson Goodman and subsequently appropriated to describe the aesthetics of some postmodern literature. Irreality can be defined as a feeling of estrangement from what is generally accepted as the real, combined with an intuition of dimensions that exceed it. Dean Swinford has argued that it is linked to changes in human understanding brought about by science, while others see it as arising from a heightened awareness of the disjunction between the finite human brain and a potentially infinite universe (Swinford 2002: 82). For M, the irreal is at the centre of L's art, which teaches her that '[t]he truth lies not in any claim to reality, but in the place where what is real moves beyond our interpretation of it. True art means seeking to capture the unreal' (Cusk 2021: 207). Here M is represented, as she is throughout the text, as L's disciple, taking inspiration from his 'elementally male' art, but of course it is Cusk herself who brings the reader to this point of illumination. In this respect, it can be argued that *Second Place* not only has the 'female authority' which the journalist sees in Joan Eardley's painting but also shares its achievement in locating 'the edge of the world itself' (Cusk 2018: 195).

Works Cited

Butler, J. (2000), *Antigone's Claim: Kinship Between Life and Death*. New York: Columbia University Press.
Cusk, R. (2001), *A Life's Work: On Becoming a Mother*. London: Fourth Estate.
Cusk, R. (2012), *Aftermath: On Marriage and Separation*. London: Faber & Faber.
Cusk, R. (2014), *Outline*. London: Faber & Faber.
Cusk, R. (2016), *Transit*. London: Jonathan Cape.
Cusk, R. (2018), *Kudos*. London: Faber & Faber.
Cusk, R. (2019), *Coventry*. London: Faber & Faber.
Cusk, R. (2021), *Second Place*. London: Faber & Faber.
Swinford, D. (2001), 'Defining Irrealism: Scientific Development and Allegorical Possibility', *Journal of the Fantastic in the Arts* 12 (1): 77–89.
Waugh, P. (2015), 'The Novel as Therapy: Ministrations of Voice in an Age of Risk', *Journal of the British Academy* 3: 35–68.

Introduction

Roberta Garrett and Liam Harrison

'Rachel Cusk Won't Stay Still'

In autumn 2022, *The Atlantic* published a profile of Rachel Cusk entitled 'Rachel Cusk Won't Stay Still'. The title referred to Cusk's decision to permanently relocate to Paris, the city in which she had been spending much of her time following the UK's controversial decision to exit the European Union in 2016. Frequent relocation has been a feature of Cusk's life. Born in Saskatoon Canada in 1967, she spent her early childhood in Los Angeles before moving to East Anglia in the UK to be educated at a private Catholic girls' school. She attended New College Oxford in the late 1980s and moved to London in the early 1990s. After having children, she moved to Bristol, Brighton and the Norfolk coast, before her recent move to Paris. In an interview with Merve Emre, that concludes this collection, Cusk reflects upon her move to France and how it relates to questions of identity, character and time in the French and Anglophone novel:

> Character is a very difficult thing to believe in or to assert the existence of in anything other than a very static set of circumstances, where character can confirm itself all the time. But now I think slightly differently, certainly, about the question of time. I wonder why I have never used my ability to slow down time and why, actually, in the Anglophone novel, it's really a rare thing for anyone to do – to make time go very, very, very slowly in a book. I've moved to France, I'm reading French novels in French all day, every day, and this is the thing that I'm most struck by: they go much more slowly. Time pauses. The book's location in time is completely different.

Cusk's approach to writing demonstrates the conflict between a restless spirit and an attention to temporal stasis – the ways in which time pauses and passes. Transition and renewal have been constant themes throughout her work, and she is an innovative, prolific and versatile writer. To date, she has produced twelve novels, three distinguished works of non-fiction, a collection of essays, short stories and numerous reviews and journalistic pieces. She has also written for theatre, creating a new version of Euripides's *Medea* in 2015. And yet, as Liam Harrison's chapter in this collection concludes, Cusk has frequently 'disparaged the forms of fiction available to her as a writer, while nonetheless continuing to write fiction'. Cusk has recently stated, 'I always think and feel that I'm coming to the end of writing as a useful occupation, which is maybe a suicidal impulse given to female creators' (Treisman 2023). The history of Cusk's literary output is one of experimentation and a desire to push against established models and forms, whether these are artistic and cultural or socio-political. There is a well-recognized historical tendency for critics and readers to over-identify the biography of the female writer with the characters and situations addressed in her novels. This has often worked to the detriment of their art, by means of diminishing and undermining its formal and imaginative achievements. As noted throughout this collection, the tendency to narrow the scope of women writers by interpreting their work in this manner has been particularly evident in critical and media responses to Cusk's fiction and non-fiction, and, in turn, has become something her work has actively sought to anticipate and complicate. As an astute observer and chronicler of modern life and consciousness, and as a woman writer whose life and work spans a period of intense and sustained debate on sexual difference and gender identity, the interplay between Cusk's life and the themes and concerns of her work are increasingly difficult to separate, especially when considering her experiments with form and narrative structure, and this difficulty is explored throughout this book from a variety of perspectives and critical approaches.

Cusk's early novels, *Saving Agnes* (1993), the debut that won her the Whitbread First Novel Award at the age of twenty-six, and *The Country Life* (1997), adopt a self-ironizing tone that still resonates with the work of young female authors over two decades later. Both are comic, protagonist-focused *Bildungsromans* that depict the trials and tribulations of young, educated, white middle-class women (Agnes Day, like Cusk, is an Oxford graduate). These novels are written in the 1990s, during a period in which career and lifestyle aspirations and expectations for certain women had shifted in comparison to the previous generation. In his essay on representations of femininity in Cusk's early work, Nicolas Boileau states that, 'her early novels depict young, successful female characters that, for some reason have failed to live up to society's expectations and end up as marginal, but conventional women' (2013: 2). In her chapter in this collection, Sonja Pyykkö, interrogates Cusk's ongoing preoccupation with femininity and failure stating that 'it is ultimately not failure per se, nor even a fear of failure, that

Saving Agnes seeks to represent, but something even more elusive: a distorted self-perception that causes Agnes to compare herself to an idealized version of herself'. The opening chapter of *Saving Agnes* captures this disjuncture between the required performance of female empowerment, what Ros Gill and Shani Orgad have more recently referred to as 'confidence culture' (2021), and the inner lives of young women in a patriarchal culture that makes few real concessions to their needs:

> Agnes usually managed to sustain the appearance of a thrusting young professional running on a tight schedule; but then someone switched on the lights, pulled off the mask, revealed the pretender for exactly who she was.
>
> Cusk 2013: 190

Pyykkö contextualizes Cusk's youthful protagonist's distorted view as symptomatic of the gradual impact of falling living standards – even for the middle class – due to neoliberal policies, alongside the conflict between female career aspiration, traditional expectations of femininity and the persistence of structural sexism. As Pyykkö details, these latter conflicts were also the basis of much female-orientated culture in the 1990s, through popularized figures such as Helen Fielding's Bridget Jones. In 1998, Cusk continued to explore the vicissitudes of attempting to acquire an acceptable version of female identity in her third novel, *The Country Life*. The tonal register of *The Country Life* is also comedic, drawing on Stella Gibbon's classic pastoral satire *Cold Comfort Farm*, and the older plot of the outsider amongst an eccentric wealthy family. The themes of alienation and estrangement continue in what might be considered the second phase of Cusk's writing career. This ranges from her first foray into non-fiction, *A Life's Work: Becoming a Mother* (2001), through the novels of the noughties: *The Lucky Ones* (2003), *In the Fold* (2005), *Arlington Park* (2006) and *The Bradshaw Variations* (2009). It also includes her second and third autobiographical works, *The Last Supper* (2009) and *Aftermath* (2012), as discussed in depth below, the latter received such negative reviews that it produced a period of 'creative death' that led to a third phase in Cusk's writing, of creative renewal.

The tonal register of Cusk's noughties' novels and non-fiction is darker and more contemplative than her early novels. Thematically, much of this work explores the tension between the desire to live fully as an intellectual, an artist and – for many of her characters – merely as an autonomous, sentient adult, while being subject to dominant cultural expectations and judgements on maternal behaviour and family life. In *A Life's Work*, Cusk states of her pregnancy, 'it is the population of my privacy, as if the door to my room were wide open and strangers were in there rifling about, that I find hard to endure. It is as if I have been arrested or called to account, summoned by the tax inspector, isolated and searched, I am not living freely but in some curious tithe' (Cusk 2001: 40) and 'motherhood, for me, was a sort of compound fenced off from the rest of the world. I was forever plotting to escape from it' (8). The five female characters in *Arlington Park* have little in common except their exasperation that marriage and motherhood has led to a greatly restricted social role. Juliet, the most openly rebellious of the wives and mothers reflects that:

> for a while she prized the idea of a house and a husband and children, as though they were a new refinement of human experience. Then she got them, and the feeling of lead started to build up in her veins, a little more each day. The time she realised that if she didn't buy food herself there would be none in the house; the time Benedict returned to work a week after Barnaby's birth and she realised she would be looking after him alone; the countless time a domestic task had fallen to her ... it was all surprising to her, outrageous almost.
>
> Cusk 2005: 39

Roberta Garrett's chapter contextualizes Cusk's response to the public culture of motherhood in terms of the increased socio-cultural intrusion into these areas that began in the late years of Conservative rule in the 1990s and continued through the period of New Labour government in the 2000s. Cusk's first memoir, *A Life's Work: On Becoming A Mother*, blends a thoughtful account of her own physical and psychological experiences of pregnancy and motherhood with reflections on the absence of critical work addressing these themes in classical literature, satirical comments on the socially-validated maternal role and some hard-hitting feminist observations on the continuation of domestic inequalities 'after a child is born the lives of its mother and father diverge, so that where before they were living in a state of equality, now they exist in a feudal relationship to one another' (2001: 11). In their analysis of the public culture of motherhood, Rachel Rosen and Katherine Twamley discuss the tendency for this to either conflate women and children (in a 'protected' but marginalized bubble) as 'motherandchild' or, if a mother desires any degree of independence or individual autonomy beyond her proscribed role, to view them as adversaries – 'motherversuschild' (2008: 1). Cusk's complex memoir narrates her attempts to negotiate a path through these polarized identities as a female writer attempting to retain an evolving but authentic sense of selfhood while also responding to her child's needs.

It is testimony to the power of the oppressive public narrative of motherhood during this period that *A Life's Work* was greeted with censorious responses from female lifestyle columnists who were determined to interpret Cusk's narrative through a 'motherversuschild' lens and ignore its exploration of ambivalence. As Garrett also details in her chapter, there had been few high-profile memoirs on motherhood in the UK and US since second wave feminism, before Cusk's controversial memoir. In contrast, the last two decades has witnessed an explosion in female authored Western life-writing on this subject. This has ranged from the more academic and sociological to playful autofictional work, such as Sheila Heti's *Motherhood* (2018) or Annie Ernaux's interrogation of parenthood in *I Remain in Darkness* (1999). It has become almost commonplace to address this subject through the blending of the personal and political that was pioneered during second wave feminism by Adrienne Rich and revisited by Cusk in the early noughties. Given the consistent attention to gendered double standards, oppressive gender roles and misogyny in her work, it is odd that Cusk has been so rarely thought of as a feminist writer. This is, in part, a historical accident. Cusk's early work fell between the critical identification of feminist writing as a form primarily associated with the self-reflexivity and metafictional qualities of much innovative women's writing of the 1980s and early 1990s and the emergence of fourth-wave confessional, autofictional feminist work in the early twenty-first century. One of the intentions of this collection is to highlight the role that Cusk's work has played in carving out space in the cultural mainstream for women writers to voice taboo ideas and emotions. As mentioned, Cusk has endured reviews that were hostile even by the harsh standards routinely applied to women writers. It seems likely that if Cusk had been more strongly identified as a feminist writer – and therefore as part of a known tribe rather than a lone warrior – this understanding of her autobiographical work would have afforded some protection from the impulse to ridicule her writing that is evident in some critical responses (epitomized by Camilla Long's savage review of *Aftermath*, in which she accuses Cusk of 'mad flowery metaphors and highfalutin creative writing experiments' (Long 2013)).

Cusk's thematic focus on privileged characters has also been held against her in a manner that has not been evident in comparison to her male contemporaries. Yet Cusk is rarely oblivious to privilege, including her own. As Pyykkö argues, in Cusk's debut, Agnes is 'saved' by becoming aware of a wider and much less rarefied world beyond her own. Garrett's analysis of Cusk novels of the early noughties, specifically *The Lucky Ones* and *Arlington Park* also highlights the 'condition of England' element of these predominantly realist texts. The reader is aware that the stifling but materially comfortable lives of the middle-class housewives who constitute the principal characters of these works, exist contemporaneously alongside the lives of the poor and dispossessed. Indeed, Cusk's allusion to Woolf's *Mrs Dalloway* through *Arlington Park*'s use of multiple narrators spanning one significant day, signals Cusk's awareness of the cruelty and insularity of certain sections of English middle-class culture. Cusk's evocation of Woolf is also salient in terms of her feminist credentials, as Peter Childs explores in his afterword. Woolf was famously dismissed by certain second wave critics – most notably Elaine Showalter – due to her interest in androgyny and her tendency to write about personal issues with a level of detachment and aloof intellectualism that was interpreted as an inability to confront her own 'painful femaleness'. Cusk is also a writer whose restrained use of emotion and experiments with narrative voice has precluded recognition of the way in which her work consistently challenges gender injustice, along with other socially validated sources of prejudice and inequality. Daniel Lea's chapter takes this view in his analysis of Cusk's critique of the restrictive values and roles of bourgeois family life in the last of her family-focused noughties' novels, *The Bradshaw Variations*. Lea argues that the novel offers a reconstituted notion of authenticity which resembles that proposed by Charles Taylor, in which romantic isolation and existential individualism is rejected in favour of a dialogic view of self and its relationship to social structures. This acknowledges the limitations of routine while also allowing for 'the possibility of moments of transcendence'. Childs examines these questions of female authenticity by bringing them back to Woolf, claiming that Cusk's 'quest for a female reality' is a 'question inherited from Woolf'. As Cusk writes in an essay on the subject of defining 'women's writing': 'In *A Room of One's Own* Woolf asserts two things: first, that the world – and hence its representations in art – is demonstrably male; and second, that a woman cannot create art out of a male reality' (*Coventry* 2019: 167).

It's All Aftermath

The third phase of Cusk's writing career was initiated by the 2012 non-fiction work *Aftermath*, a memoir about her divorce from her second husband, Adrian Clarke. 'Nothing belongs to me any more. I have become an exile from my own history,' Cusk writes, 'I no longer have a life. It's an afterlife; it's all aftermath' (2019: 91). As with her fictional work, *Aftermath* is intensely concerned with gender expectations, who holds narrative power, and how relationships and lives blend into each other, alongside the moral difficulties which arise when conflicting narratives take place. Early in *Aftermath*, Cusk sets up the stakes of her project, describing the battleground of her divorce:

> My husband believed that I had treated him monstrously. This belief of his couldn't be shaken: his whole world depended on it. It was his story, and lately I have come to hate stories. If someone were to ask me what disaster this was that had befallen my life, I might ask if they wanted the story or the truth. I might say, by way of explanation, that an important vow of obedience was broken. I might explain that when I write a novel wrong, eventually it breaks down and stops and won't be written any more, and I have to go back and look for the flaws in its design. The problem usually lies in the relationship between the story and the truth. The story has to obey the truth, to represent it, like clothes represent the body.
>
> 2019: 2–3

Aftermath raises many pressing questions – about artistic representation, the relationship between objectivity and subjectivity, and the ethical stakes of form – as Cusk asks us to reflect upon what shape each narrative takes and who gets to do the telling, especially in relation to gender roles. These questions are interrogated throughout Cusk's writing, as the chapters in this collection explore, and her work frequently returns to the conflict between 'the story and the truth' that *Aftermath* poses.

Aftermath received a vitriolic critical response for the candid and partial way that it portrayed the breakdown of Cusk's marriage. Indeed, just as *Aftermath* raised many artistic questions that have informed Cusk's later work, the criticism she faced has also had a significant effect on Cusk's writing style. Echoing the criticism that, several years earlier, was directed at *A Life's Work*, *Aftermath* was dismissed as 'whiny, pretentious and self-indulgent'. In *The Sunday Times*, Camilla Long condemned Cusk, this time as 'a brittle little dominatrix and peerless narcissist who exploits her husband and her marriage with relish' (2012). Joanna Biggs summarized the complaints, while adding some of her own: '*Aftermath*, has brought Cusk charges of self-absorption, narcissism, condescension, commercialism, cruelty towards her children, too much revelation, not enough revelation, naivety, grandiloquence, ice in her heart and a lack of a sense of humour' (2012). The critical focus on Cusk's work has therefore predominantly been evaluative and highly personal. This collection recomplicates these evaluative responses to Cusk, by examining her writing in various historical, cultural, and artistic contexts, analysing how she has confounded critics and readers alike, and considering how this relates to the diffuse renderings of subjectivity, gender and identity in her work. Moreover, we can see how Cusk has subverted the impulse to read her work biographically, by disrupting the biographical foundations and narrative expectations of the novel.

From the criticisms listed above, we can see how Cusk was portrayed after writing *Aftermath*; self-indulgent, narcissistic, condescending, exploitational, pretentious, and, perhaps more than anything, cruel. Indeed, Emre has suggested that Cusk is perhaps 'the cruel[l]est novelist at work today' (2018), based on the relationships she cuttingly depicts in her novels, rather than a judgement on Cusk's own personality. What the criticism of Cusk's character tends to ignore or dismiss, however, is how Cusk self-consciously highlights these negative qualities within her writing, accentuating her own fallibility in non-fiction works like *Aftermath* for dramatic effect, with a degree of self-reflexivity that is both pronounced and difficult to gauge. As readers we end up asking ourselves when encountering Cusk's cruelty: how deliberate, self-aware and self-critical is it? As Melissa Schuh states in her chapter, Cusk's understanding of self is 'contingent, unfinished and multi-faceted' thereby eluding conventional moral judgements. However, responses that conflate the analysis of cruelty in her work – whether emanating from 'Cusk as character' in her autobiographies or manifested through the behaviour of her fictional characters – with Cusk herself, suggest a gender-biased critical tendency that is inadequate in dealing with the complex revisioning of selfhood in her work.

Cusk's work has received more attention from the media than from literary critics, and there is a striking dearth of academic criticism which this collection aims to redress, while also noting some of the potential causes. As detailed throughout these chapters, Cusk has been especially reviled for her memoirs, *A Life's Work* and *Aftermath*, which expose the ambivalence of maternal subjectivity and the visceral pain of divorce, leading to the personal and gendered criticism of her – as a mother, (ex-)wife and writer. Indeed, Patricia Lockwood has noted how it is a commonplace confession to dislike Cusk, and she expresses surprise that no one has ever begun a review of her work with: 'I, too, dislike her' (2018). Writing about *A Life's Work* and *Aftermath* several years after publication, Lockwood also reflects on the affective experience of reading these memoirs, arguing that 'these books are notorious not for their actual content but for the degree to which they seemed to leave readers feeling thwarted. We know what we want from memoirs, and she did not give it to us – too much of her mind and not enough of herself' (2018). Cusk's response after *Aftermath*, as several chapters examine, is to evacuate the self almost completely, drawing variously on minimalism, silence and questions of authenticity to render a diffuse and complicated portrayal of selfhood. This collection also examines why Cusk's work has prompted such critical hostility. On the one hand, Cusk's characters are often privileged middle class white people, who fail to interrogate their social status, as Pyykkö explores in Cusk's portrayals of failure in *Saving Agnes*. On the other hand, the discomfort Cusk causes may be generated by her perceptive interrogation into the societal and cultural narratives that we live by.

Cusk described her own state of mind after writing *Aftermath* and the backlash directed at her as a kind of 'creative death'. 'That was the end,' Cusk claimed, 'I was heading into total silence – an interesting place to find yourself when you are quite developed as an artist' (Kellaway 2014). 'I was depleted to the point of not being able to create anything,' Cusk explains, linking this exhaustion to her own sense of selfhood: 'There seems to be some problem about my identity. But no one can find it, because it's not there' (Thurman 2017). Here was an established author at a creative impasse. On the one hand, the prospect of writing novels felt 'fake and embarrassing', and Cusk proposed that 'once you have suffered sufficiently, the idea of making up John and Jane and having them do things together seems utterly ridiculous' (Kellaway 2014). On the other hand, Cusk confessed that 'my mode of autobiography had come to an end. I could not do it without being misunderstood and making people angry' (ibid.). Cusk declared that the form of writing which had epitomized her previous non-fiction, *A Life's Work*, *Aftermath* and *The Last Supper* was exhausted (Cusk was sued for defamation over *The Last Supper*, and the first print run had to be pulped). While she also rejected the notion of writing another social novel, such as *Arlington Park* or *The Bradshaw Variations*, which had defined the second phase of Cusk's fiction writing career. This creative impasse resulted in the novel *Outline* (2014), later followed by *Transit* (2016) and *Kudos* (2018), eventually forming the *Outline* trilogy.

Life and Writing

The *Outline trilogy* breaks down boundaries between fiction and life writing, as the narrator and protagonist, Faye, appears to be a lightly fictionalized version of Cusk. And yet, Cusk's work does not neatly fall into the burgeoning, albeit tenuously defined category of autofiction, just as her writing career has often eschewed fixed genres. As Lorrie Moore notes, despite the comparisons, 'her work is not the autofiction of Karl Ove Knausgaard and Sheila Heti, whose own voices and personalities cram their pages; nor is it the meditative flâneurie of W. G. Sebald or Teju Cole; it is something more peculiar and thrilling and Cusk's own' (2018).[1] And yet, while Cusk's work does not comfortably sit amidst this growing corpus of writing or nascent genre, Schuh's chapter draws on the conceptual litheness of autofiction to analyse Cusk's autobiographical experiments in the *Outline* trilogy. Schuh suggests that autofiction, as a 'combination of fictional modes of representation and autobiographical impulses, offers possibilities' of revealing a kind of representation through absence. By considering the trilogy's preoccupations with the 'boundaries between life and imagination, fact and fiction, [...] questioning established autobiographical tropes of "truth", unity, coherence and closure', Schuh unpacks how Cusk 'advances an understanding of self and life that is characterized by ongoing reflection and affirmation of complexity and contradiction'. Put more simply, Schuh argues that while '"Faye" is not quite interchangeable with "Rachel Cusk" [...] Cusk is still inseparable from Faye'. This blurring between biographical and fictive selves can also be read as a pointed response to the previously noted conflation between women writers and their creations, complicating this relationship through formal innovation. As Clare Hanson states in her foreword, there is a 'tight interplay between substance and form' in Cusk's work and it is animated by 'the mutual imbrication of life and writing'. Or as Kevin Brazil has suggested, situating Cusk in a new period of literature, 'Cusk's work, as in many interactions between life-writing and fiction after postmodernism, is haunted by the distance between life and literary form while pursuing their ever closer fusion' (2019: 96).

Cusk's work frequently returns to the significance of narrative and stories, in terms of how identities, society and culture are constructed, and how narratives attempt (and often fail) to connect individual experience with social structures. This tension is stretched to its limits in the *Outline* trilogy, which strives for what Cusk calls a 'purity of narrative' (Kellaway 2014), through a series of one-sided conversations. In all three novels, Faye is mostly silent and instead acts as conduit for the stories and confessions of other people. In place of narrative development, the trilogy relays a series of encounters between Faye and an assortment of

---

[1] Cusk has frequently commented on and distanced her work from the term autofiction: 'I don't think that I write "autofiction," though I admire the people who do, and essentially wish that I did. I think it's an evolution beyond what I'm doing. I'm perhaps stuck in the past, trying to work out the past. I don't think I'm in any way as free as the writer of autofiction. I don't think that anything I do is revolutionary in that way. I have a moral agenda, a willingness to commit myself to morality, that feels extracted at great cost from the "novel," as we define it currently. The autofiction writer can access that instantly through the legitimacy of the self. So maybe I'm working away on something basically bankrupt. But I enjoy the work and sometimes feel sustained by it – very much so in the case of "The Stuntman"' (Treisman 2023).

friends, acquaintances and strangers, such as fellow plane passengers, her hairdresser, her builders, her creative writing students, rich philanthropists, businessmen, writers, organizers at literary festivals, and so on. In each encounter, Faye (whose name is only announced once in each novel, adding to her sense of anonymity and withdrawal) appears to be largely detached from the stories and anecdotes relayed to her, intervening only enough to keep the other people talking. These characters rarely appear more than once, preventing a linear narrative or character development from taking shape. This sense of stalled progression adds to Cusk's 'extension of what modernist experimentation began', as Ella Ophir argues, through Cusk's 'means of disabling the twinned vectors of character and plot development before they can start' (2022: 4). The more the trilogy progresses, as Ruth Franklin notes, the more 'the monologues circle and spiral around one another, their layering and patterning creating a form of profound complexity, like a seashell' (2016). While these novels are predicated on the absence of the narrator and subjective withdrawal, they are the work that, paradoxically, saw Cusk finally recognized as a major writer. This success also prompted Cusk's back catalogue to be republished with uniform covers by her UK publisher, Faber & Faber, emphasizing a shift in reputation, as she was now recognized as a 'serious' writer – marketed and stylized as modernist inheritor rather than chick-lit, raising many questions of gender and reception unpacked in the chapters by Garrett and Ricarda Menn. Indeed, considering Cusk's use of metaphor, Menn proposes that while 'the Faber covers may suggest a uniformity of writing across Cusk's writing career, the serial continuity in the content of her work is predicated upon discontinuities of selfhood'.

Violence and Silence

While the *Outline* trilogy fictionalized her own life, albeit in a formally fraught and complicated manner, Cusk's next novel, *Second Place* (2021), tackles biographical innovation by repurposing the art patron Mabel Dodge Luhan's 1932 memoir about D. H. Lawrence, *Lorenzo in Taos* (1932), to create a novel that explores gender relations, artistic freedom, identity and, more obliquely, the conditions of confinement and lockdown. Like the *Outline* trilogy, *Second Place* similarly dwells on the dissolution of a linear identity, as Cusk claimed after writing *Aftermath*, 'I have lost all interest in having a self. Being a person has always meant getting blamed for it' (Thurman 2017). In *Second Place*, Cusk continues her radical experimentation with narrative perspective, ventriloquizing the voice of Luhan and reworking the memoir *Lorenzo in Taos* into a first-person fictional form, as well as portraying her 'hero' D. H. Lawrence (although as Cusk notes in her interview with Emre, *Second Place* is about 'chucking D. H. Lawrence, getting him out of my life. I will survive without D. H. Lawrence. I turned against him and got rid of him'). Without wishing to exaggerate Lawrence's influence on Cusk, it bears noting how she writes about Lawrence in terms that acutely capture her own creative practice: 'Lawrence does more than part company with the Victorian modes of narration – he destroys them by completely inverting the literary and actual function of "man" as a representative of "mankind"' (2019: 203).[2] Cusk similarly takes a destructive attitude towards previous forms of narration and character, as she subverts the notion that a unified sense of self is required to render subjectivity, and complicates what the novelistic and non-fictional 'I' is capable of representing – whether in the evacuation of narrative selfhood in the *Outline* trilogy, or the recasting of Luhan and Lawrence in *Second Place*. These ideas also raise questions surrounding influence and legacy, as Childs notes in his afterword, *Second Place*, 'in one simple sense accords first place to Luhan's memoir', and thereby 'interrogates the abiding question of precedence and what, or who, is displaced into a second "place", understood as location, role, or status'. Cusk's D. H. Lawrence stand-in, L, is given the last line on the matter in the novel, in the fitting form of a posthumous letter to M, writing that 'I miss your place', before pronouncing how his current location, the hotel room in which he will die, 'is a bad place' (Cusk 2021: 207).

Cusk revisits the 'discontinuities of selfhood', which Menn detects across her serialized reading of Cusk's corpus, in the short story 'The Stuntman', published in *The New Yorker* in 2023, and incorporated into Cusk's latest novel, *Parade* (2024). The story, once again, explores a diffuse sense of selfhood, and what it might mean to delegate difficult experiences to an 'alternate or double self whose role it was to absorb and confine them so that they played no part in the ongoing story of life' (Cusk 2023). This repressive or inoculating method (depending on your reading of it) is analogized in the form of a 'stuntman': 'this alternate self took the actual risks in the creation of a fictional being whose exposure to danger was supposedly fundamental to its identity' (2023). The narrator of the story is assaulted on the street in a random attack, in a narrative tactic (as well as a biographical event which actually happened in Cusk's own life) that disrupts the withdrawal of selfhood trialled by the *Outline* trilogy, as the narrator notes 'the

---

[2] We can also hear echoes of Lawrence's famous letter to Edward Garnett, 'You mustn't look in my novel for the old stable ego of the character' (Lawrence 1981: 183).

violence and the unexpectedness of the incident in the street had caught my stuntman unawares' (2023).³ While the *Outline* trilogy subverts many conventional expectations of presence – in terms of plot, character and narrative – 'The Stuntman' and its central act of violence epitomizes 'the inversion of representation while being ultimately representative'. The story ends on a contrapuntal note of 'violence and silence' (2023) that is explored extensively throughout the chapters that follow, as this collection examines how these twinned vectors function throughout Cusk's work, often through subtle and inverted measures.

The essays in this book frequently return to and excavate the 'creative death' that Cusk claims to have suffered after the publication of *Aftermath*, and the artistic possibilities contained therein. Menn unpacks how Cusk's generic turn from memoir to autofiction is directly influenced by the preceding series of memoirs and the impact of their reception. Moreover, Pyykkö notes how Cusk's writing contains a kind of 'post-mortem' inflection, and describes life 'rendered almost unrecognizable by some perfectly ordinary but no less destructive disaster'. As Cusk notes in her interview with Emre, 'somehow death or exhaustion or not being defined attains a weird adverse value'. Nonetheless, the essays in this collection are also alert to the limitations of metaphorical exile, especially in comparison with the very real experiences of exile in its historical and contemporary iterations. Cusk's styles of self-criticism and self-condemnation are put under the microscope. Harrison's chapter explores how Cusk's vein of self-deprecation attempts to protect her work from any future criticism, pre-empting the kind of backlash she received after *Aftermath* by 'interposing such criticism into her self-reflexive prose'. As Harrison details, Cusk's work complicates any easy parsing of her work by repurposing muted qualities of silence and withdrawal into something powerfully expressive, through her distinctively, 'discrepant style'. Pieter Vermeulen, alternatively, considers criticism of Cusk in the context of developments in British fiction since the apparent 'hysterical realism' and 'maximalism' of the early 2000s. Vermeulen's chapter pushes back against the classist and elitist charges often directed at Cusk, noting how the portrayal of the downstairs neighbours in *Transit*, 'The Trolls', offers 'an entirely more conflicted politics than the self-righteous embodiment of bourgeois values' that

---

³ In an interview with *The New Yorker* discussing the story, Cusk reveals that the attack is based on personal experience: 'It's true that I was brained in the street in Paris, completely randomly, and the difficulty for me as a writer lay in the use of a personal experience that was so anomalous.'

many critics have condemned Cusk for. As with many chapters in this collection, Vermeulen's critical approach pays attention to the importance of style, unpacking the political and cultural resonances of Cusk's pared back prose in *Transit*, to explore how 'the psychology, the economics, and the aesthetics of minimalism are deeply connected; through the insistent presence of the neighbours', while also suggesting Cusk's style draws attention to rather than reaffirms 'minimalism's problematic exclusionary politics'. By detailing how 'the aspiration of minimalism is dependent on class and citizenship', Vermeulen claims that '*Transit* checks the privilege it performs', as its 'performance of minimalism is a self-critical one'. We can thereby trace a common thread throughout Cusk's writing career – challenges of irony, representations of failure, and moral conflations between art and author – that speak to the hermeneutic difficulty and pleasure of encountering Cusk's work.

Cusk has spoken about the challenges she sets her readers, noting of the *Outline* trilogy: 'for these books to work, the reader needs to play at least some role in the "writing" of them, since there's no conventional narrator. It's an active rather than passive reading experience' (Zafiris 2017). The active reading experience speaks to how these novels (un)dramatically unfold, how the various narratives accumulate, which is perhaps more significant than what they literally describe. Rachel Kushner has recently countered one criticism frequently applied to Cusk's work, by stating 'I don't read for relatability' (2023). Situating Cusk amidst 'strangely, unapologetic novelists from the upper echelons', Kushner claims that Cusk and her peers 'tend to be especially good at writing about class, [...] their own class, because they have nothing to prove, or to obscure' (2023). We see this in the self-criticism of *Aftermath*, as Cusk mistreats her au pair with demonstrable disdain for her own actions, as Harrison examines in his chapter. Garrett's reading of *The Lucky Ones* also examines Cusk's skill in exposing the more serious consequences of social privilege combined with ethical indifference by interweaving the story of a young, poor, incarcerated pregnant woman with that of the lawyer that fails to properly represent her.

Cusk's writing contains elements of the 'new audacity' that Jennifer Cooke traces across contemporary feminist life-writing, as a series of intersectional feminist literature that draws on innovative forms of expression to challenge ongoing structures of oppression. The new audacity, in Cooke's terms, 'experiment[s] by testing the boundaries of autobiographical conventions', exhibits 'boldness in style and content', and explores 'difficult and disturbing experiences', resonating with the formal innovations of Cusk's hybrid writing (2020: 2). Writing about the French author Annie Ernaux in 2023 – whose work also captures the kind of 'new audacity' described by Cooke – Cusk uses language that perhaps more accurately describes her own work. On the one hand, Cusk considers writing 'as a sphere where the self, the soul, is entitled to find refuge' (2023). On the other hand, Cusk claims that Ernaux's 'art bears no relation to a privileging of personal experience; on the contrary, it is almost a self-violation' (2023). In this sense, Cusk's work explores 'the relationship between fate and freedom', as Emre notes in the interview with Cusk that concludes this collection, as well as the relationship between 'silence and violence' which is explored in 'The Stuntman'. Harrison touches on the creative possibilities of silence as it functions as an expressive mechanism for Cusk's style throughout her essays and fiction, a style which may lead to new forms of artistic liberation. Silence also speaks to Cusk's interest in the visual arts, which she has frequently written about, as Harrison notes: 'visual art appeals to Cusk because of its silence [...] and it provides a correlative for her own style, which is deeply entangled with the limitations of language'. Cusk, in her interview with Emre, similarly concludes, 'If there is a desire for freedom, it is freedom from language.'

While there is often a line drawn between different phases of Cusk's writing career, as sketched above, especially her pre- and post-*Outline* writing, Lea's chapter pushes back against this dichotomy, tracing similar concerns with authenticity, domesticity and 'the representation of selfhood' in *The Bradshaw Variations* and the *Outline* trilogy. Lea examines the social and cultural pitfalls that Cusk's novels explore, analysing how she 'portrays her characters *in situ*, embedded, and often trapped within domestic relationships that govern the outline of their identity'. The protagonists in these narratives 'largely reconcile themselves to the narrative identities from which they have striven to break free', Lea contends, and proposes that they 'discover some solace in the familiarity of their compromises'. Pyykkö also notes common concerns that span Cusk's writing career, tracing a thematic concern with failure across Cusk's debut novel, *Saving Agnes*, and *Second Place*. 'True art means seeking to capture the unreal' (Cusk 2021: 180), M writes, while confessing she only possesses the 'more common ability to read the surface of life' (54). Pyykkö traces a similar fixation on surfaces with Agnes Day, albeit in the trials and tribulations of the *Bildungsroman*, as opposed to the stasis of M's Norfolk marshes. Considering both Agnes and M, Pyykkö contends that for Cusk's 'novels to succeed as works of art, their protagonists must fail'. Distinguishing Cusk's work into neat phases, then, may be as complicated as the depictions of selfhood and biographical innovations of the Outline trilogy and *Second Place*, as her work continues to subvert and confound readerly and critical expectations, and refuses to stay still.

Works Cited

Biggs, J. (2012), 'Clytemnestra in Brighton', *London Review of Books*, 22 March. Available at: https://www.lrb.co.uk/the-paper/v34/n06/joanna-biggs/clytemnestra-in-brighton (accessed 20 July 2023).

Boileau, N. P. (2013), 'Not feminine enough? Rachel Cusk's highly-feminised world and unfeminine characters in *Saving Agnes* and *The Country Life*'. *Anglistik: International Journal of English Studies* (hal-01306511).

Brazil, K. (2019), 'Form and Fiction, 1980–2018', in Peter Boxall (ed.), *The Cambridge Companion to British Fiction: 1980–2018*. Cambridge: Cambridge University Press.

Cooke, J. (2020), *Contemporary Feminist Life-Writing: The New Audacity*. Cambridge: Cambridge University Press.

Cusk, R. ([1997] 2019), *The Country Life*. London: Faber & Faber.

Cusk, R. (2003), *The Lucky Ones*. London: Harper Collins.

Cusk, R. ([2005] 2019), *In the Fold*. London: Faber & Faber.

Cusk, R. (2006), *Arlington Park*. London: Faber & Faber.

Cusk, R. (2008), *A Life's Work: On Becoming a Mother*. London: Faber & Faber.

Cusk, R. (2009), *The Last Supper. A Summer in Italy*. London: Faber & Faber.

Cusk, R. (2009), *Bradshaw Variations*. London: Faber & Faber.

Cusk, R. ([2012] 2019), *Aftermath*. London: Faber & Faber.

Cusk, R. (2013), *Saving Agnes*. London: Faber & Faber.

Cusk, R. ([2014] 2018), *Outline*. London: Faber & Faber.

Cusk, R. ([2016] 2018), *Transit*. London: Faber & Faber.

Cusk, R. (2018), *Kudos*. London: Faber & Faber.

Cusk, R. (2019), *Coventry*. London: Faber & Faber.

Cusk, R. (2021), *Second Place*. London: Faber & Faber.

Cusk, R. (2023), 'The Stuntman'. *The New Yorker*, 17 April. Available at: https://www.newyorker.com/magazine/2023/04/24/the-stuntman-fiction-rachel-cusk (accessed 20 July 2023).

Cusk, R. (2023), 'Annie Ernaux Has Broken Every Taboo of What Women Are Allowed to Write'. *The New York Times*, 5 July. Available at: https://www.nytimes.com/2023/05/02/magazine/annie-ernaux-delphine-de-vigan.html (accessed 20 July 2023).

Cusk, R. (2024), *Parade*. London: Faber & Faber.

Emre, M. (2018), 'Of Note'. *Harper's Magazine*. 1 June. Available at: https://harpers.org/archive/2018/06/of-note/ (accessed 20 July 2023).

Franklin, R. (2016), 'The Uncoupling'. *The Atlantic*, 13 December. Available at: https://www.theatlantic.com/magazine/archive/2017/01/the-uncoupling/508742/ (accessed 28 August 2023).

Gill, R. and S. Orgad (2022), *Confidence Culture*. Durham, NC: Duke University Press.

Kellaway, K. (2014), 'Rachel Cusk: "Aftermath Was Creative Death. I Was Heading into Total Silence"'. *The Observer*, 24 August. Available at: https://www.theguardian.com/

books/2014/aug/24/rachel-cusk-interview-aftermath-outline (accessed 20 July 2023).

Kushner, R. (2023), 'Disappear Here'. *Harper's Magazine*, April. Available at: https://harpers.org./archive/2023/04/the-shards-bret-easton-ellis-rachel-kushner-review/ (accessed 28 August 2023).

Lawrence, D. H. (1981), 'Letter to Edward Garnett of 5 June 1914', in George J. Zytaruk and James T. Boulton (eds.), *The Letters of D. H. Lawrence, Vol. II*. Cambridge: Cambridge University Press.

Lockwood, P. (2018), 'On Rachel Cusk "Why Do I Have to Know What McDonald's Is?"'. *London Review of Books*, 10 May. Available at: https://www.lrb.co.uk/the-paper/v40/n09/patricia-lockwood/why-do-i-have-to-know-what-mcdonald-s-is (accessed 20 July 2023).

Long, C. (2012), 'Aftermath: On Marriage and Separation by Rachel Cusk'. *The Sunday Times*, 4 March. Available at: https://www.thetimes.co.uk/article/aftermath-on-marriage-and-separation-by-rachel-cusk-xn0xgt0lsp9 (accessed 20 July 2023).

Moore, L. (2018), 'The Queen of Rue'. *The New York Review of Books*, 16 August. Available at: https://www.nybooks.com/articles/2018/08/16/rachel-cusk-queen-of-rue/ (accessed 28 August 2023).

Ophir, E. (2022), 'Neomodernism and the Social Novel: Rachel Cusk's Outline Trilogy'. *Critique: Studies in Contemporary Fiction*, 64: 2. Available at: https://doi.org/10.1080/00111619.2021.2021133.

Rosen, R. and K. Twamley (2018), 'Introduction', in R. Rosen and K. Twamley (eds.), *Feminism and the Politics of Childhood: Friend or Foe?* London: University College London.

Thurman, J. (2017), 'Rachel Cusk Gut-Renovates the Novel'. *The New Yorker*, 7 August. Available at: https://www.newyorker.com/magazine/2017/08/07/rachel-cusk-gut-renovates-the-novel (accessed 20 July 2023).

Treisman, D. (2023), 'Rachel Cusk on the Self in Visual Art'. *The New Yorker*, 17 April. Available at: https://www.newyorker.com/books/this-week-in-fiction/rachel-cusk-04-24-23 (accessed 20 July 2023).

Zafiris, A. (2017), 'Rachel Cusk'. *BOMB Magazine*, 16 February. Available at: https://bombmagazine.org/articles/rachel-cusk/ (accessed 20 July 2023).

1

Life Style

Rachel Cusk and the Critique of Minimalism

Pieter Vermeulen

After Maximalism

By many accounts, the twenty-first century in British literary fiction began on 27 January 2000: 'Early in the morning, late in the century, Cricklewood Broadway. At 06.27 hours on January 1, 1975, Alfred Archibald Jones was dressed in corduroy and sat in a fume-filled Cavalier Musketeer Estate face down on the steering wheel, hoping judgement would not be too heavy upon him' (Smith 2000: 3).[1] The opening sentence of Zadie Smith's *White Teeth* exemplifies the zany and overly informative narrative mode through which millennial literary fiction reconciled the exigencies of postmodern self-reflexiveness and the demands of readerly connection. Nor was this mode restricted to Britain. Nine months later, arguably the most celebrated American novel of the year began as follows: 'In later years, holding forth to an interviewer or to an audience of aging fans at a comic book convention, Sam Clay liked to declare, apropos of his and Joe Kavalier's greatest creation, that back when he was a boy, sealed and hog-tied inside the airtight vessel known as Brooklyn, New York, he had been haunted by dreams of Harry Houdini' (Chabon 2000: 1). Michael Chabon's Pulitzer Prize-winning *The Amazing Adventures of Kavalier and Clay*, like *White Teeth*, indulges

---

[1] It is almost a commonplace to position *White Teeth* (published on 27 January 2000) as the endpoint of 1990s British literature and the start of its next phase. See Bentley 2015; Vermeulen 2018. Tew claims that *White Teeth* made Smith 'the first quintessentially British twenty-first-century writer' for her capacity to capture 'a millennial zeitgeist' (2010: 21). Because of its fortuitous publication date in early 2000, *White Teeth* is often the earliest work to be included in courses on twenty-first-century literature or scholarly surveys of the period.

narrative detail, complexity and storyworld excess in a way that can, without too much controversy, be termed *maximalist*.[2]

The more familiar signifier for this mode of writing, however, is a different one. In a sprawling review of Smith's novel, critic James Wood infamously (and deaf to the gendered history of ascriptions of hysteria) diagnosed her 'big, ambitious novel' as a form of what he termed 'hysterical realism'. This realism is 'lively and varied and brightly marked'; it is 'a perpetual-motion machine that appears to have been embarrassed into velocity'. At the beginning of the millennium, novel-writing, for Wood, had become information management rather than character elaboration: 'Information has become the new character,' and this means that one can read these loud novels without encountering 'anything really affecting, sublime, or beautiful' (2000: n.p.).

Two decades later, this is no longer the most valorized mode of writing (not even Chabon or Smith write like that anymore). Indeed, the critical labels that joined hysterical realism in the attempt to capture the contemporary novel's propensity for relatedness and profusion after postmodernism (New Sincerity, metamodernism, post-irony) have in their turn been superseded. In retrospect, 2000 was the end rather than the beginning of something new (Jonathan Franzen's *The Corrections*, perhaps the last major work to fit the hysterical and maximalist moulds, was published exactly ten days before 9/11, a key signifier for the irrevocable end of the end of history).[3] Today, literary sophistication is measured by the leaner and sparser conventions of autofictional writing (Wasserman 2022: 561–4), which shares the literary spotlight with the widely discussed turn to genre (McGurl 2015); to the extent that narrative excess and hyperattention to detail are indulged in autofiction, they are kept in check by the referential pull of authorial identity and realist setting – a marked difference

---

[2] The notion of literary maximalism is less extensively studied than that of minimalism, arguably because it lacks the latter's overlap with dominant pedagogical creative writing practices that emphasize craft and constraint (McGurl 2011: 294). Ercolino defines the maximalist novel as a distinctive genre of postwar literature with ten specific characteristics (2014: xiii–iv); for Levey, maximalism applies to 'writing that values the pursuit of detail, specificity, and comprehensiveness' over other literary purposes (2017: 2). My use of the label 'maximalist' here straddles Levey's and Ercolino's more sustained accounts. McGurl identifies maximalism with the impulse 'to say all there is to say,' which results in 'crowdedness of characterization, complexity of plot, and relatively long length' (2021: 202–3).

[3] The idea that 9/11 spelled the end of 1990s fantasies of the triumph of capitalism and the end of conflict (the features that Francis Fukuyama infamously saw as inaugurating the end of history) is a commonplace: the association with 'the end of the end of history' was already codified in a *Newsweek* article with that title that appeared on 23 September 2001. See Wegner 2009 for the most elaborate literary critical case for the impact of (the end of) the end of history.

from hysterical realism's 'excess of storytelling' (Wood 2000: n.p.).[4] In literary studies, this shift from hysterical realism to autofiction has coincided with a shift from postmodernism to neoliberalism as the dominant periodizing category, to the extent that autofiction's literary winnowing is often cast as an effect of the neoliberal colonization of literature and of the lived experiences on which it draws (De Boever 2019; Lorentzen 2021). In recent years, autofiction has emerged as the literary mode of compulsory authorial self-branding and of the growing indistinction between life and work under neoliberalism (Konstantinou 2021); autofictional leanness, then, is a reflex of the stark realities of over a decade of enforced austerity and shrinking economic and existential prospects.[5]

Rachel Cusk's *Outline* trilogy effortlessly fits this description of the new literary austerity. The three novels are narrated by a rigorously self-effacing writer, whose job to a large extent determines the coordinates of her life – as a creative writing teacher (an assignment that brings her to Greece, the icon of twenty-first-century austerity, in *Outline*), as a reluctant speaker at literary festivals (where she is talked over and groped by toxic men in *Transit*), or as an interviewee after the publication of her book (which brings her back to the European mainland in *Kudos*). Especially in the first volume, Cusk's narrative set-up positions Faye (her name occurs exactly once in each of the volumes) in the background and gives centre stage to the voices of her mansplaining and oversharing interlocutors, whose words are conveyed without overt judgement.

---

[4] Because of the unique combination of individual scope, monumental length, and excessive focus on detail, Knausgaard's *My Struggle* series, which in the early 2010s announced the shift to autofiction as a new dominant, takes a peculiar position in this shift to minimalism. As the fifth book of the series describes Knausgaard's project: 'What my aim was, well, it was to escape from the minimalistic, into the maximalistic, something bold and striking, baroque, Moby Dick, but not in an epic way, what I had tried to do was take the little novel, about one person, where there is not much external action, and extend it into an epic format' (quoted in Van De Ven 2019: 91). It is safe to say that the restriction to 'one person' (its minimalist dimension) has had a more enduring afterlife in contemporary autofiction than the monumental size (the maximalism) of Knausgaard's work.

[5] While I ground the shift from a maximalist to a minimalist dominant in altered political economic circumstances, it is also possible to gloss this shift as a dynamic intrinsic to literary history. Nor do I want to oversell the link between economic and literary developments, which risks flattening out the distinctions between very different writers who adopt autofictional lean forms – think of Ben Lerner, Claire-Louise Bennett, Sheila Heti, Tao Lin, Teju Cole and others. Still, all these writers explicitly reflect on the neoliberal contexts in which they live, and all of them directly reflect on its impact on their formal choices (this self-reflexivity is, of course, intrinsic to the genre). See Ercolino 2014: 65–70 for a consideration of the '*cyclical corrections of excess*' that have always marked literary and art history and the conclusion that maximalism and minimalism are forever '*dialectically coexistent*'. In the US context, minimalism gained prominence in critical discourse in the 1980s, where it began to refer to a more restricted set of 'dirty realist' or 'populist minimalist' works rather than to the more encompassing and less exclusively US-based 'aesthetic of omission, reduction, or simplicity' (Doherty 2014: 88) I am interested in, if only because it is that latter aesthetic that informs Cusk's practice. See Doherty 2014: 79–82 and 87–9, Hoberek 2010: 102–8 and Jones 2020: 301–6 for the critical career of minimalism in the US in the 1980s.

To the extent that there is exuberance and expression, then, its legibility is muffled by the self-effacing and nonobtrusive mediations of the narrator. The *Outline* trilogy, in other words, performs a *deliberate* curtailment of hysteria and excess; its tenor and aesthetic are not just *different* from the zany exuberance of hysterical realism – it is a determinate, even programmatic negation of it. Cusk's trilogy still operates on the terms Wood established: the books are emphatically works of information management, in which the narrator carefully filters her interlocutors' verbal excretions; arguably, nothing 'affecting, sublime, or beautiful' transpires in them, as the novels instead make visible how carefully they have excised such excessive emotion. This investment in affective curtailment, verbal condensation and information sparsity, together with the trilogy's diegetic focus on the mundane life of only one character, undeniably qualifies it as a *minimalist* work.

Minimalism is not just the name of a literary style: it names a twentieth-century aesthetic mode that also ranged over sculpture, architecture, design and the visual arts, and that has, on many accounts, morphed into a globally commodified and eminently Instagrammable lifestyle in the twenty-first century (and to be clear, this commodified minimalism is not customarily linked to autofiction; the link, I argue, is established in Cusk's trilogy). As Kyle Chayka notes, while minimalist lifestyles initially became ubiquitous in the wake of the 2008 financial crash as an 'aesthetic of necessity' in the 'faux-blue-collar hipsterism' that spread through social media, it has since been transformed into a kind of 'high-gloss consumer minimalism' – an aesthetic of white walls, Apple products, and isolated pieces of (faux-)design furniture in open spaces (2020: 13). This lifestyle minimalism is morally and politically problematic. As Chayka argues, its visual austerity typically goes together with an ascetic morality informed by a sense that 'the surrounding civilization is excessive [...] and has thus lost some kind of original authenticity that must be regained' (14). At the same time, this commodified minimalism is marked by an unacknowledged class privilege; in Michael Dango's analysis, minimalism's emphasis on control and curtailment feeds a fantasy of 'detoxification', in which style constitutes a gesture for 'expung[ing] environmental otherness' and the 'radical and globally dispersed interdependence' marking contemporary life (2019: 657–8). Twenty-first-century minimalist style, that is, naturalizes a hygienic divorce between a privileged constituency and the rest of the human and nonhuman world.

In this chapter, I argue that this broader artistic heritage and these moral and political challenges are crucial for understanding Cusk's trilogy's peculiar deployment of minimalist style. Far from uncritically adopting such a posture of self-curtailment, the trilogy, I argue, gradually sheds its own drive for detoxification and purity, which Cusk's work after the trilogy will transform into a minimalism-inspired deployment of literary form to reconnect to (rather than divorce from) the world. Through a reading of *Transit*, the instalment of the trilogy that most emphatically links Cusk's signature minimalist *literary* style with minimalist *lifestyle* through the subplot of a home renovation, I show how Cusk's project in the trilogy can productively be read as dramatizing the attractions and pitfalls of minimalism. This critique mobilizes literary minimalism to connect to what Chayka identifies as a countertradition of minimalism that is less interested in reduction and control than in 'seeking unmediated experiences, giving up control instead of imposing it, paying attention […] accepting ambiguity' (2020: 221). It is Cusk's first work of fiction after the trilogy, *Second Place*, that most ambitiously activates this countertradition, even if it adopts a stylistic register that is, in many ways, the obverse of that in the trilogy. While stylistically, *Second Place* no longer qualifies as a minimalist work, it instantiates a way of mobilizing a less obsessive minimalist ethos for literary fiction that is less interested in anxious or hysterical information management than in encountering the real world.

Aspirational Austerity

Transit's opening sentence immediately announces its aesthetic of reticence and privacy: 'An astrologer emailed me to say she had important news for me concerning events in my immediate future' (Cusk 2018: 1). The news, it turns out, is only available '[f]or a small fee'; nor is it quite human: the message as well as the astrologer herself sound as if they had been generated by an algorithm. It seems, the narrator notes, as if 'the faux-human was growing more substantial and more relational than the original' (3). Cusk's opening recalls Georg Lukács' classic *Theory of the Novel*, which famously begins by celebrating 'those ages when the starry sky is the map of all possible paths – ages whose paths are illuminated by the light of the stars' (1974: 29). The modern age, of course, is no such happy age, as the 'old parallelism' between 'the form-giving subject and the world of created forms' has been destroyed (40–1). For Lukács, the novel is the genre that addresses the 'fundamental dissonance of existence' that follows from this destruction (62) – what he calls a condition of 'transcendental homelessness' (41). As a way of signalling its serious engagement with the affordances of the novel today, *Transit* takes the metaphor of homelessness literally as it develops a sustained reflection on the place of home-making and house-ownership in the novel genre's negotiation of the relation between life and form.

Early in the novel, Faye encounters Gerard, a former lover with whom she once shared a flat. The flat had been 'a big, rambling network of rooms on the upper storeys of an Edwardian villa' (Cusk 2018: 12). But not any longer: after they broke up, Gerard decided to 'knock down all the internal walls in the flat to create one enormous space' so he would be able 'to stand at the windows at one end of his flat and see all the way through the windows at the other' (35). The aesthetic Gerard aims for is that of the 'aspirational austerity' of typical minimalist condos (Chayka 2020: 57); it implements the '[m]inimalist decorative formula' of a minimal amount of clutter in an open space (61). Architectural minimalism in *Transit* promises the transparency that, in the terms of the novel's Lukácsian opening, is no longer available in the relation between the individual and the outside world. In an analogy between psychology and architecture that runs through the novel, Gerard's renovation frenzy is transparently also a mind-clearing exercise – it is a prosthetic form of psychotherapy that (in an association that the opening reference to commodified cosmic wisdom already announced) is also inevitably a sound business investment: the renovation is 'a great opportunity' (Cusk 2018: 36). Later in *Transit*, Amanda, a friend of Faye's, describes how her parents made money by serially renovating houses in order to later sell them with a profit: 'Her childhood memories were of living in houses that were effectively building sites, houses that were always in the process of transformation' (173). Twenty-first-century 'transcendental homeless', then, is always also a matter of houses being temporary occasions for debt and investment rather than anchors of stability (McClanahan 2017: 143–83).

Much of the plot of the novel is taken up by the fairly hopeless renovation project through which Faye hopes to find her footing again in London. The apartment she buys is in a former council house; the people living in the basement flat (directly exposed to the sounds of Faye's and her children's footsteps and the noise of the renovations) are the last council tenants; as such, they are not active participants in the economy of renovation and speculation. The flat's previous inhabitant, a Ghanaian woman, was: having launched her children on profitable careers in the UK, her job contributing to the aspirations of upward mobility is done, and she decides to return to Ghana (Cusk 2018: 43). Faye's renovation project is emphatically minimalist, even if only in contrast with the clutter that surrounds her: the neighbour's part of the garden is 'full of things that were all at different stages in the process of decay, so that the boundary between ornament and junk had been obscured' (37–8); Faye's apartment itself features 'shelves wobbl[ing] loose on their brackets' and walls 'covered in thick paper with a rash-like raised design' (40). This chaos and clutter requires the demolition of walls (176) and insulation – radical measures to insulate Faye's life against the smells and noises of the downstairs neighbours, who serve as insistent reminders of the economic inequality that powers the life that twenty-first-century minimalism serves to detoxify. Crucially, literary style and lifestyle reinforce one another, as Cusk's signature technique for establishing setting, which consists in describing a room by enumerating a few bare essentials, is conducive to such a minimalist design aesthetic. When a room is described as 'very warm, and furnished with things I didn't recognize from [a character's] former existence: modern, cuboid sofas; a vast glass-and-steel coffee table; a rug made of an animal's pelt' (213), the very sparsity and precision of the descriptive style exemplifies architect Philip Johnson's minimalist formula to 'pick very few objects and place them exactly' (quoted in Chayka 2020: 61).

Both through its sparse style and its thematic choices, *Transit* shows how the psychology, the economics and the aesthetics of minimalism are deeply connected; through the insistent presence of the neighbours – disabled, alcoholic, racist – it also signals minimalism's problematic exclusionary politics. The neighbours are less fully-fledged individuals than cyphers for the socioeconomic realities that minimalist aesthetics aim to hide behind its shiny and slick surfaces. Late in the novel, Faye refers to them as 'a force, a power of elemental negativity that seemed somehow related to the power to create' (Cusk 2018: 195). The lower-class neighbours are a disavowed part of an infrastructure of creativity – they are 'crouch[ing] malevolently in the psyche' as instances of evil, which the passage defines as 'the relinquishing of effort, the abandonment of self-discipline in the face of desire' (195–6). The ethos that the novel (self-critically) proposes against such careless indulgence is that of a deliberate self-restraint and rigorous self-control – an ethos embodied in the trilogy's trimmed style and the minimalist visual aesthetic it evokes in its spatial descriptions (as when a hair salon is described as 'a lofty, white, brilliantly lit room with white-painted floorboards and baroque, velvet-upholstered furniture' (61)). By consistently emphasizing the tension between this clean aesthetic and the disorderly lives of the neighbours, the novel qualifies its own investment in minimalism as a way of managing repression – as part of a psychological dynamic different from that of hysteria. It is no coincidence that Chayka refers to Marie Kondo, the icon of contemporary decluttering, as a Freudian who teaches audiences to confront 'repressed feelings in the form of hidden mountains of clothes, papers, and books' (2020: 34).

Clothes, papers and books: these kinds of 'excess stuff' can be disposed of, but neighbours can't (and least of all when they are council tenants). If Cusk's novel evokes and performs the attractions of minimalism, by so emphatically including the stubborn reality of the neighbours, it at the same time scrutinizes the exclusions that this style is designed to render invisible. In Dango's analysis of minimalism's practice of detoxification, he show how minimalism's aesthetic of constraint and reduction performs an exclusion of undesirable realities – environmental threats, but also social forces that threaten the homogeneity of a dominant identity (2019: 647); minimalism, on this account, is 'a practice of detoxification that reorients and creates a space in which multiple kinds of perceived toxicity [...] are conflated and then, fantastically, eliminated' (2019: 646). By interrupting the composure of the novel with the smells, sounds and vibes of the neighbours, *Transit* foregrounds this eliminative dimension of its own aesthetic and shows it to be deeply problematic. Its performance of minimalism is a self-critical one.

In *Transit*, the house is simultaneously an allegory of mental space and an economic investment; in that way, it is inevitably implicated in the complexities of global life that it seeks to offer a refuge from. Dango emphasizes that minimalism is unsettled by 'a continued anxiety' about global interdependence (2019: 658); Chayka notes that minimalism's slick design 'encourages us to forget everything a product relies on', while in fact, minimalist life relies on a 'maximalist assemblage' of globally interdependent forces and infrastructures (2020: 43). In *Transit*, this assemblage materializes as the lead contractor taking on the renovation project, on whose work and judgement Faye finds herself to be fully dependent. The contractor notes how he is often reduced to a contraption in his clients' mental ecology – he feels like 'the representative of someone else's aims and desire', like 'an extension of [people's] own will' (Cusk 2018: 49, 53). The novel links the contractor to the clutter and confusion it associates with the lower-class neighbours when the contractor opens the door of his van and Faye sees it is 'full of empty cardboard coffee cups and discarded food packaging and scraps of paper' (58). For the contractor, as a mere cog in the wheel of global capitalism, minimalist decluttering is an unattainable aspiration: 'if it was up to me, increasingly I imagine living somewhere completely blank, somewhere where all the angles are straight and the corners squared and where there's nothing, no colours or features, maybe not even any light' (55). Here also, by showing how the attainability of the aspiration of minimalism is dependent on class and citizenship, *Transit* checks the privilege it performs.⁶

Minimalist Contraction and the Great Outdoors

Transit not only engages with contemporary minimalist design, it also directly refers to the twentieth-century minimalist artistic tradition. The lead contractor's fantasy of featureless living is not even the most minimalist fantasy in the novel: Pavel, one of his aides, explains how he has built a house in the woods for himself in Poland with 'enormous windows' that stretch 'from the ceiling to the floor': 'the forest was so visible that you almost felt you were living in the open air' (Cusk 2018: 180). The aide notes that his 'transparent box' is inspired by 'a house in America' that 'was made almost entirely of glass' (181–2). The reference is clearly to architect Philip Johnson's Glass House, which he constructed in Connecticut in the years following the Second World War. Customarily considered a minimalist masterpiece, the Glass House is a one-floor pavilion marked by principled transparency and ruthless economy in furnishing a liveable space – including a living room, a kitchen, a bedroom, a bathroom – that offers an uninterrupted 360-degree view of the surrounding landscape. Just like Pavel's house, the house is designed 'so that in certain places you could see all the way through it, out into the forest on the other side' (182). As Chayka notes, '[t]he Glass House turns interior and exterior into meaningless terms. The walls don't do the work of obscuring what's inside, nor do they keep anything external out' (2020: 65).

Isn't there a contradiction between minimalism's relentless expunction of 'environmental otherness' (Dango 2019: 657) and the Glass House's erosion of the borders between inside and outside? This contradiction is only apparent when we realize that the surroundings of the Glass House were nothing like 'environmental otherness' – they were simply Johnson's estate, on which he continued to build other constructions and which he carefully rendered invisible from the street and the gaze of others. The landscape, in Johnson's own words, is simply 'expensive wallpaper'. Once we appreciate the Glass House's location on a

---

⁶ *Transit*'s representation of the downstairs neighbours is one the main exhibits in Sally Rooney's argument that Cusk's trilogy simply acts out its 'revulsion' at lower-class life (Rooney: 2018: n.p.). My argument aims to demonstrate that a more generous reading of *Transit* reveals an entirely more conflicted politics than the self-righteous embodiment of bourgeois values that Rooney (and with her, many other readers) finds in it.

carefully controlled estate, minimalism again emerges as a gesture of exclusion and control; Johnson's minimalism is a moralized performance of living with less that aspires to be admired without surrendering control. It testifies to what Chayka calls a 'megalomaniacal possessiveness' (2020: 68).

Transit's encrypted reference to the Glass House continues its critique of minimalism's disavowed moralization and class politics. Pavel's Polish glass house is not situated on an estate – it is situated in the woods, exposed to passers-by, which draws his father's ridicule, as he goes about town 'telling people that if they went out to the forest, they could stand there and watch Pavel shitting' (Cusk 2018: 183). The idea that transparency without possession leads to vulnerability also inflects the real estate trajectory of Gerard, Faye's former lover. He recalls a time living in a community of artists in Toronto in a house that 'had once been a shop and the large glass shopfront had been retained, so that the inhabitants could be viewed from the outside' (26). Gerard reflects that living on this 'illuminated stage,' in these 'human tableaux,' would be unthinkable in London because '[t]here's too much irony [...] everything is already an imitation of itself' (26).[7] This fateful theatricality also afflicts Faye when she walks by the hair salon at night and observes how '[f]rom the darkness of the street it was almost like a theatre, with the characters moving around in the bright light of the stage' (75). *Transit*'s encrypted deconstruction of the Glass House is concluded when a boy leaving the salon accidentally throws the 'big glass door' against 'the tiers of glass shelving where the haircare products stood,' which then 'collapse [...] in a tremendous shrieking cascade of breaking glass' (81).

Minimalism, for all its attractions, is untenable in a social world where ethnic and economic difference cannot simply be drowned out but need to be confronted and accommodated. I have elsewhere analysed *Outline*, the first volume of Cusk's trilogy, as a feminist gesture of rationing affect that refuses readers, in David James's words, 'the conventional gratifications of empathetic identification' (2021: 138). *Outline* is situated in Greece, the battle zone of the Eurozone's austerity dictates in the second decade of the century, and Cusk's narrator's affective and communicative austerity can be seen to repurpose imposed austerity into a strategy of refusal (Vermeulen 2021). *Transit*'s narrator is less rigorously self-effacing, and this goes even more for the narrator of *Kudos*.

---

[7] Gerard's claim about London life was exposed to an empirical test it did not survive when owners of luxury flats with floor to ceiling windows near Tate Modern lost a privacy case complaining that one of the museum's popular top-floor terraces exposed them to near constant surveillance in 2019. According to the law, living in 'human tableaux' in London is possible after all.

I suggest we read this careful loosening of narrative restraint over the span of the trilogy as a gentle self-critique – as the reflex of a growing awareness of the problematic politics of the first novel's programmatic minimalism. I have been arguing that *Transit* channels that self-critique through an engagement with different dimensions of minimalist art and lifestyle. Indeed, *Transit*'s narrator comes close to saying as much when she connects her changed attitude to the home renovation project – the event that activates the book's more conscious engagement with the aesthetics of minimalism. Late in the novel, the narrator remarks that she has come to appreciate the limits of a way of living 'as though living were merely an act of reading', as though life were 'something that had already been dictated'; this way of living as if 'it was only through absolute passivity that you could learn to see what was really there' recalls nothing so much as the mode of narration that *Outline* sustains, but that *Transit* modifies because the narrator's 'decision to create a disturbance by renovating [her] house [awakes] a different reality' – a reality marked by complex negotiations of power and desire (Cusk 2018: 198). The narrator can no longer hide in her own stylistic glass house, impotent and passive, as she has realized that she is not protected by a safe estate around it but exposed to a world that does not cease to intrude. *Transit*'s explicit engagement with the valances of minimalism, I argue, repositions the narrative austerities of *Outline* in a field of power and exclusion where stylistic choices, whether literary or existential, have a political import. If this 'different reality' was rigorously bracketed in *Outline*, *Transit*'s more self-critical minimalism more consciously acknowledges it. It will fall to Cusk's post-trilogy work to give that desire for reality a less minimalist and more determinate shape.

Minimalist Depth

Cusk's self-critique of minimalism still resonates in the first novel she published after the trilogy. While *Second Place* stylistically no longer counts as a work of minimalism, it promotes a position that, I argue, can still productively be linked to the minimalist tradition. From its long, sprawling, and excessively metaphorical opening sentence (which exuberantly refers to an evil 'that rose up and disgorged itself over every part of life'; Cusk 2021: 1), the novel announces its stylistic difference from the trilogy. The novel is set up as a long letter to a person named Jeffers, and this positions the narrator in the monological position (speaking without response) into which the narrative set-up of *Outline* forced Faye's interlocutors; this device exposes her as oversharing, affected, and fairly obnoxious and self-obsessed, an assessment from which the trilogy's stylistic minimalism shielded Faye. The event that kickstarts the narrative (about the narrator and her husband inviting L, a famous but erratic painter, to stay with them 'on the marsh'; (4)), the narrator feeling 'summon[ed]' by a painting during an exhibition in Paris (11), echoes a very similar event that was attributed to Jane, one of Faye's interlocutors in *Transit* (Cusk 2018: 142). This underscores the impression that the more recent novel is narrated by someone very much like Faye's interlocutors – and this time with Jeffers as the self-effacing mediator. Clearly, this exposure of an oversharing character is not an instance of minimalist style.

Nor is the narrator's disposition a minimalist one, as the novel tells us by featuring another home renovation project (which again underscores that *Second Place* consciously revises the trilogy). The title, while also signalling the struggle for primacy and secrecy that the novels' narrative mode dramatizes, refers to a renovated cottage close to the narrator's house. The cottage is conceived as a site of creativity and art: it is to be used 'as a home for the thing which weren't already here – the higher things,' to establish 'some degree of communication [...] with the notion of art and with the people who abide by these notions' (Cusk 2021: 22–3). For the narrator's husband, who is in charge of the renovation, that assignment requires something very much like the minimalist aesthetics we discussed before: the renovated cottage features windows 'from the floor to the ceiling,' which allows the suggestion that 'the huge horizontal bar of the marsh and its drama' is 'right there in the room with you' (24). The narrator, however, objects to this minimalism: she does not want the place to feel 'all clinical and squared off in the way that some new places feel,' and this involves hanging up 'beautiful curtains made of a thick pale linen' (26). For the narrator, privacy trumps transparency – as if the tenuous balancing act between exposure and performance dramatized in *Transit* can simply be neutralized and overcome.

The narrator's impatience with minimalism resonates with the novel's more maximalist – indeed, more self-consciously hysterical – narrative mode; both complement the self-critique of minimalism that overtook the trilogy. Still, the fate of the cottage hints at something more interesting than a mere renunciation of minimalism. The curtains are not appreciated by L's young girlfriend, who, to the narrator's dismay, refers to the place as 'a cabin in the woods, straight out of a horror story' (Cusk 2021: 57); soon the narrator finds that the curtains are removed because, for L, they obstruct the traffic between inside and outside

(102–3). The narrator's next visit to the cottage reveals that the furniture has been moved around, that L and his girlfriend are dancing around almost naked, and that they have begun to paint on the walls – a kind of 'hellish' Garden of Eden (160–1). The place has now truly become a site of creativity – even if this means that the walls have been repurposed as canvases, not unlike the way the windows in Johnson's Glass House were reassigned as expensive wallpaper. Opening the curtains restores the relation between inside and outside and reconfigures the relation between life and form.

In his study of minimalism, Dango qualifies it as typically an 'obsessive' style for dealing with the fear of losing control. One problem with this obsession, he notes, is a 'phobia of nature' and a concomitant 'need for "containment"' (Dango 2021: 104). Dango notes how there is a countertradition of minimalism, consisting of Ernest Hemingway rather than Raymond Carver (in literature), John Cage rather than Steve Reich (in music), and van der Rohe and Corbusier rather than John Pawson (in architecture), that deployed minimalist techniques not to expunge but to open human forms up to nature; for these 'deeper' minimalists (the term is Chayka's), style is 'a practice of conservation, housing natural environments or sublimating the human or created work into natural proxies' (Dango 2021: 105). Chayka, also, points to Cage's 4'33" as a work that constitutes less an escape from contingency and environment than 'a kind of conditioning for heightened awareness' (2020: 146); he also points to Case Study House #8, the L.A. house where modernist designers Charles and Ray Eames lived for most of their lives, as a less totalitarian and obsessive and ultimately less superficial kind of minimalism than that on display in Johnson's Glass House. In Case Study House #8, the Mondrian-inspired geometrical panels and panes of glass reflect a fundamental openness to difference and contingency; unlike the Glass House, it is not surrounded by the architect's property, but by a meadow occupied by three other Case Study Houses; with its driftwood, colourful paintings, bird sculptures and rice-paper lanterns, the main living area is 'crowded and haphazardly curated', 'an eclectic symphony of sights and reference points' (Chayka 2020: 45–6), rather than a display of austere limitation. In this way, Chayka notes, the house emblematizes 'the appreciation of things for and in themselves, and the removal of barriers between the self and the world' (46). It does not seem too far-fetched to see L in *Second Place* redesigning the cottage as a site for such a deep minimalist attunement between inner and outer realities – for the valorisation of a range of objects and experiences that the twenty-first-century shift from literary maximalism to minimalism might seem to have relegated from the remit of the novel and that *Second Place*, I argue, is allowing back in. This is not a simple return to maximalism, but a trajectory *through* minimalism that aims to overcome its obsessiveness from within.

The novel's narrator does not simply accept L's invitation for a less obsessive and more welcoming minimalism. She feels tempted to bury the mural 'beneath layers of whitewash', but realizes that that would turn the cottage into a fake, as it would amount to 'a betrayal of the truth of memory' (Cusk 2021: 168). Near the end of the novel, when the painter has left the cottage after a turbulent stay, the mural is painted over after all, the curtains are rehung, but without totally obliterating the memory of art, as she offers the cottage to her daughter who put the painting that L gave her in there – as a kind of sublimation of the mural that overwhelmed the space. That painting, one of a series of night paintings completed while L was staying in the second place, evokes the tension between 'two half-forms', which, to the narrator's mind, might represent herself and her daughter on the night L caught them swimming (206). Or perhaps not. What is key, it seems, is the restored tension between self and thing, between inside and outside, between life and form; this restoration is achieved by abandoning obsessive self-curtailment and an almost gimmicky insistence on simplicity *without* abandoning a minimalist commitment to the importance of style as mediation of the outside world. Such a commitment to style, it seems, is the ethic and aesthetic that *Second Place* puts forward as a less compromised minimalist gesture than the one the trilogy gradually shed.

Conclusion: Raising the Curtain on Minimalism

The development of twenty-first-century fiction so far can reductively be described as a shift from an inclusive and hysterical maximalism to an austere minimalism. This essay has argued that in the work of Cusk, that minimalism has performed a self-critique that has moved it from (what in retrospect appears to be) a potentially obsessive and exclusionary minimalism to a more worldly minimalism that restores and refines some of the connections to the outside world that an overly austere minimalism had renounced. And perhaps this looser minimalism is not confined to the work of Cusk alone. One of the oeuvres that Chayka puts forward as an example of a deeper minimalism is that of Donald Judd, whose name is customarily identified with sculptural minimalism (even if he himself, like many minimalists, renounced the label). Judd's steel boxes and polished rectangles have become almost synonymous with minimalism's refusal of intention, symbolism and emotion – with what critic

Michael Fried influentially condemned as its literalism and mere objecthood. For Fried, minimalism's theatricality – its explicit concern with 'the actual circumstances in which the beholder encounters literalist work' (1998: 153) – famously disqualifies it as art ('the literalist espousal of objecthood amounts to nothing other than a plea for a new genre of theater, and theater is now the negation of art' (153)). Rather than withdrawing from the audience and folding back on its own intention, the minimalist work, for Fried, assures that '[e]verything counts – not as part of the object, but as part of the situation in which its objecthood is established and on which that objecthood at least partly depends' (155). Judd's work, for Fried, is marked by a fateful combination of concentration and worldly connectedness.

In light of Cusk's minimalist self-critique, this combination of concentration and connection appears as a strength. As Chayka notes in his book, Judd famously relocated from New York to Marfa, which he turned 'into his own artistic laboratory and a shrine to his entire career' (2020: 95). This location, which feature hangars' full of seemingly random stuff, drives home the essential worldliness of Judd's seemingly austere objects: '[t]he whole place was a machine for finding inspiration and making art – the objects [...] were challenging, shocking, and discomfiting as well, reminders of the wider world outside' (96). While Cusk's work does not explicitly engage with Judd's, the fact that her negotiation of minimalism operates through the hanging, opening, closing, removing and rehanging of curtains at least hints at the implication of a deeper minimalism with theatricality; a deeper minimalism, it seems, is one that self-consciously opens and closes its window on the world. That her trilogy as well as *Second Place* so clearly operate through forms of address (giving the floor to a series of interlocutors in the trilogy; performing an almost dramatic monologue-like letter in *Second Place*) that include the reader in a 'circuit of storytellers, narrators, readers, friends, sisters, and neighbours' (Valihora 2019: 30) qualifies her work as an oeuvre that, like Judd's work, makes the reader part of the situation in which the works is constituted. As Marc Botha notes in his *Theory of Minimalism*, '[m]inimalist narrative time is marked by a strong sense of immanence, drawing both narrator and reader onto what appears to be a common ground' (2017: 51). Cusk's programme is then also minimalist in the sense articulated by Judd and (albeit critically) Fried.

Cusk's work shares this combination of autofictional concentration and readerly address with Ben Lerner's *10:04* – a work that is increasingly being elevated in literary criticism as a key reference in the recent ascendence of autofiction. Like Cusk's work, *10:04* is limited to the perspective of one author-character, but it uses that limitation to explore a promiscuous range of worldly connections. It also features an excursion to Marfa, where Lerner's novelistic stand-in spends a residency. His initial response is not positive: 'The work of [Judd] I'd seen – always in museums or small gallery installations – had left me cold' (Lerner 2014: 178). But seeing the work in Marfa changes everything, as the objects stop being things one might as well encounter 'by walking through a Costco or a Home Depot or IKEA' (178), and become objects that, while being 'located in the immediate, physical present,' are also 'tuned to an inhuman, geological duration' (180). The objects offer an encounter with 'all those orders of temporality – the biological, the historical, the geological' (180). Minimalism, then, emerges as a site of worldly connection. Neither 'hysterical' nor obsessive, this simultaneous refusal of both maximalism and principled austerity might open up the bandwidth within which contemporary literature might yet overcome its autofictional renunciations.

Works Cited

Bentley, N. (2015), 'Rewriting National Identities in 1990s British Fiction', in N. Hubble, P. Tew and L. Wilson (eds), *The 1990s: A Decade of Contemporary British Fiction*, 67–94. London: Bloomsbury Academic.

Botha, M. (2017), *A Theory of Minimalism*. London: Bloomsbury Academic.

Chabon, M. (2000), *The Amazing Adventures of Kavalier & Clay*. New York: Random House.

Chayka, K. (2020), *The Longing for Less: Living with Minimalism*. London: Bloomsbury.

Cusk, R. ([2016] 2018), *Transit*. London: Faber & Faber.

Cusk, R. (2021), *Second Place*. London: Faber & Faber.

Dango, M. (2019), 'Minimalism as Detoxification', *Modern Fiction Studies*, 65 (4): 643–75.

Dango, M. (2021), *Crisis Style: The Aesthetics of Repair*. Stanford: Stanford University Press.

De Boever, A. (2019), 'What is "the" Neoliberal Novel? Neoliberalism, Finance, and Biopolitics', in S. Baumbach and B. Neumann (eds), *New Approaches to the Twenty-First-Century Anglophone Novel*, 157–74. Cham: Palgrave Macmillan.

Doherty, M. (2014), 'State-Funded Fiction: Minimalism, National Memory, and the Return to Realism in the Post-Postmodern Age', *American Literary History*, 27 (1): 79–101.

Ercolino, S. (2014), *The Maximalist Novel: From Thomas Pynchon's* Gravity's Rainbow *to Roberto Bolaño's* 2666. London: Bloomsbury Academic.

Fried, M. (1998), 'Art and Objecthood', in *Art and Objecthood: Essays and Reviews*, 148–72. Chicago: University of Chicago Press.

Hoberek, A. (2010), 'Foreign Objects, or, DeLillo Minimalist', *Studies in American Fiction*, 37 (1): 101–25.

James, D. (2021), 'Affect's Vocabularies: Literature and Feeling after 1890', in D. Mao (ed.), *The New Modernist Studies*, 129–51. New York: Cambridge University Press.

Jones, S. (2020), 'Minimalism's Attention Deficit: Distraction, Description, and Mary Robison's *Why Did I Ever*', *American Literary History*, 32 (2): 301–27.

Konstantinou, L. (2021), 'Autofiction and Autoreification', *The Habit of Tlön*, 6 February. Available at: https://www.leekonstantinou.com/2021/02/06/autofiction-and-autoreification/

Lerner, B. (2014), *10:04*. London: Granta.

Levey, N. (2017), *Maximalism in Contemporary American Literature: The Uses of Detail*. Abingdon: Routledge.

Lorentzen, C. (2021), 'The Vying Animal: The Life of Philip Roth and the Art of Literary Survival', *Bookforum.com*, March. Available at: https://www.bookforum.com/print/2801/the-life-of-philip-roth-and-the-art-of-literary-survival-24390.

Lukács, G. (1974), *The Theory of the Novel*. Cambridge, MA: MIT Press.

McClanahan, A. (2017), *Dead Pledges: Debt, Crisis, and Twenty-First-Century Culture*. Stanford: Stanford University Press.

McGurl, M. (2011), *The Program Era: Postwar Fiction and the Rise of Creative Writing*. Cambridge, MA: Harvard University Press.

McGurl, M. (2015), 'The Novel's Forking Path', *Public Books*, 4 January. Available at: https://www.publicbooks.org/the-novels-forking-path/

McGurl, M. (2021), *Everything and Less: The Novel in the Age of Amazon*. London: Verso.

Rooney, S. (2018), 'Buried in Bourgeois Life', *Slate.com*, 25 May. Available at: https://slate.com/culture/2018/05/rachel-cusks-kudos-reviewed-by-sally-rooney.html.

Smith, Z. (2000), *White Teeth*. New York: Vintage.

Tew, P. (2010), *Zadie Smith*. London: Palgrave Macmillan.

Valihora, K. (2019), 'She Got Up and Went Away: Rachel Cusk on Making an Exit', *ESC: English Studies in Canada* 45 (1–2): 19–35.

Van De Ven, I. (2019), *Big Books in Times of Big Data*. Leiden: Leiden University Press.

Vermeulen, P. (2018), 'The 1990s', in P. Boxall (ed.), *The Cambridge Companion to British Fiction 1980–The Present*, 32–46. Cambridge: Cambridge University Press.

Vermeulen, P. (2021). 'Against Premature Articulation: Gender, Empathy, and Austerity in Rachel Cusk and Katie Kitamura', *Cultural Critique* 111: 81–103.

Wasserman, S. (2022), 'Critical Darlings, Critical Dogs: Joseph O'Neill and What Contemporary Criticism Doesn't Want', *American Literary History* 34 (2): 561–85.

Wegner, P. (2009), *Life Between Two Deaths, 1989–2001: U.S. Culture in the Long Nineties*. Durham: Duke University Press.

Wood, J. (2000), 'Human, All Too Inhuman', *The New Republic*, 24 July. Available at: https://newrepublic.com/article/61361/human-inhuman

2

Mother Courage and Mother Shaming

Rachel Cusk's Contribution to Maternal Feminism

Roberta Garrett

In the foreword to this edition, Clare Hanson notes the 'formal and stylistic shifts in Cusk's writing, which are deftly related to the far-reaching socio-cultural and philosophical transitions of the last thirty years'. As many of the chapters in this book demonstrate, Cusk's status as a distinguished stylist is now widely recognized. Cusk's fiction and creative non-fiction has been described as neo-modernist in approach (Ophir 2022) as it focuses on the rendering of consciousness and eschews the interiority and theory-led self-reflexivity of the previous generation of (postmodernist) writers' experiments in style and form. In Cusk's work, style is always aligned to the investigation of the subject's relation to ethical, moral and ontological questions. This gives it the monumental, timeless quality that we ascribe to canonical modernist writers. But like the work of Lawrence, Woolf, Kafka and other key influences, Cusk's novels and creative non-fictions are also highly attuned to the way in which ontological and ethical questions are refracted through socio-political ideologies of gender, class and nation.

It is these latter issues that will be explored in this chapter. More specifically, the chapter will examine Cusk's engagement with the public discourse of good motherhood and how this continues to restrict women and bolster other forms of prejudice and oppression. Fictional and autobiographical works that express the view that socially validated conceptions of motherhood can be oppressive to women are not a recent phenomenon: this has been a key theme in women's writing from the nineteenth century onwards. However, the chapter argues that Cusk's sharp-sighted observations on the policing of maternal and female identities does important feminist work in exposing the contradictions and 'normative cruelties'[1]

---

[1] I'm drawing here on Jessica Ringrose and Emma Renold's research on school bullying cultures which enforce gender normativity but it also applies to the treatment of adult women, particularly those who are mothers.

associated with this discourse at a moment in which it takes on a particularly insidious form.

Cusk in Context: Parenting Discourse in the Noughties

The domestic and maternal have been a key focus of interest throughout Cusk's work, but the fictional and non-fictional texts which take the deepest dive into these areas were written in the early to mid-noughties: *A Life's Work: On Becoming a Mother* in 2001, *The Lucky Ones* (2006) and *Arlington Park* (2006). As her autobiographical work demonstrates, Cusk's thematic concern with these areas was fuelled by her own experience of raising children throughout her thirties and forties. It was also part of a more widespread renewal of interest in the domestic and the maternal by female writers that occurred in the latter years of the twentieth century.

In broad terms, much celebrated contemporary women's writing from the late seventies to early nineties tended towards the production of either counter-histories and mythological metafictions (Angela Carter, Toni Morrison, Anita Desai, A. S Byatt, Jeannette Winterson) or the rewriting of traditional male genres through a female lens (such as science fiction or the hard-boiled crime novel).[2] As the literary and critical preference for postmodernist fiction waned, new cycles and forms appeared that interrogated late twentieth and early twenty-first century Western models of domestic life and maternal behaviour across the high/low literary spectrum. These included comic mum's lit, the dysfunctional family novel, domestic noir, the childhood trauma autobiography (sometimes referred to as the misery memoir) and the maternal memoir (Garrett 2021: 4–20). The emergence of these forms and cycles was, at least in part, a response to an increasingly heavy-handed and intrusive state and media approach to parenting issues in the UK and US. In the UK, this began in earnest in the early 1990s with Tory attacks on teenage single mothers (Fox Harding 1999), but it was continued in more subtle ways by the centre-left New Labour government, elected in 1997. New Labour were less censorious towards non-traditional families but were no less concerned with policing parental behaviour. In line with more general shifts towards neoliberal socio-political culture in Western countries, their intention to clamp down on teenage anti-social behaviour and their oft-repeated mantra of 'education, education, education' as a means of social mobility, held failing parents accountable for a variety of social ills – such

---

[2] My 2021 monograph contains a much more detailed analysis of these cycles.

as poverty, educational inequality and crime – that might otherwise have been viewed as the responsibility of the state (Gillies 2006: 6–10; Jensen 2018: 74–83).

This coincided with an explosion of cheap reality television shows that shamed incompetent parents, a vast expansion of parenting manuals and the emergence of internet parenting sites. As many sociologists and cultural critics have argued, much of this advice was condescending or critical (Furedi 2001: 175–90; Bristow 2009; Jensen 2018: 53–72). Faux-scientific ideas derived from dubious scientific evidence, such as 'infant determinism' i.e. the belief that the quality of parenting in the first three years determines brain development and the emotional well-being and academic success of the child throughout their lifetime, were widely reported in the media (Guldberg 2009: 129–47; Macvarish, Lowe and Lee 2016). The gender-neutral term 'parenting' became more widespread, but the intense state and media interest in the quality of British parenting and its potential consequences and social outcomes weighed far more heavily on mothers (Jensen 2018: 78–9; Glaser 2021: 14–15; Orgad 2019: 63–71). The discourse on fathers hailed the *perceived* increase in 'hands-on' fathers and celebrated their contribution to parenting and household tasks, while mothers were subject to an expanding list of regulations concerning their behaviour and its potential effect on their offspring. As feminist critics have argued, the cultural bias of the moment was clearly in favour 'natural' childcare practices and round-the-clock 'intensive' motherhood (Hays 1996: 8; Douglas and Michaels 2004: 2–27; Badinter 2011). This was presented as compatible with a modernizing, progressive centre-left agenda as it was justified on behalf of the welfare of what Zelizer refers to as 'the priceless child' (1985: 57) and the government preoccupation with child safety and raising educational outcomes, rather than a belief in female subordination to male authority within the domestic realm.

As mentioned above, the late 1990s/early 2000s cluster of maternal memoirs, *Life After Birth* (Kate Figes 1997), *Misconceptions* (Naomi Wolf 2001), *Making Babies* (Ann Enright 2004), *Love Works Like This* (Lauren Slater 2003) and Cusk's *A Life's Work* (2001) emerged as a response to this discourse. Given the context described above, it is not difficult to see the factors that precipitated their production. All were published by novelists and academics, such as Cusk, who had been raised with the benefits of higher education and a relative degree of autonomy. By the 1990s, mainstream media representations of women had begun to accept, and even promote, female empowerment and independence (albeit mainly in terms of consumerism) but this discourse was largely targeted at young, childless, single women (McRobbie 2007). It did not extend to mothers, who became the target of a state and media campaign to call out sloppy and neglectful parenting. It is not the purpose of this chapter to compare these memoirs, as they all contributed to the re-emergence of feminist writing on motherhood. However, Cusk's work, which combines cultural commentary, literary analysis and subjective experience, received the most praise and the most vitriolic criticism.

In the longer term, it has been widely accepted as a landmark text on modern motherhood. It has been promoted as an enlightening text for expectant mothers on the National Childbirth Trust website for some years now and was awarded sixteenth place in the *New York Times* list of fifty best memoirs. More significantly, in the last fifteen years, there has been an explosion of popular feminist and academic texts addressing the themes raised by Cusk, such as the continuation of gendered inequalities in parenting culture and the socio-political desire to police and criticize mothers (Douglas and Michaels 2004; Warner 2006; Asher 2011; Badinter 2013; Rose 2018; Orgad 2019; Lockman 2019; Agarwal 2021; Glaser 2021; Brearley 2021). With the exception of Sharon Hays' *The Cultural Contradictions of Modern Motherhood* (1996) these were all published after Cusk's controversial and widely circulated memoir. Cusk's publication of *A Life's Work: Becoming a Mother* was therefore a significant step in bringing maternal experience back into the mainstream of contemporary feminist debate.

It begins with observations that leave no doubt as to the feminist-materialist frame in which the memoir is constructed:

> The issue of children and who looks after them has become, in my view, profoundly political [...] It is well known that in couples where both parents work full-time, the mother generally does far more than her fair share of housework and childcare, and is the one to curtail her working day in order to meet the exigencies of parenthood.
>
> Cusk 2008: 11

Later in the introduction she states that,

> Looking after children is a low-status occupation. It is isolating, frequently boring, relentlessly demanding and exhausting. It erodes your self-esteem and your membership of adult world. (13–14)

And concludes that:

> childbirth and motherhood are the anvil upon which sexual inequality was forged, and the women in our society whose responsibilities, expectations are like those of men, are right to approach it with trepidation. (15)

Twenty years later, in the aftermath of #me too, fourth wave feminism and the publication of the many popular feminist texts on motherhood listed above, Cusk's statements don't appear particularly controversial or provocative.

However, in the context of the early noughties, she was kicking against a state and media preoccupation with child welfare that regarded mothers with the utmost suspicion.

As critics such as Rosalind Gill and Angela McRobbie demonstrated, the popular noughties discourse of 'post-feminism' also consigned 'angry' critiques of gender roles to a prior moment of confrontational feminist politics (Brunsdon 2005; Gill 2017; McRobbie 2007). This was deemed dated and unnecessary, as the mainstream view was that women had succeeded in obtaining equality in education and the workplace and men were now fully engaged with childcare and domestic labour. If modern mothers embraced domesticity and scaled down their careers, in mainstream culture this was viewed as a positive choice rather than a necessity due to continuing workplace prejudice and lack of childcare support from fathers (Hakim 2001). Unfortunately, the resolutely upbeat noughties equality discourse existed in marked contradiction to all available data produced at the time. The statistical evidence showed very clearly that while an increasing percentage of women with young children were returning to the workforce after becoming mothers, their careers stalled, pay dropped and – crucially – they were still shouldering the majority of childcare and housework responsibilities (Garrett 2017: 121–53)

By drawing attention to uncomfortable truths, Cusk pierced the continued 'conspiracy of silence' around the realities of what has been more recently termed 'the motherhood penalty' (Brearley 2021) and highlighted the void between the public discourse of gender equality and the lived experience of pregnant women and mothers. *A Life's Work* then moves from the broader socio-historical story to a more specific analysis of the structures of state care that patronize and dehumanize women at a time when they are undergoing profound physical change. Cusk draws attention to the direct 'policing' of pregnant bodies in the US through prosecutions and custodial sentences for drug and alcohol consumption and wonders 'how the body can become public space, like a telephone box, and can vandalise itself' (Cusk 2001: 35) In her chapter on pregnancy, '40 Weeks', she analyses the more subtle and oblique forms of control and judgement that pregnant women are still routinely subject to by doctors, midwives and health visitors in the UK. When asked if she has been given a copy of a particularly patronizing handbook doled out to all pregnant women entitled *Emma's Diary*, Cusk pithily comments that, 'it is patently not a reference to Jane Austen' (30). She continues to highlight the gulf between the level of intelligence normally assumed of any reasonably educated young woman in the noughties and the mode of address adopted towards expectant mothers in NHS approved material and satirizes the tension between the superficially 'chummy', cosy, feminine address of such texts and their tendency to deliberately fuel anxiety and guilt:

> Like a bad parent, the literature of pregnancy bristles with threats and promise of reprisal, with ghoulish hints at the consequences of thoughtless actions [...] Eat blue cheese and your baby will get listeria, a silent and symptomless disease that will nonetheless leave your baby hideously deformed [...] don't use saunas, have hot baths, or for that matter don't wear a jersey at any point in pregnancy lest your baby be hideously deformed. Don't drink or smoke, you murderer.
>
> Cusk 2008: 35

Cusk notes that the approved NHS handbook presents 'Emma', the fictitious expectant 'mum-to-be' as a white, married, age-appropriate woman, whose every thought echoes the diktats of midwives, health visitors and doctors. She also highlights the text's tendency to reinforce sexist and racist attitudes about 'good' motherhood and functional and dysfunctional relationships by presenting unmarried couples as prone to conflict, black fathers as lazy and chauvinistic and only married white fathers as willing participants in domestic labour and childcare:

> She has two friends, both of whom are also pregnant. The first is an unmarried good time girl with a wavering boyfriend. The second is an older black woman with an unreconstructed husband and two daughters [...] Emma reports that her unmarried friend is arguing a lot with her boyfriend. I'm so glad Peter and I don't do that! Her other friend's husband, meanwhile, is copping off the childcare. I'm so glad Peter and I have agreed to share everything equally!
>
> Cusk 2008: 32

The most vitriolic reviews of Cusk's book were produced by female lifestyle columnists, such as India Knight and Gill Hornby, in right-wing newspapers that endorsed precisely the kind of racist, sexist, heteronormative assumptions about family life and motherhood that Cusk is critiquing. India Knight wrote that:

> Cusk's book is a timely manifestation of all that is wretched about grotesquely self-obsessed about modern parenting ... Frankly, you are a self-obsessed bore, the epitome of the 'me! me! me!' attitude you despise in little children.
>
> Knight 2001

While Gill Hornby, suggests that:

> if everyone were to read this, the propagation of the human race would virtually cease, which would be a shame. Because, believe it or not, quite a few people enjoy motherhood. But, in order to do so, it is important to grow up first.
>
> Hornby 2001

That such vicious personal attacks (which refuse to engage with either Cusk's socio-political arguments or her complex account of her own experience of pregnancy and early motherhood) were published in mainstream newspapers, tells us much about the prevailing anti-feminist currents of the period. Hornby and Knight are also both writers of 'comic' mum's lit novels: a conservative sub-cycle of popular women's fiction that depicts mothers of young children as naturally bitchy and competitive and assiduously avoids any references to workplace prejudice, lack of engagement by fathers or the socio-cultural demands placed on mothers (Garrett 2013; 2021: 45–69).[3]

After being directly accused of narcissism and even child cruelty – for merely stating that she spent a lot of time in her kitchen when her daughter was learning to walk – Cusk continued to explore the relationship between gender, class, motherhood and patriarchy from the more distanced perspective of her fictional work. However, rather than retreating from the feminist-materialist critique of contemporary parenting norms that frames *A Life's Work*, the wider cast of characters in *The Lucky Ones*, published two years later, allows for a fuller exploration of parenthood and childrearing from a range of socio-cultural and psychological perspectives.

Although not as experimental as her later *Outline Trilogy* (discussed in this volume by Pieter Vermeulen, Melissa Schuh and Daniel Lea), Cusk breaks with the conventional novel form as *The Lucky Ones* comprises five chapters that also work as standalone short stories. Minor characters from one story appear as major characters in the next and the final chapter loops back to themes and characters in the first chapter. The novel is both an analysis of the gendered experience of modern parenting and a millennium 'condition of England' piece. Its broad social critique is made possible by the wider range of characters allowed through the construction of semi-independent narratives and different story worlds. *The Lucky Ones* examines parenting from the point of view of a young, incarcerated pregnant woman, a new father, a childless woman,[4] a grandmother and a mother of young children. Throughout, Cusk reads the marginalization and devaluing of pregnant women and new mothers as an index of an increasingly callous, individualistic society that abuses the vulnerable and validates masculine

---

[3] In keeping with this view, Hornby's novel, *The Hive*, is built on an extended beehive metaphor that proposes that the formation of strict, hierarchical social groups is biologically hard-wired female behaviour.

[4] This story, 'The Sacrifices' is not discussed in this chapter, but it contributes to Cusk's critique of reproduction as an area of patriarchal privilege as the central female character wants a child but her partner, who has a child from a previous relationship, does not.

power and agency over feminine connectivity and nurture. While Cusk's work is generally located in the *milieu* of middle to upper middle-class English society, *The Lucky Ones* begins with a story that shows intersectional class/gender oppression at its most brutal. 'Confinement' is a harrowing account of a young, single, heavily pregnant woman, Kirsty, who is incarcerated and in the early stages of labour. Kirsty has been wrongly convicted of an arson attack on a boyfriend's wife and family that was committed by a man known to be dangerous by those on the underfunded rural council estate (The Barrows) that Kirsty was raised on. Published during a period in which young, poor single mothers were castigated in the popular media as hardened, workshy benefit frauds (Tyler 2008), Cusk depicts Kirsty as a vulnerable, sensitive girl who is dehumanized by a justice system that actively discriminates against the poor.

In contrast to the popular media view of impoverished, young single mothers as incapable of finer feelings, Kirsty's narrative also emphasises the formal and informal forms of support that women provide for each other on the estate, 'The women held the Barrows together' (Cusk 2003: 22) and in prison. She pines for her mother, idolizes her aunt, has a warm relationship with the woman she was wrongly convicted of attacking and is cared for and supported by Michelle, her cellmate. Michelle has also been badly let down by the care system as a child and was convicted after killing her abusive husband in self-defence.[5] Cusk's representation of Michelle also offsets the negative stereotypes of young people who have grown up in care, as she has used her time in prison to study law in an attempt to overturn her and Kirsty's convictions. It says much about Cusk's critique of English class relations that the sole connection between the two convicted women and the middle-class class characters who dominate the rest of the novel is Victor, a compassionate barrister who specializes in miscarriage of justice cases. Victor is the only male figure in *The Lucky Ones* who exhibits any concern for those less privileged than themselves. It is therefore also significant that he is a background figure, who only gains a speaking part in the last chapter, shortly before his death. In 'Confinement' Victor is too ill to visit Kirsty in prison and a younger female colleague, Jane, is sent in his place. This connects the reader to the more affluent characters in the next story, who exhibit varying levels of entitlement and class prejudice. Unlike Victor, Jane seems unconvinced by

---

[5] In 2019, Sally Challen, who killed her husband after decades of mental and physical abuse, was freed after a long campaign by her sons to reduce her charge from murder to manslaughter. The case generated much interest in the legal position of women who are imprisoned under similar circumstances.

Kirsty's innocence and refuses to acknowledge her as a legitimate or valid maternal subject:

> She could almost hear her thinking '*thief, liar, whore, Murderer*' Victor wasn't like that [...] Jane wouldn't look at her stomach, her eyes kept hitting it then and bouncing off. Kirsty watched her, waiting to see her give the stomach a proper look but she wouldn't. It hurt her that she wouldn't. She imagined her tick-tacking around her life in her little shoes, around London and her posh lawyer's office, fragile and efficient, controlling, doing everything the right way. (15)

Jane also exhibits more general middle-class prejudices towards those from council estates. When Kirsty enquires whether the man who is responsible for her crime will be arrested, Jane responds in a dismissive manner, 'I'm afraid I don't know. You know what it's like in the Barrows' (16). This comment is followed by a lengthy passage of free indirect discourse that interrupts the flow of the narrative and seems close to authorial commentary:

> Kirsty did know what it was like: you got in trouble for everything you didn't do and nothing that you did. She'd grown up thinking that the police were crooks, that juries were bent, but now she'd been through the justice system she understood that it was simply that people thought the life they lived on the Barrows was bad, and that it didn't matter much what you were accused of, if you came from the Barrows you were guilty of something. (16)

The Lucky Ones then swerves away from the poorest characters, but Kirsty's powerful excoriation of intersectional class/gender injustice casts a long shadow over the more privileged lives described in the rest of the novel. Jane is a minor character, but, as an educated, childless, professional woman, her indifference to Kirsty's plight can be viewed as a commentary on the mainstream neoliberal interpretations of feminism[6] as female individualism and professional success rather than a movement that challenges broader social inequalities. Due to Jane's lack of empathy and her professional inaction, Kirsty's child is taken from her and she is left to rot in a cell. The reader cannot help but note the contrast between Michelle and Kirsty's desperate lives and those of the professional middle-classes described in the following story, 'The Way You Do it'. Jane is now off skiing with affluent friends before starting her new job at a high paid city firm, stating of her legal aid work:

---

[6] See Catherine Rottenberg's *The Rise of Neoliberal Feminism* (2018) for a historicized analysis of this phenomena.

> 'I got tired of it,' said Jane, 'it was all so squalid.' [...] 'You just spent all your time worrying about people,' said Jane. 'They'd come into your office wanting to offload their terrible lives onto you. And half the time you couldn't make any difference, you know, even if you got them off the odds were stacked against them. They still had to go back to these awful lives'. (36)

Jane's desire to avoid the poor and vulnerable is echoed by other characters, such as her friend Lucy:

> 'It's so hard, isn't it,' said Lucy, 'to stick by your principles [...] before I had the twins, I was absolutely certain that I wouldn't educate my children privately, but now, whenever I walk past our local primary school, I get this sort of pain in my stomach at the thought of having to send them their one day. It looks like a remand centre. (36)

Lucy's light-hearted comparison between the local state primary school and 'a remand centre' emphasizes the more serious effects of the class bias that has helped to convict innocent people in the previous story. Cusk satirizes Jane and Lucy's snobbery and lightly discarded ethical concerns, but the more consistent target of the chapter is their friend Martin, who has accepted an invitation to ski despite being the father of a three-week old baby. Unlike Lucy and Jane, Martin does not make ignorant comments about the economically disadvantaged. He also 'rescues' Lucy when her domineering husband leaves her tearful and terrified on dangerous ski run. But in a manner that anticipates the double-voiced discourse of the *Outline* trilogy, in which Faye's engagement with many of the male characters consists of silently listening as they unwittingly reveal the misogynist attitudes and behaviours that lie behind their self-justifying narratives,[7] Martin appears tone deaf to the needs of his wife and baby:

> Dominique, always tired or in pain or somehow unhappy, always in the end victimised by the things she had created, seemed to exist more and more in a state of unrestrained emotion. The baby got on her nerves – that was the sort of thing she had started to say. (44)

It is left for the reader to note that Martin's reflections on his wife's fragile mental state do not prevent him from leaving her to struggle with the baby alone. Moreover, Martin nearly skis off a precipice in his desire to re-establish the agency and autonomy that he feels have been thwarted by becoming a father:

---

[7] See Mary Holland's analysis of Cusk's use of narrative voice and her critique of misogyny in the *Outline* trilogy.

he skied under the ropes at the edge of the *piste* and headed off into the wilderness. This is what he liked best, skiing in the trees. Today he skied dangerously, wildly dodging rocks, hurtling down unmarked valleys. It was still cloudy and he could see only a few feet in front of him. He felt a vicious carelessness of himself. He revelled in his skill and his right to expend himself. (53)

The sequencing of these chapters, the first in which a young, working-class mother – who gives birth while shackled – fights to keep her baby, the second in which an affluent young father willingly puts his life at risk while brooding on the responsibilities of new parenthood, tells us much about class and gender privilege. An unjust legal system that discriminates against the poor deprives Kirsty of the loving bond that could give her life meaning, while Martin wallows in existential angst due to the curtailment of his freedom: 'Now that a baby had come his life would be lived against a mounting force of limitation' (56).

He is also disappointed that his wife hasn't morphed into a 'earth mother' through childbirth and continues to dehumanize her through metaphors that imagine her as a form of creeping, poisonous vegetation:

> He had thought that she possessed some secret knowledge, that a mysterious fund of femininity lay beneath her like a pale root [...] Instead she had spread herself like frantic ivy over every available surface; she had covered him in needy tendrils. (52)

In *A Life's Work*, Cusk calls out the gendered double standard on parenting whereby male columnists are permitted to voice ambivalence – even paternal fury – but women are required to toe the line by expressing only benign maternal feelings (2001: 131–6). Martin's story exposes the same dynamics at work. Not only does Martin escape judgement for leaving his wife to cope alone with their newborn daughter, he is pitied for having to deal with them at all. During a discussion on breastfeeding, one of the women in the party states,

> 'at least take pity on this poor guy then,' said Josephine, clapping a hand lightly on Martin's arm. 'He's come all the way to Switzerland to get away from all that stuff.' (49)

By exposing the gendered double-standard and encouraging the reader to judge disengaged fathers rather than struggling mothers, Cusk offers a corrective to the dominant culture of noughties mother-shaming discussed above. In another act of authorial retribution, a later story, 'Mrs Daley's Daughter' – the central story in the collection – features Josephine herself as a vulnerable new mother struggling with the demands of a tiny baby. The novel's depiction of Jane's behaviour towards Kirsty and Josephine's willingness to dismiss Martin's wife and child – prior to becoming a mother herself – illustrates women's collusion with the misogynist attitudes that marginalize and disempower pregnant women and new mothers. 'Mrs Daley's Daughter' explores this theme in more depth through its analysis of the relationship between Josephine and her abusive mother. Focalized through Mrs Daley, a brittle, bitter, status-obsessed, grandmother, Cusk again uses a double-voiced discourse to construct a far more monstrous figure with minimal self-awareness. Unlike Martin, as a post-war wife and mother, Mrs Daley has endured a life of minimal agency and status:

> she found that when she opened her mouth in public it was her husband's feelings rather than her own that came out of it. It was not because she was cowed that this happened; but rather than in matters of the world she judged herself to be her husband's inferior in both intelligence and information.
>
> Cusk 2003: 110

Mrs Daley compensates for her lack of worldly recognition through becoming a self-appointed authority on childcare, 'In matters concerning children Mrs Daley expected her husband to bow to her, as she did to him in everything else' (115). As the chapter demonstrates, the authority invested in this role is no challenge to patriarchy. It is far more likely to lead to conflict between women, and specifically, intergenerational conflict between mothers and grandmothers, as they have been subjected to opposing schools of thought by (largely male) childcare experts.

Cusk's rendering of Mrs Daley's internal thoughts demonstrates how *The Lucky Ones* explores the callousness and hypocrisy of certain sections of the post-war generation of parents. Mrs Daley seeks power by undermining her fragile daughter's attempts to comply with contemporary baby-care wisdom, situating herself as the defender of babies via her investment in the 'common sense' parenting advice doled out to the prior generation of mothers:

> 'Well haven't you washed her hair?' cried Mrs Daley.
> 'No,' said Josephine. 'We haven't bathed her yet. You're supposed to wait till the cord drops off. And it's bad for their skin. Don't worry, it won't do her any harm.'
> 'But babies love their bath!' said Mrs Daley. 'You can't take that away from her!'

Echoing the concerns of the right-wing press during this period, she disapproves of Josephine's plans to continue working, her unmarried state, her partner's stepchildren and their urban existence:

> unclean forces arrayed themselves around the baby in much the same way as the filthy reaches of London did. Mrs Daley had a desire, which when the baby was older might become a plan, to pluck the child from her unsavoury setting, to convert her back to what was proper and good and right if it wasn't, as by then it might be, too late. (145)

She is furious when Josephine suffers an emotional collapse and seeks the shelter of her parents' home. Her desire to physically punish her adult daughter for suffering from post-natal depression brings back repressed memories of her own abuse of Josephine as a child:

> she felt a tremendous pity for herself, even as she recalled, very fleetingly, that the room had been Josephine's, in the old house and that it was she, Barbara Daley, who had struck the child again and again. (145)

Cusk's rendering of the tension between the idealisation of the 'perfect' childhood (understood by Mrs Daley as rural-based and experienced within a conventional nuclear family) and her cruelty to Josephine, evokes Barbara Almond's psychoanalytic work on maternal ambivalence. Almond's work concludes that the more mothers are publicly required to conform to notions of maternal self-sacrifice and benevolence, the higher the likelihood that one of their children will be viewed as a 'problem' child and will become the repository of their repressed rage (2011: 38–51).

In more general terms, the chapter explores the phenomena whereby mothers from the last 'pre-feminist' generation might seek revenge for their own repressed and unacknowledged historical wounds by tormenting the next generation of mothers. The cultural hostility towards mothers of young children explored in *The Lucky Ones* reaches its apotheosis in the final chapter 'Matters of Life and Death'. This is set in the small village where the Daleys' reside, but it also returns to the first chapter as Victor, the legal aid barrister, and his lifestyle columnist wife, Serena, have relocated there due to his illness. The protagonist of the story, Vanessa, is a fulltime mother who has embraced the neo-traditionalist, maternal role. Again, Cusk invites us to question the central character's internalisation of normative roles:

> she had attained a state of refinement, and of abasement, too, of humility before the task of motherhood. It was a part of this humility that she felt entitled to

judge other mothers. When she saw them shout, or smother, or complain or draw attention to themselves, the full weight of her sacrifice bore down on her.

2003: 186

When the urbane Serena suggests to Vanessa that her role places her in a position of dependence and inequality, Vanessa tells her that:

> there are things I really like about being at home with the children. Nobody tells me what to do; I'm pretty free to do as I like [...] I've got more independence here than I'd have in some office [...] I'm more than equal. I'm the lucky one. (178)

As the title of Cusk's novel is clearly ironic, we are not surprised when this chapter exposes the fraudulent basis of this widely held justification for women's exclusion from the paid workforce. Vanessa later learns that her husband, Colin, is intending to abandon his family and eject them from their home. Colin rubs salt in the wounds by bragging that his new female partner has, 'her own money. He couldn't help himself from sounding proud. She runs her own company. She's very successful' (213). The damage Colin inflicts is not limited to his plan to divorce her: he also causes a car accident that leaves Vanessa disfigured and blind in one eye. Colin is forced to parent the boys in her absence while she undergoes a process of physical and psychological change 'she had looked in the mirror and she had not cried, in spite of the fact that she didn't recognise her own face. [...] It was the face she'd always suspected lay beneath the face she'd had before' (217).

The 'new face' clearly symbolizes the birth of a more perceptive and authentic Vanessa, despite her loss of sight, 'She was getting stronger all the time. She was slowly filling with life. Yet she knew she would never go back to the children: the mornings at nursery would remain, like a fence around her heart' (227). Cusk ends the novel on an uncharacteristically hopeful note. Victor, the ethical lawyer, whose illness leaves Kirsty at the mercy of an unsympathetic legal system in the first chapter, has died, but Vanessa has chosen to befriend Kirsty and take up her cause. Vanessa evolves from playing the role of the socially-validated 'good mother', who cares only for her own family, to an expanded horizon of social responsibility that extends beyond her own privileged circle.

The Desperate Housewives of *Arlington Park*

Cusk's subsequent novel, *Arlington Park*, extends her contextualized exploration of contemporary parenting and gender roles from the transition to parenthood and the early years to the lives of women with older children who have, grudgingly, accepted the limitations that marriage and motherhood have imposed on them. The story unfolds over one day, passing through the successive minds and capturing the thoughts and emotions of different women who live in the same affluent suburb of a provincial city. It culminates in a dinner party in which all five female characters are present with their husbands.[8]

Like *The Lucky Ones*, *Arlington Park* highlights both the oppression of women through motherhood and domesticity and the cruelty and ethical indifference that the privileged show towards the vulnerable and dispossessed. The novel's structure and themes allude to Woolf's *Mrs Dalloway*, but its tone is both darker and more satirical. Woolf's characters experience moments of elation and wonder alongside despair. In contrast, the female residents of *Arlington Park* exist in a fog of permanent disappointment. This is suggested by *Arlington Park*'s opening description of the provincial city that has more in common with Woolf's *To The Lighthouse*, with its post-human description of the destruction of the war years, than *Mrs Dalloway*'s rich, urban vision of 'life, London, this moment in June'.

> The clouds came from the West: clouds like dark cathedrals, clouds like machines, clouds like black blossoms flowering in the arid starlit sky [...] Unseen they grew like a second city overhead, thickening, expanding, throwing up their savage monuments [...] the wind picked up. It faintly stirred the branches of the trees, and in the dark, empty park the swings moved back and forth a little. A handful of dried leaves shuffled.
>
> Cusk 2006: 3

Setting the tone in which the mothers view their alienating lives, the story begins with an allusion to Kafka's *Metamorphosis*, as the first character, Juliet, wakes from a nightmare in which she has a giant cockroach in her hair:

> What a horrible dream – horrible! Juliet clutched her head and frantically searched her hair. The cockroach both was and wasn't there. She was full of its presence and yet she couldn't touch it.
> [...] All she could think of now was that Benedict hadn't helped her. He had pitied her, but he had accepted her fate. (8–9)

Cusk's allusion to a text famously associated with isolation and existential dread expresses Juliet's horror at being laughed at and verbally threatened at

---

[8] *The Lucky Ones* is divided into five chapters that also constitute freestanding stories. *Arlington Park* has ten chapters but is focused on the lives of five different women. Both novels also follow the rising action/falling action structure of a five-act play.

dinner by a friend's bullying, misogynist husband for defending his female employee's right to extend her maternity leave. Juliet, herself a high achiever in her youth, has had her career ambitions curbed by marriage and motherhood and has returned to her home city to become a teacher at a private girls' school, reproducing the education that she wrongly assumed would take her into a higher status job. She now relies on minor rebellions, such as questioning received ideas about women's lives through a reading group for her the pupils and cutting off her long hair, to restore her sense of lost agency. In a similar manner, full-time mother, Amanda is bored and misses her sales job, regaining a sense of agency only through the more 'masculine' act of driving a powerful car: 'her car was her true companion: it was clean and spacious and mechanically discreet, and it did her bidding powerfully, efficiently and with silent approval of her style of command' (43). Yet she still suffers from panic attacks, 'there were mornings when she had driven around weeping, sweating, palpably distressed' (45).

Arlington Park is scattered with allusions to maternal enervation and impotence. Maisie, another full-time mother, ruminates on the loss of youthful drive and ambition: 'When she thought of her life before – of her twenties and London, and work [...] she saw herself always animated by a nameless dissatisfaction: it had filled her out, like the wind fills out a sail, and propelled her along' (189). We are also told 'she was like a boat in a harbour where the tide has gone out, lying helplessly on her side in the mud with the neutered fin of the rudder drying in the still air' (190). Solly, a mother pregnant with her fourth child, describes herself as 'a sack full of children, a woman who had spent her life until there was none left' (134) and is envious of her lithe and stylish Italian nanny, who is divorced and has left her child with her husband.

The only mother who voices the more socially palatable view that non-working mothers are 'the lucky ones' and should be grateful for their lot, is the upwardly mobile and outspoken dinner party host, Christine. Cusk's reimagining of the refined Mrs Dalloway as a blunt, upwardly mobile working-class character whose speech patterns are distinguished from the wealthier characters by banter and constant rhetorical questions, suggests an irreverent attitude towards the canonical *ur*-text. However, like her literary predecessor, Christine is determined to savour life's pleasures, 'You've got to love, just being alive' (246), and rebels against the stifling atmosphere of the middle-class, couples' dinner party. After being asked by one of her guests if she was enjoying the party, Christine offers a blunt response:

'I was thinking what a frigging hassle it all is [...] Do you know what I mean?' She upended the wine bottle over her glass so that the wine came gushing out and made a foaming whirlpool that sent a wave over the rim. 'I mean why aren't we all dancing? Why are we sitting here like the district council discussing a frigging planning application?' (241)

She longs to energize and unite her companions, but her less appealing beliefs are also in keeping with Woolf's protagonist. While Mrs Dalloway famously states that, 'she could feel nothing for the Albanians, or was it the Armenians?' Cusk updates the uncaring attitudes of the privileged in line with contemporary anti-immigrant prejudices. For example, when the conversation with other mothers drifts away from the domestic and into global problems, Christine responds with clichés and callousness:

> 'When you think of all the terrible things happening in the world,' Christine said, 'when you think of those earthquake victims in Indonesia. We can't complain can we?' 'Or those people in the lorry' [...] 'What lorry?' 'You know,' Stephanie said. 'They opened the back of a lorry at Dover and found about fifty people in it, all dead' [...] 'Did they?' Christine wore an expression of distaste. Presently she said, 'actually I don't mind it so much when it's something people have brought on themselves.' (111)

Arlington Park thus critiques neo-traditionalist gender roles and satirizes the middle English view of those that are vulnerable or different from themselves (Christine is also irritated by Gypsies, dislikes what she identifies as non-white names and has an openly racist husband). It therefore continues Cusk's analysis of the cultural interconnections between the low value awarded to carers and care-work and the callousness of the dominant neoliberal logic of greed, individualism and self-interest. As stated earlier, the period in which Cusk produced *A Life's Work*, *The Lucky Ones* and *Arlington Park* was one in which the dominant socio-political discourse idealized a neo-traditionalist 'intensive' maternal role as the means of raising educational outcomes, lowering crime and improving the nation's health. In her book on cultural attitudes towards mothers, Jacqueline Rose (2018) explores the psychic and political drives behind the culture of mother-blaming and proposes that mothers become objects of 'licensed cruelty' in a culture in which health and education systems are semi-privatized and notions of the common good, social responsibility and community support are displaced by self-congratulatory individualism. She argues that the media is dominated by:

'increasingly shrill voices, telling us that our greatest ethical obligation is to entrench our national and personal borders, to be unfailingly self-regarding and sure of ourselves. It is a perfect atmosphere for picking on mothers, for branding them as uniquely responsible for both securing and jeopardising this impossible future.

Rose 2018: 7

Conclusion: Cusk as 'Feminist Killjoy'

As Cusk illustrates in *The Lucky Ones* and *Arlington Park*, mothers often internalize harsh attitudes towards themselves, other mothers and the more vulnerable sections of society. However, there are also those – such as Juliet or Vanessa – who challenge them. In *The Feminist Killjoy's Handbook* Sara Ahmed considers the scene from *Arlington Park* in which Juliet calls out a powerful man over his treatment of a new mother (Ahmed 2023: 22). Juliet receives no support from her husband and is blamed for spoiling the evening, leading to the Kafkaesque nightmare that begins *Arlington Park*. Ahmed uses the scene to demonstrate the courage required of women who adopt the role of the 'feminist killjoy' (1–43) and the hostility they face for speaking truth to power. In a wider sense, Cusk's autobiographical and fictional work of the noughties embodies the spirit of the feminist killjoy in the celebratory sense described by Ahmad. For Ahmad, a feminist killjoy is a female figure who won't shut up about injustice, despite being subjected to a range of belittling responses. To identify feminist killjoys, Ahmad poses the question, 'Do you just have to open your mouth for eyes to start rolling?' (2). It would be fair to say that Cusk has been subjected to an unprecedented degree of critical eye-rolling and deserves recognition and praise as an unrepentant feminist killjoy.

By drawing attention to the misogyny, cruelty and prejudice that lay behind socially-validated views of motherhood in the noughties, Cusk paved the way for a new generation of critical and interrogative writing on the maternal and continues to provide reference points for contemporary feminist scholars such as Ahmed. Twenty-odd years later, in the midst of the 'culture wars' and increasing political hostility towards vulnerable groups – such as immigrants – it is evident that Cusk also offered a prescient warning as to the coarsening effects of a dominant discourse that values only strength, crushes the vulnerable and devalues care and care-work.

Works Cited

Agarwal, P. (2021), *(M)otherhood: On the Choices of Being a Woman*. Edinburgh: Canongate.
Ahmed, S. (2023), *The Feminist Killjoy Handbook*. London: Allen Lane.
Almond, B. (2010), *The Monster Within: The Hidden Side of Motherhood*. California: University of California Press.
Asher, R. (2011), *Modern Motherhood and the Illusion of Equality*. London: Harvill Secker.
Badinter, E. (2011), *The Conflict: How Modern Motherhood Undermines the Status of Women* (trans. Adriana Hunter). New York: Metropolitan Books.
Brearley, J. (2021), *The Motherhood Penalty: How to Stop Motherhood Being the Kiss of Death for Your Career*. London: Gallery.
Bristow, J. (2009), *Standing Up to Supernanny*. Exeter: Societas.
Brunsdon, C. (2005), 'Feminism, Postfeminism, Martha, Martha, and Nigella'. *Cinema Journal*, 44 (2): 110–16.
Cusk, R. (2003), *The Lucky Ones*. London: Harper Collins.
Cusk, R. (2006), *Arlington Park*. London: Faber & Faber.
Cusk, R. (2008), *A Life's Work: On Becoming a Mother*. London: Faber & Faber.
Cusk, R. (2012), *Aftermath*. London: Faber & Faber.
Douglas, S. and M. Michaels (2004), *The Mommy Myth: The Idealisation of Motherhood and How it Has Undermined All Women*. New York: Free Press.
Enright, A. (2004), *Making Babies: Stumbling into Motherhood*. London: Jonathan Cape.
Figes, K. (1997), *Life After Birth*. London: Penguin.
Fox Harding, L. (1999), 'Family Values and Conservative Government Policy: 1979–97', in G. Jagger and C. Wright (eds), *Changing Family Values*. London and New York: Routledge.
Furedi, F. (2001), *Paranoid Parenting: Why Ignoring the Experts Might Be Best For Your Child*. London and New York: Continuum.
Garrett, R. (2013), 'Novels and Children: "Mum's Lit" and the Public Mother/Author'. *Studies in the Maternal*, 5 (2): 1–28. DOI: 10.16995/sim.25.
Garrett, R. (2017), 'A Terrible Deal for the Western Parent: Maternal Memoirs, Mother-Shaming and Neoliberal Parenthood', in K. Launis and J. Ahlbeck (eds), *Fragile Subjects: Child Figures in Western Modernity*. Abingdon: Routledge.
Garrett, R. (2021), *Writing the Modern Family*. London: Rowman & Littlefield.
Gill, R. (2017), 'The Affective Cultural and Psychic Life of Postfeminism: A Postfeminist Sensibility 10 Years On'. *European Journal of Cultural Studies*, 20 (6): 606–26.
Gillies, V. (2006), *Marginalised Mothers: Exploring Working-Class Experiences of Parenting*. Abingdon: Routledge.
Glaser, E. (2021), *Motherhood: Feminism's Unfinished Business*. London: HarperCollins.
Guldberg, H. (2009), *Reclaiming Childhood: Freedom and Play in an Age of Fear*. New York: Routledge.

Hakim, C. (2001), *Work Lifestyle Choices in the Twenty-First Century*. Oxford: Oxford University Press.

Hays, S. (1996), *The Cultural Contradictions of Motherhood*. New Haven: Yale University Press.

Holland, M. (2023), 'Rachel Cusk's New Realism: Gender, Power, Voice and Genre in the *Outline* Trilogy'. *Contemporary Women's Writing*, 17 (1).

Hornby, G. (2001), 'Mother's Ruin', *The Times*. 1 September.

Jensen, T. (2018), *Parenting the Crisis: The Cultural Politics of Parent Blame*. Bristol: Policy.

Knight, I. (2001), 'Who Are They Trying to Kid?' *Sunday Times*. 9 September.

Lockman, D. (2019), *All the Rage: Mothers, Fathers and the Myth of Equal Parenting*. New York: HarperCollins.

Macvarish, J., P. Lowe and E. Lee (2016), 'Understand the Rise of Neuroparenting', in R. Garrett, T. Jensen and A. Voela (eds), *We Need to Talk About Family: Essays on Neoliberalism, Parenting and Popular Culture*. Newcastle: Cambridge Scholars.

McRobbie, A. (2004), 'Post-feminism and Popular Culture', *Feminist Media Studies* 4 (3): 255–64.

McRobbie, A. (2007), 'Top Girls?' *Cultural Studies*, 21 (4–5): 718–37. DOI: 10.1080/09502380701279044.

Ophir, E. (2023), 'Neomodernism and the Social Novel: Rachel Cusk's *Outline* Trilogy'. *Critique: Studies in Contemporary Fiction*, 64 (2): 353–64, DOI: 10.1080/00111619.2021.2021133.

Orgad, S. (2019), *Heading Home: Motherhood, Work and the Failed Promise of Equality*. New York: Columbia University Press.

Ringrose, J. and E. Renold (2010), 'Normative Cruelties and Gender Deviants: The Performative Effects of Bully Discourses for Girls and Boys in School'. *British Educational Research Journal*, 36 (4): 573–96. DOI: 10.1080/01411920903018117.

Rose, J. (2018), *Mothers: An Essay on Love and Cruelty*. London: Faber & Faber.

Rottenberg, C. (2018), *The Rise of Neoliberal Feminism*. Oxford: Oxford University Press.

Slater, L. (2003), *Love Works Like This: Travels Through a Pregnant Year*. London: Bloomsbury.

Tyler, I. (2008), '"Chav Mum, Chav Scum": Class Disgust in Contemporary Britain'. *Feminist Media Studies*, 8 (1): 17–34.

Warner, J. (2006), *Perfect Madness: Motherhood in the Age of Anxiety*. London: Vermillion.

Wolf, N. (2001), *Misconceptions: Truth, Lies and the Unexpected on the Journey to Motherhood*. London: Vintage.

Zelizer, V. A. (1985), *Pricing the Priceless Child: The Changing Social Value of Children*. Princeton: Princeton University Press.

3

Serial Metaphors

Revising and Rewriting in Rachel Cusk's Life Narratives

Ricarda Menn

Rachel Cusk is not only a prolific novelist but also author of three memoirs and a trilogy of autofictional texts, the *Outline* trilogy. Upon their initial publication, Cusk's memoirs, *A Life's Work: On Becoming a Mother* (2001), *The Last Supper: A Summer in Italy* (2009) and *Aftermath: On Marriage and Separation* (2012), were not labelled as part of a series or serial, unlike the coherent cover designs of the *Outline* trilogy in both the UK Faber & Faber editions and the US Macmillan edition. However, the Faber 2019 re-issues of the memoirs, as well as her entire oeuvre of novels, outwardly impose a serial frame upon the texts by re-furnishing them in the distinctive style of the *Outline* trilogy covers. This style consists of an image surrounded by a white frame and black block letters that show the title on the upper half of the cover. As Lauren Oyler describes the design, these covers contain 'striking photographs and set in a modern sans serif font, the sort of objects that might look good in Cusk's home' (2020).

In *Gender and Seriality: Practices and Politics of Contemporary US Television* (2021), Maria Sulimma devotes a chapter to the importance of paratexts for authorizing serial narratives. She considers paratexts, and especially serial paratexts, as 'prime examples of serial texts' feedback loop, requiring author figures to turn their authorship performance into a serial project enacted in paratexts' (155). Paratexts enhance and reinforce serial connections between parts of a series, and further demonstrate authors' awareness of their engagement in serial practices. Faber's branding of Cusk's books in an idiosyncratic, uniform style could be seen as a marketing mechanism, steering readers of the highly successful *Outline* trilogy towards her other work. More programmatically, this homogenous branding could bestow a sense of causal connectedness and thus possibly a paratextual, serial continuity between heterogeneous texts. However, while paratextual factors are one way to render texts as serial, strategies of serialization in and among Cusk's corpus of work are more complex and warrant closer scrutiny.

For one, this homogenous branding runs counter to the heterogeneous nature of Cusk's writing: she has published novels, memoirs, autofictions – hybrids of autobiography and fiction – and essays (collected in *Coventry*). The borders between these forms and genres are not always clear-cut, for example, an extract from *Aftermath* is included in her essay collection *Coventry*. While her earlier novels are stand-alone texts, the *Outline* trilogy is closely connected through the same central character-narrator, Faye (see also Melissa Schuh's chapter). Her three memoirs are published as independent texts, but together and especially in connection with Cusk's autofiction contribute to the narrated and partly fictionalized experience of Cusk's authorship. Her memoirs clearly reference her lived experience, and the *Outline* trilogy includes implicit parallels with Cusk's autobiographies alongside reflections on literary authorship. I understand this multiplicity of different self-referential practices as a form of serial life writing, a genre that shows how authors experiment with multi-volume textual self-scrutiny to counter autobiographical norms and ideas of textual closure and unity (cf. also Stamant 2014; Menn and Schuh 2022).

Cusk's narratives call for an adapted conceptualization of seriality. The three parts of the *Outline* trilogy consist of marginally connected stories and conversations. Told by a first-person narrator who relays and thereby mediates conversations with other people, these texts do not give direct insight into the narrator's perspective but only indirectly create an 'outline' by relying on external sources. Cusk's memoirs, despite preceding the trilogy, can be read as tangibly related to this process, in the sense that they can be understood as a *series* of thematically and stylistically linked but self-contained texts (see also Menn and Schuh 2022). Both her autofictions and her memoirs, despite their formal and creative differences, are preoccupied with questions of authorship and its continuities and disruptions, explored in ways that are unambiguous in her memoirs and externalized and elusive in the autofictional trilogy. Ultimately, the memoirs and the trilogy sketch an idea of an author or a textual self that is disrupted over time instead of narrated in a unifying, chronological or linear manner.

Fiona J. Doloughan observes how a preoccupation with narrating female identity and particularly 'the positioning of and response to professional middle-class women; family life and societal expectations' (2023: 142) structures Cusk's writings and particularly her memoirs and her autofictions. The departure from

Cusk's memoirs to the experimental and indirect style of the *Outline* trilogy is often read as a response to the harsh criticism Cusk received for her earlier writings. At the same time, such a turn to a different style for self-presentation can be seen as an indispensable aspect of feminist autobiography, as Smith observes, a female autobiographer 'may even create several, sometimes competing stories about or versions of herself as her subjectivity is displaced by one or multiple textual representations' (1987: 47).

Fiction and multi-volume publication can therefore counter patriarchal norms towards an all-encompassing autobiography and instead centre on self-displacement and self-masquerade. Both autofiction and serial forms of life writing can undermine canonical ideas of a single autobiographical volume being representative of an author's life. By employing different forms and degrees of conveying self-reference, Cusk's serialized writings indicate how even a variety of narrative forms and genres does not establish a complete view of the narrated life. Instead, narrativizations are dispersed in terms of style and form, a dispersal which is taken up in revising her former style. Ultimately, the engagement in different subgenres of life writing and the use of partly unifying, partly contrastive strategies for self-narrative show that Cusk's idea of a textual self rather resides in multiplicity and revision rather than uniformity.

This chapter posits Cusk's engagement in such diverse practices of self-reference as a form of *serial revision*. Her stylistic turn to a very distinct and elusive way of self-presentation may be reflective of a response to the criticism she received for her memoirs *A Life's Work* (2001) and *Aftermath* (2012). This chapter will examine how two key aspects of seriality – repetition and variation – impact on aspects of personal and authorial (re)-imagination in Cusk's work. A number of contributions in this volume analyse aspects of the *Outline* trilogy (see Pykköö) as a self-contained project or focus on their impetus of transgressive seriality and genre experimentation (Schuh). My primary focus in this chapter is on Cusk's memoirs and their act of serial self-reimagination, although certain connections can only be illuminated when considering the overlapping relationships between her memoirs and autofictions. I will trace narrative strategies – such as spatial metaphors and motifs that reflect on authorship and writing – that recur throughout Cusk's memoirs and partly her autofictions. Ultimately, this chapter proposes that Cusk's multi-volume explorations into self-scrutiny are structured by a sense of continuity alongside the impetus to revise and rewrite the narrated self. In this context, I will also consider how metaphors can be read as both serial connectors but also as points of re-imagination, which facilitate Cusk's probing of selfhood.

Memoirs and Metaphors

As mentioned, Cusk's series of memoirs includes *A Life's Work: On Becoming a Mother*, *The Last Supper: A Summer in Italy* and *Aftermath: On Marriage and Separation*. In the respective paratexts, the texts are labelled as memoirs. Memoir is a form of life writing that stresses the importance of other people, and/or particular events or a sequence of events for a life story (Smith and Watson 2010: 274). Couser defines one basic difference between autobiography and memoir: 'autobiography is more comprehensive, memoir more limited, in scope' (2012: 23). Cusk's three life narratives do not present an entire life course and instead encompass episodes and their respective impacts on the life of the narrator and her family. They are further told by a first-person author-narrator who mostly puts forth a retrospective evaluation of past events and includes occasional detours to the narrated present. *Aftermath* only departs from this perspective in its last chapter, 'Trains', in which a third-person narrator gives an outsider's perspective on the divorce.

Crucially, all three texts make use of the same title pattern: the main title is succeeded by an explanatory subtitle, which in two instances begins with 'On'. The subtitles introduce the topic of each text: motherhood, travel and the end of marriage. Even though the three memoirs are not labelled as a serial, they use complementary narrative strategies of autobiographical recollection. Both *A Life's Work* and *Aftermath* foreground processes contributing to autobiographical self-constitution and storytelling, including symbols, metaphors and commentaries. In the opening section of *Aftermath*, the author-narrator introduces the image of the jigsaw, which structures the entire text: 'Recently my husband and I separated, and over the course of a few weeks the life we'd made broke apart, like a jigsaw dismantled into a heap of broken-edged pieces' (Cusk 2012: 1). The author-narrator equates the state of divorce to a broken, unmade jigsaw: quite literally, the shared life has broken apart, and individual pieces of this jigsaw appear as 'broken-edged', suggesting a state beyond repair. 'Broken' is mentioned twice in close syntactic succession and refers to both the jigsaw and the divorce, and the jigsaw returns several times as a motif throughout *Aftermath*. The process of textually (re)assembling personal identity structures *Aftermath* as a whole, with readers following the author-narrator as she adapts to her new situation as a divorced single mother and attempts to regain her own, individual identity.

In a passage at the beginning of *Aftermath*, Cusk considers the nature of storytelling:

> It was his story, and lately I have come to hate stories. If someone were to ask me what disaster this was that had befallen my life, I might ask if they wanted the story or the truth. I might say, by way of explanation, that an important vow of obedience was broken. I might explain that when I write a novel wrong, eventually it breaks down and stops and won't be written any more, and I have to go back and look for the flaws in its design. The problem usually lies in the relationship between the story and the truth. The story has to obey the truth, to represent it, like clothes represent the body. The closer the cut, the more pleasing the effect. Unclothed, truth can be vulnerable, ungainly, shocking. Over-dressed, it becomes a lie.
>
> 2021: 2–3

This passage lends itself to closer scrutiny for declaring Cusk's view on autobiographical storytelling and truth. The narrative segment 'I might + verb' is repeated three times in close syntactic alignment. It first occurs within a sentence and begins two phrases in direct succession. The repetition of 'might' problematizes a distinction between story and truth: 'might' as a subjunctive form signifies how storytelling is always imbued with various possibilities. First, this meditation on narrative capacities ties in with Cusk's occupation as a writer of literary fiction, which she mentions in passing ('when I write a novel'). Second, the author-narrator puts forth a distinction between story and truth. She presents disagreeing with her former husband's version of events as hating 'his stories'. In this reading, stories symbolize highly subjective viewpoints, which run counter to 'the truth' as oriented towards an objective promise.

In this context, the metaphorical comparison of storytelling to the act of wearing 'clothes' underlines the difficulty of this relation. Truth in and of itself ('unclothed', naked) has the potential to shock and displease, whereas an 'overdressed' (falsified, extenuated) story runs the risk of turning into a lie, misrepresenting the truth. Storytelling in this interpretation oscillates between adequate representation and overstatement. The analogy 'like clothes represent the body' links storytelling to self-fashioning, for just as clothes are chosen to express moods or stage a self in a certain way, so too can stories be adapted to certain needs and purposes. The metaphor of clothing truth foregrounds processes of textual construction and thereby reminds readers of the text's own subjective nature. In light of Cusk's ongoing preoccupation with self-referential texts, this metaphor illustrates how texts – and by extension narrative self-presentation – are not stable but contingent, subject to alterations and revisions. In this sense, continuities and discontinuities in Cusk's work precisely underline this process of stories as 'clothes' that are adapted to certain needs. *A Life's Work* also includes strategies that illustrate underlying poetic principles. A central passage contrasts the book's aesthetic agenda with those of self-help and advisory books:

> Books about pregnancy go into this process of transformation, or sublimation, in sinister detail. You are offered a list of foods to eat, recipes for how to combine them, and occasionally photographs of the finished result, with captions such as *Salad* or *Bowl of Granola*. You are told, with the help of illustrations, how to get into bed, how to lie in it, and how to get up again. You are told, again with illustrations, how to make love. Possible conversations you might have with your partner concerning the impending birth and parenthood are detailed. You can conduct these over a cocktail if you like; non-alcoholic for you, of course. Find recipes for non-alcoholic cocktails on page 73.
>
> Cusk 2001: 28

Alongside switching to the second-person perspective, the author-narrator uses two forms of imperative to mimic the advisory (and condescending) tone of guidebooks: first, in the form of an active imperative using infinitive forms ('Find recipes'), and second in the compound of passive indicative ('You are told'), which in conjunction with the iterative 'how to' sounds like an imperative. Moreover, this style posits an antipode Cusk's narrative exploration of her pregnancy and impending motherhood: they precisely list those elements of pregnancy books that are absent in her account: she does not give advice, but just states her very subjective experience (see also Roberta Garrett's chapter on the often condescending treatment of pregnant women and Cusk's response to it).

Throughout her memoirs, Cusk uses symbols and metaphors to reflect on self-narrativization and comment on autopoetic processes. Additionally, her memoirs build heavily on metaphors that foreground the subjective and ultimately constructed nature of autobiography. Alongside Cusk's engagement in several genres of self-narrative, such strategies underline how self-narrativization is not a linear process but rather one that is invested in re-writing and re-visiting the self at different times of life and through different forms of expression. In this sense, Cusk's metaphors – whether focusing on space or on storytelling – contribute to an overarching endeavour of open-ended, non-uniform self-presentation. While the Faber covers may suggest a uniformity of writing across Cusk's writing career, the serial continuity in the content of her work is predicated upon discontinuities of selfhood.

Metaphors of the (Narrated) Self

Delineating the importance of metaphor for autobiography, James Olney in *Metaphors of Self* remarks that 'The self expresses itself by the metaphors it creates and projects, and we know it by those metaphors' (1972: 34). Terms and strategies of autobiographical representation affect autobiographical self-constitution, and in this regard, metaphors can be seen as textual stand-ins of the self but also reveal the constructed nature of those stories. Metaphors achieve their associations by a comparison that builds on what Paul Ricoeur, following I. A. Richards, terms as '*tenor* and *vehicle*' ([1975] 2003: 85), a transfer from a source that is dissimilar to the target expression. For David Punter, an effect of such comparison is that metaphor 'seeks to "fix" our understanding, but at the same time it reveals how any such fixity, any such desire for stability and certainty, is constructed on shifting sands' (2007: 10). Metaphors can be understood as integral to self-narrativization and signify the constructed nature of a life story.

Spatial metaphors epitomize the main narrative themes in all three of Cusk's memoirs. In *The Last Supper*, a dichotomic contrast between the portrayals of England and Italy underlines the family's travel and the author-narrator's reflections on art, for instance a treatment of Piero della Francesca's house and his art ('But after his death it was destroyed, like so much of his work', Cusk 2009: 58). Metaphors of confinement accentuate the author-narrator's ambivalent experiences of motherhood and pregnancy in *A Life's Work*. In *Aftermath*, a house visualizes the author-narrator's exclusion from (hetero)normative expectations on life courses (see also Roberta Garrett, 'Cavorting in the Ruins' (2016)). Kerstin Wilhelms notes that in autobiographies, life courses are constructed around pivotal spaces like school or hospitals (2017: 35), and Cusk's texts stand in such a lineage of self-narrativization immersed in spaces and spatial metaphors.

The spatial reconstruction of a life is particularly pronounced in *The Last Supper*, which has rarely been subjected to in-depth analysis, compared to Cusk's other memoirs. The main exception is Isabelle Rannou, who reads *The Last Supper* as a travel narrative reflecting on art, as the text includes paintings and holiday photographs and thereby intertwines mundane activities and aesthetic meditations (Cusk 2013: 6). The book's material space incorporates different textual and visual layers of the narrative and the journey. Space recurs as a driving force of both the metaphorical construction of the story and the textual, typographical set-up of the published book. In terms of its intermediality and its essayistic inquiry of art and aestheticism, *The Last Supper* takes on a unique position in Cusk's body of work, as it is her only travelogue.

Autobiography and travel writing are closely intertwined, as Smith and Watson attest: 'it [travel writing] can be read as a major mode of life narrative, in this case the reconstitution of the autobiographical subject in transit and encounter' (2010: 150). Laura Marcus observes that alongside the parallel development of autobiography and leisure travel (2018: 29), 'in much modern travel writing [...] the story is both that of a journey to a place and into the self' (38). Autobiography and travel writing tend to share an impetus of joining self-discovery and spatial exploration. Indeed, the personal journey has a long tradition in autobiographical writing, not least in Johann Wolfgang von Goethe's *Wilhelm Meisters Wanderjahre* (1821, 1829) or William Wordsworth's *The Prelude* (1799) (Marcus 2018: 29–30). Further examples include Dorothy Richardson's semi-autobiographical modernist sequence of novels, *Pilgrimage*, and specifically its first volume *Pointed Roofs* (1915), in which the coming-of-age story of authorial alter-ego Miriam is interfused with her travel to Germany to work as an English teacher.

Cusk's account of her travel to Italy ties in with this tradition of autobiographical travel narratives. In this text, she conceives of England as the start of the trip and Italy as its destination in dualistic, contrasting terms:

> We have closed the door on England as one would close the door on a dark and cluttered house and walk out into the sun. It is this release, from the feeling of interiority, that I relish the most. Yet I love this darkness and clutter, its shady labyrinths of memory and emotion. They give rise to feelings of outward misshapenness, but they have their own value, the heavy metal coins of Englishness that strain and bulge through the fabric of the purse. But now the purse is empty: it is flat and light.
>
> Cusk 2009: 29–30

Whereas Italy is positively associated with a 'release' 'into the sun', England is equated to a 'dark and cluttered house'. This negative comparison is enhanced by the metaphor of 'shady labyrinths'. The tenor of the labyrinth is transferred to the vehicle of personal remembering owing to the syntactic alignment of 'memory and emotion'. The labyrinth does not appear as an actual space to walk through but evokes the author-narrator's mindset. Despite this dualistic set-up between a negative past and a promising future, the author-narrator feels ambivalent about this very contrast: even though she 'relishes' the release from 'inferiority', she 'loves' those negative sentiments associated with England. The imagery of coins and purse furthers this paradoxical value: past and personal identity are equated to 'heavy metal coins of Englishness', which occasionally pierce through the 'fabric' of consciousness. Even though the current state is perceived as 'flat and light', the impact of memory still lurks beneath the surface, which is enhanced by the ascription as 'heavy', suggesting material importance and equally symbolizing mental impact.

This passage spatializes recollections and simultaneously comments on personal remembering. Just as the act of narrating a life story is invested in overcoming and ordering the past, so too is it concerned with delineating its importance for the present. The author-narrator's travel to Italy is inextricably linked to her past life and the desire to overcome it. Glimpses of the past reappear occasionally and involuntarily, just as remembering is an involuntary endeavour triggered by seemingly random events. Hence, the personal journey embraces the spatial, actual travel and, in a further step, entails a mental process of encountering the labyrinthine mechanisms of memory. In this sense, the journey as depicted in *The Last Supper* corresponds to an established autobiographical topos of spatial travel leading to self-discovery. At the same time, spaces are used as integral metaphors for narrative self-construction. Across Cusk's work, *The Last Supper* most strongly relies on spaces and motifs of journeys, however the notion of travel recurs to various degrees, such as in *Transit* and *A Life's Work*.

A Life's Work is characterized by spatial metaphors contributing to recollection. Due to its focus on pregnancy, birth and motherhood, metaphors and images illustrate the ambivalence underlying these experiences and their narrativization. In a central passage, the author-narrator remarks:

> for motherhood is a career in conformity from which no amount of subterfuge can liberate the soul without violence; and pregnancy is its boot-camp. My arrival in this camp is mediated but not uninformed. I know about pregnancy only what everybody knows about it, which is what it looks like from the outside. I have walked past it many times. I have wondered what goes on behind its high walls. Knowing the pain which every inmate must endure as the condition of their release, I have imagined it to be a place in which some secret and specialised process of preparation occurs.
>
> Cusk 2001: 15–16

The difficult and negative experiences of motherhood and pregnancy are saturated with military language and associated spatial denominations, including 'camp', 'boot-camp' and 'inmates'. These comparisons are metaphorical in that they rely on semantic word fields usually not associated with pregnancy and motherhood, evoking severe connotations. In this description, birth is equated to a 'release' so that pregnancy is by and large conveyed in negative terms inducing not happiness but suffering, pain and ultimately imprisonment. The expressions 'outside' and 'behind [...] high walls' situate pregnancy as an experience that can only be understood from within. At the same time, the combination of 'outside' and 'high walls', suggests inaccessibility, as these spatial demarcations hinder insight. In *Memories of a Catholic Girlhood*, Mary McCarthy too draws on the concept of the camp by comparing the methods of her upbringing to 'techniques [...] [which] are common in concentration camps and penal institutions' ([1957] 2006: 63). This drastic allusion enhances the miserable conditions of her childhood and upbringing.

For Alice Braun, Cusk's metaphors and imagery attest to an ambivalence involved in chronicling and narrativizing pregnancy and motherhood. Descriptions like 'camp' and 'imprisonment' equate pregnancy to an 'ideology', which is implicitly compared to a 'fascist regime' (Braun 2017: 8). Hence, the 'imagery of totalitarianism' articulates the author-narrator's scepticism of this ideology, a suspicion caused by a 'traumatic' experience of motherhood (ibid.). Women's autobiographies and memoirs have often been analysed as part of discourses on trauma. Accordingly, Ruth Quiney reads *A Life's Work* in the context of feminist confessional writing and its responses to trauma(s) of birth. She surveys how a range of contemporary authors narrate their experiences of motherhood and subvert public discourses on gendered expectations by commenting on 'the conundrums of maternal ambivalence, and of cultural ambivalence about maternity' (Quiney 2007: 23). One could suggest that Cusk narrates birth and motherhood as traumatic events and that this is why her texts were initially negatively received. However, her harsh metaphors echo Quiney's observation on 'cultural ambivalences', illustrating an unresolved conflict between individual experience and cultural norms and expectations.

In the second half of *A Life's Work*, the author-narrator uses spatial metaphors to underscore a contrast between mother and daughter: 'It [motherhood] is like a new house, a new project. I'll be lucky if I ever find the time to make the long journey back to myself, to the old ruin, and hurl a coat of paint over it before the winter of middle age sets in' (Cusk 2001: 134). Syntactically, 'the old ruin' is preceded by 'myself' and readers can gather that the author-narrator compares her identity and emotional state to a ruin, a building incomplete and in need of repair. By linking the spatial tenor of a ruin to the vehicle of the author-narrator's identity, the spatial and material importance of that identity is emphasized and further likens the ruin to mental and bodily matters. The contrast to the daughter as a 'new house' establishes a dichotomy between youth and age. Since the ruin is ultimately the destination of a 'journey back to myself', this description induces a mental journey of adapting to the role as a mother as well as a physical transformation of 'hurl[ing] a coat of paint over it', of attempting to improve physical and bodily appearance. Cusk here offers a variation of the personal voyage which characterizes *The Last Supper*. Despite their different thematic angles, both texts return to a common repertoire of autobiographical metaphors, which are centred on space and personal movement contributing to a life course. It is interesting to note that motifs of both actual and mental journeys alongside the importance of domesticity and (re)making a home feature strongly in *Transit*. I suggest that Cusk's spatializing metaphors are linked to narrative self-construction, depicting textual selves as interwoven with their material and spatial connections. Since these metaphors reappear, to different degrees and often with variations, across her work, they can therefore be read as serial metaphors, in that they establish formal and thematic continuities. At the same time, the metaphors are re-imagined and re-written – as in *Transit* – so that the alteration underlines the process of self-re-imagination across different texts.

Inside versus Outside

Metaphors too are a prominent strategy of *Aftermath*, a text which Rachel Robertson describes as 'stuffed with metaphors and analogies that aim to convey the pain and confusion of post-separation life' (2012: 78). While a further analysis of the abundance of analogies and metaphors could be interesting, I will focus on how these metaphors and narrative strategies connect Cusk's memoirs and autofictional works, and underpin her over-arching concerns with authorship and self-expression. In this context, *Aftermath* introduces a tension between inside and outside. Spatial constellations of inside and outside symbolize normative expectations of domesticity and family life and the author-narrator's exclusion from these after her divorce:

> [...] now I notice the unbroken home, the unified lives that I see through lit windows. When I lived behind those windows I wondered about what was outside. Now that division has been externalised again, has become actual, like the geographical division of my youth. I am no longer a participant: once more, I am an observer.
>
> Cusk 2021: 64

The author-narrator implements a dichotomy between inside and outside to mirror her physical and social exclusion. The windows are lit, casting the outer realm in its shadow. By disclosing a contrast between inside and outside, this scene appears to signify inclusion and exclusion from social norms; the house is equated to an 'unbroken home', which contains 'unified lives'. The building's physical intactness correlates with the idea of a happy, intact family life. For the author-narrator, this observation leads her to reflect on her past situation living a shared life 'behind those windows'. *Aftermath* illustrates the effects of divorce on her life and identity by placing her – literally and metaphorically – outside normative life courses. This exclusion means that she comes to realize those very distinctions between intact family and single mother only once she has become aware of their discriminating, excluding power, 'that division has become externalized'.

Evaluating the position of the narrated presence, the author-narrator remarks that she is no longer a 'participant' but an 'observer', and the spatial exclusion from an intact home illustrates her changed social role. This outside perspective ultimately informs the style of the *Outline* trilogy, which entirely relies on an externalization of subjectivity. Faye is the narrator of the trilogy, but personal information or comments on her part can, for the most part, only be deduced from her use of externalization.

Faye shares some conspicuous autobiographical details with Cusk. These become uttered in one of those rare moments in which Faye – albeit briefly – speaks about her personal situation:

> He began to ask me questions, as though he had learned to remind himself to do so, and I wondered what or who had taught him that lesson, which many people never learn. I said that I lived in London, having very recently moved from the house in the countryside where I had lived alone with my children for the past three years, and where for the seven years before that we had lived together with their father.
>
> Cusk 2014: 11

Both Faye and Cusk (at the time of writing the *Outline* trilogy) are divorced mothers of two children, authors – as we learn throughout the trilogy – and based in London after having lived in the countryside. Faye does not spell out the events leading up to the divorce: 'It was impossible [...] to give the reasons why the marriage had ended: among other things a marriage is a system of belief, a story' (Cusk 2014: 12). This statement echoes her memoir on the aftermath of her divorce, in which she too conceives of marriage as a story (Cusk 2012: 2–3) and similarly does not 'give the reasons' or explanations for the divorce. Next to this intertextual allusion to *Aftermath*, this passage includes an implicit connection: Faye mentions her very recent move to London, which is the topic of the second volume of the *Outline* trilogy, *Transit*. Since the trilogy so rarely includes overt self-descriptions of Faye, those few instances in which she does reveal something about herself emphasize these autobiographical references. One such scene occurs in *Outline*, when Faye witnesses a happy family on a boat and ponders:

> And likewise I was beginning to see my own fears and desires manifested outside myself, was beginning to see in other people's lives a commentary on my own. When I looked at the family on the boat, I saw a vision of what I no longer had: I saw something, in other words, that wasn't there.
>
> Cusk 2014: 75

Precisely because readers learn so little throughout the *Outline* trilogy, a special emphasis is put on such rare – albeit indirect – ways of commenting on the narrator's life. The happy family she observes reminds the narrator of her past situation and makes her aware of an irretrievable loss on her part, 'a vision of what I no longer had'. Indirectly, this passage thus posits Faye's current family state of affairs (children, divorced) in parallel to the experience of divorce in *Aftermath*. Alongside their separate names, there are discrepancies between their life courses: most notably, Cusk is mother to two daughters, while Faye has two sons. The *Outline* trilogy thus relies on a paradox of evoking yet simultaneously undermining autobiographical reference, which sustains an autofictional paradox that Gérard Genette describes as 'It is I and it is not I' (1993: 77). Even though the trilogy features a first-person narrator, readers get little insight into her subjectivity. Hence, Genette's autofictional paradox structures Faye's use of externalization as a primary central narrative strategy of the *Outline* trilogy.

In this sense, the aesthetic principle of the serial is to only devise outlines of events and persons, hence the fitting serial title (see also Schuh's chapter). Besides the fragmentary chapter structure, the trilogy inhabits an autofictional style that disavows textual unity and refutes linear structures. Instead, the externalization of self-description and the serializing of episodes appear as a revision of her earlier employed autobiographical style. The trilogy's second central strategy of observing and commenting on the literary industry and its gender dynamics provide a textual positioning of authorship that ties in with Cusk's initial responses to the criticism of her memoirs.

Cusk's memoirs have attracted ambivalent responses: some reviewers have evaluated them favourably, but others have judged them as too intellectual or too self-centred (see Craig 2009 and Jordan 2009, who both criticized *The Last Supper*; see Robertson 2012 for a summary of *Aftermath*'s reception). Arguably, their reputation has grown, in light of a resurgent interest in autobiographies written by authors of fiction (see also *Radical Realism* by Fiona Doloughan 2023). In some cases, readers have even formulated harsh, personalizing statements attacking not the text but the author Rachel Cusk. Because autobiographical texts are not fictional but referential, readers associate certain norms of truth or factuality with the genre. Even though her autobiographies do not flaunt generic standards, some readers seem to expect universalizing representations of topics like pregnancy or marriage so that departures from these expectations are condemned (see in particular debates on Mumsnet). In other words, had Cusk's text been labelled as novels instead of memoirs, they would presumably not have attracted such harsh, personalizing and even moralizing responses.

The impact of reception is, in Cusk's case, particularly relevant since this criticism has affected her writing. Facing what she has termed a 'creative death' following the publication of *Aftermath*, Cusk only overcame this creative crisis by turning to a new style for continuing her preoccupation with autobiography, which she considers 'the only form in all the arts' (Kellaway 2014). I suggest that her turn from memoir to autofiction is directly influenced by the preceding series of memoirs and the impact of their reception. Autofiction – a hybrid of autobiography and fiction – endows authors with enhanced possibilities to experiment with referential storytelling and autobiographically informed content. Unlike autobiography, autofiction is not associated with normative expectations of truth. As a reflection on the circumstances of literary authorship, the *Outline* trilogy can thus not only be said to include strategies of textual positioning contributing to (and complicating) the self-presentation of a literary author, and is also, in turn, another of Cusk's work in a serial of reflections concerning the literary industry and creative practices.

Conclusion: Serial Autofiction and Revision

The conjunction of autofictional and serial segmentation in the *Outline* trilogy underscores a dissatisfaction with claims to narrative, autobiographical unity. As Hywel Dix observes: 'Drawing attention to discontinuities, lacunae, inconsistencies and contradictions [...] autofiction is a means of serializing multiple fictive aspects of the narrating self' (2018: 13). Autofiction embraces fiction as a means to overcome limits of autobiographical memory and can involve serialization as a strategy to articulate these divergent versions of the self. Smith understands processes of self-fictionalization and self-serialization as indispensable aspects of feminist autobiography (1987: 46):

> Involved in a kind of masquerade, the autobiographer creates an iconic representation of continuous identity that stands for, or rather before, her subjectivity as she tells of this 'I' rather than of that 'I'. She may even create several, sometimes competing stories about or versions of herself as her subjectivity is displaced by one or multiple textual representations.
>
> Smith 1987: 47

Fiction and multi-volume publication shed light on self-displacement and impressions of self-masquerade, which, in Cusk's case, formulate a strategy of feminist self-presentation to respond to patriarchal norms of autobiography. Both autofiction and serial forms of life writing undermine canonical ideas of a single autobiographical volume being representative of an author's life (see Pascal 1960; Gusdorf 1980). As I have detailed in this chapter, Cusk uses a recurring set of metaphors to foreground and reflect on processes of self-narrativization. Some of these motifs – for instance the notion of travel, which features heavily across the trilogy – occur as a form of variation in her autofictional works, so that Cusk's work embraces seriality's two premises of repetition and difference (Eco 1990) in both continuities but also forms of re-writing and re-imagination. By employing different forms and degrees of conveying self-reference, Cusk's series and her serial indicate how even this variety of narratives does not suffice to establish a complete view of the narrated life. Instead, Cusk's turn to a different style, where she only implicitly relays autobiographical references, shows how serial life narrative is not a straight-forward process but rather an experiment with different strategies of self-presentation.

Works Cited

Braun, A. (2017), '"A compound fenced off from the rest of the world": Motherhood as the Stripping of One's Self in Rachel Cusk's A Life's Work: On Becoming a Mother'. *Études britanniques contemporaines. Revue de la Société, 53*. Available at: http://journals.openedition.org/ebc/3802 (accessed 19 August 2019).

Couser, T. (2012), *Memoir. An Introduction*. Oxford: Oxford University Press.
Craig, A. (2009), 'The Last Supper, by Rachel Cusk', *The Independent Online*, 15 March. Available at: https://www.independent.co.uk/arts-entertainment/books/reviews/the-last-supper-by-rachel-cusk-1642884.html (accessed 10 April 2021).
Cusk, R. (2001), *A Life's Work. On Becoming a Mother*. New York: Picador.
Cusk, R. (2009), *The Last Supper. A Summer in Italy*. London: Faber & Faber.
Cusk, R. (2012), *Aftermath: On Marriage and Separation*. London: Faber & Faber.
Cusk, R. (2014), *Outline*. London: Faber & Faber.
Dix, H. (2018), 'Introduction: Autofiction in English: The Story So Far', in H. Dix (ed.), *Autofiction in English*, 1–23. Basingstoke: Palgrave Macmillan.
Doloughan, F. J. (2023), *Radical Realism, Autofictional Narratives and the Reinvention of the Novel*. London: Anthem Press.
Eco, U. (1990), *The Limits of Interpretation*. Bloomington: Indiana University Press.
Garrett, R. (2016), 'Cavorting in the Ruins? Truth, Myth and Resistance in Contemporary Mumoirs', in R. Garrett, T. Jensen and A. Voela (eds), *We Need to Talk about Family: Essays on Neoliberalism, The Family and Popular Culture*, 224–44. Newcastle: Cambridge Scholars Publishing.
Genette, G. ([1991] 1993), *Fiction & Diction*, trans. C. Porter. Ithaca and London: Cornell University Press.
Gusdorf, G. (1980), 'Conditions and Limits of Autobiography', in J. Olney (ed.), *Autobiography. Essays Theoretical and Critical*, 28–48. Princeton: Princeton University Press.
Jordan, J. (2009), 'The good, the bad and the ugly', *The Guardian Online*, 7 February. Available at: https://www.theguardian.com/books/2009/feb/07/rachel-cusk-italy-travel-memoir (accessed 10 April 2021).
Kellaway, K. (2014), 'Interview with Rachel Cusk: "Aftermath was creative death. I was heading into total silence"', *The Guardian Online*, 24 August. Available at: https://www.theguardian.com/books/2014/aug/24/rachel-cusk-interview-aftermath-outline (accessed 10 April 2021).
Marcus, L. (2018), *Autobiography. A Very Short Introduction*. Oxford: Oxford University Press.
McCarthy, M. ([1957] 2006), *Memories of a Catholic Girlhood*. London: Vintage.
Menn, R. and M. Schuh (2022), 'The Autofictional in Serial, Literary Works', in A. Effe and H. Lawlor (eds), *The Autofictional: Approaches, Affordances, Forms*, 101–18. Basingstoke: Palgrave Macmillan.
Olney, J. (1972), *Metaphors of Self. The Meaning of Autobiography*. Princeton: Princeton University Press.
Oyler, L. (2020), 'Rachel Cusk Questions Everything', *New Republic Online*, 20 February. Available at: https://newrepublic.com/article/156388/rachel-cusk-reinvention-review-coventry-book-essays (accessed 11 November 2022).
Pascal, R. (1960), *Design and Truth in Autobiography*. London: Routledge.
Punter, D. (2007), *Metaphor*. London: Routledge.

Quiney, R. (2007), 'Confessions of the New Capitalist Mother: Twenty-first-century Writing on Motherhood as Trauma'. *Women: A Cultural Review*, 18 (1): 19–40.

Rannou, I. (2013), '"Like journeying through a painting": Travel Writing and the Exploration of Textual Boundaries in Rachel Cusk's The Last Supper'. *E-rea-Revue électronique d'études sur le monde Anglophone*, 10 (2): 1–19.

Ricoeur, P. ([1975] 2003), *The Rules of Metaphor. The Creation of Meaning in Metaphor*. London: Routledge.

Robertson, R. (2012), 'The Air that Falls: ethics and aftermath'. *Westerly*, 57 (2): 71–87.

Smith, S. (1987), *A Poetics of Women's Autobiography. Marginality and the Fictions of Self-Representation*. Bloomington: Indiana University Press.

Smith, S. and J. Watson (2010), *Reading Autobiography. A Guide for Interpreting Life Narratives*, 2nd edn. Minneapolis: University of Minnesota Press.

Stamant, N. (2014), *Serial Memoir. Archiving American Lives*. Basingstoke: Palgrave Macmillan.

Sulimma, M. (2021), *Gender and Seriality. Practices and Politics of Contemporary US Television*. Edinburgh: Edinburgh University Press.

Wilhelms, K. (2017), *My Way. Der Chronotopos des Lebenswegs in der Autobiographie (Moritz, Fontane, Dürrenmatt und Facebook)*. Heidelberg: Winter.

4

Perceptions of Failure in Rachel Cusk's *Saving Agnes* and *Second Place*

Sonja Pyykkö

Rachel Cusk's success as an author owes a great deal to her skill at depicting failure: from the 'failure *extraordinaire*' of Agnes Day, the heroine of her debut novel *Saving Agnes* (1994), to M, supposedly the *artiste manquée* in her latest novel, *Second Place* (2021), Cusk's fiction and memoirs are overflowing with representations of failure. Failure in Cusk's writing is figured both as a real threat – like the crack that spreads slowly across Agnes's living room wall, signifying 'a tiny manifestation of a larger slippage, almost like a gravitational force' (Cusk 1994: 101) – and as a distortion of self-perception that causes her protagonists, Agnes and M included, to see themselves as failures even when nobody else would. Even though such failure-obsessed characters appear with remarkable predictability in Cusk's fiction, this chapter's focus on *Saving Agnes* with *Second Place* reveals differences in how these faulty perspectives function to delude and entrap those who possess them. In *Saving Agnes*, Agnes struggles to establish the kind of self-distance that she needs to rid herself of the belief that even with nothing outwardly wrong with her, she is an extraordinary failure – a self-distance, moreover, that seems, at the end of the novel, to promise her success as an author. In *Second Place*, by contrast, the middle-aged author M faces a different problem: M knows perfectly well that her self-perception is distorted, but this knowledge brings her no closer to freeing her from the vision of seeing herself as a failure, coming in at 'second place'. *Saving Agnes* and *Second Place* offer nuanced treatments of failure, not only as a motif – a recurring idea, or *idée fixe* – but also as an aesthetic, as a set of principles that govern the novel's portrayal of its theme. By recognizing that failure functions as an aesthetic that only becomes more refined and pronounced when moving from Cusk's early novels to her later work, this chapter seeks to contribute to the growing number of studies exploring Cusk as a 'neo-modernist' author, by Nicolas Pierre Boileau

(2013), Liam Harrison (2022), Ella Ophir (2022) and others. As Matthew Sandler notes in an essay on Gertrude Stein and 'failure studies', it was scholars of modernism who first suggested that 'while failure is endemic to modernity, failed art might provide for aesthetic possibility' (2017: 191).[1] In *Second Place*, this chapter contends, it is not failed art, exactly, but a failed artist, M, who reveals the aesthetic possibility that failure provides in Rachel Cusk's work – for her novels to succeed as works of art, their protagonists must fail.

'Failure *Extraordinaire*': Subjectivity and Authorship in *Saving Agnes*

Saving Agnes's first chapter concludes with a comical image of its young female protagonist shooting around 'trying to sustain the appearance of a thrusting young professional running on a tight schedule' one minute, and the next revealed for all the world as 'none other than Agnes Day: sub-editor, suburbanite, failure *extraordinaire*' (Cusk 1994: 12). Not only beauty but also success and failure lie largely in the eye of the beholder, Cusk indicates by providing her readers with glimpses into Agnes's hypercritical self-perception using internal focalization. Shifting between the subjective and the objective viewpoints highlights the irony between how others perceive Agnes – a recent Oxford graduate with a job in publishing, two loving parents, her own life in London, and a house share with university friends who are just as privileged as she is – and how Agnes has learned to perceive herself since she was a teenager. This is when she first became aware of the 'appellatory misfortune', the fact that her name is pronounced the same as 'Agnus Dei', Lamb of God, though nobody else seems to have noticed the coincidence, which had initially given her the impression that failure was written into her fate: 'that what would have been a success by any other name was fast becoming a failure by her own', and even 'that reality meant failure, ugliness and self-contempt' (Cusk 1994: 13–16). This kind of comic exaggeration highlights Agnes's blissful unawareness of how minor

---

[1] The study of failure in the arts is today often associated with the work of Jack Halberstam, who proposed in *The Queer Art of Failure* (2011: 88) that failure constitutes a valid response, perhaps the only valid response, to the techno-optimism and growth mentality that belong integrally to capitalism. As Sandler notes, however, Halberstam owes this orientation to scholars of modernism, such as John Berger (1989), Peter Bürger (1984), Suzi Gablik (2004), and Andrew Ross (1986), who first begun using the notion of failure to explore 'modernism's reaction to modernity' (Sandler 2017: 191).

her struggles are, but there is more at stake in *Saving Agnes* than a satire of the cluelessness of white middle-class youth. This is because it is ultimately not failure per se, nor even a fear of failure, that *Saving Agnes* seeks to represent, but something even more elusive: a distorted self-perception that causes Agnes to compare herself to an idealized version of herself – 'Grace', the alter-ego she developed as a teenager – which causes Agnes to believe that she has somehow failed at the simple task of being herself. Reading *Saving Agnes* as a *Bildungsroman*, as this chapter proceeds to, reveals a developmental trajectory that transforms Agnes into a promising young woman who is learning to observe herself and her surroundings with greater objectivity – this, Cusk implies, is a skill that she will need if she is to become an author. At stake in the novel, I suggest, is the initial development of an authorial subject who possesses a distinct and unique perspective on the world, but isn't too trapped in her subjective field of vision to perceive the universal 'pattern' or 'picture' that emerges when her personal failures and private anguish are viewed from the proper 'distance' (1994: 217).

Saving Agnes kickstarted a decades-spanning literary career that made Cusk one of the most widely acclaimed authors writing in English today. Winner of the prestigious Whitbread first novel award, it was reviewed in leading newspapers on both sides of the Atlantic, anticipating Cusk's later international success. Had Cusk chosen to write her debut in the first-person singular, it might have more eagerly been interpreted as an autobiographical novel, and perhaps later as autofiction, but it seems significant that she chose *not* to do this. Through a fictional protagonist, whose experience is more representative than individual, *Saving Agnes* depicts challenges that young people in general, and particularly those from a middle-class background, face as they strive to find their place in society. This is a common theme in the *Bildungsroman*, also known as a 'novel of development' or a 'novel of apprenticeship', which depicts its bourgeois protagonist's journey from youth to adulthood as a series of 'false starts' that concludes when the protagonist has become fully adjusted to society's demands and is therefore able to become a productive member of it, as Susanna Howe argued in an early study of the genre (1930: 4). 'Youth', Franco Moretti has more recently observed, 'acts as a sort of symbolic concentrate of the uncertainties and tensions of an entire cultural system, and the hero's growth becomes the narrative convention or *fictio* that permits the exploration of conflicting values' (1987: 185). Through the form of the *Bildungsroman*, *Saving Agnes* depicts Agnes's struggle to overcome her fear of failure as she begins her first job as an assisting editor for a weekly newspaper and tries her hand at relationships with various, more or less abusive, boyfriends. By representing Agnes's plight as a combination of her private neuroses and of real obstacles standing in the way of young women trying to succeed, or merely to survive, in a patriarchal society, *Saving Agnes* offers a subtly feminist take on failure and femininity in the early 1990s – a time that has been associated with what feminist critic Susan Faludi (1993) termed the postfeminist 'backlash'. The novel also provides a nuanced, class-conscious portrayal of growing up in a faltering capitalist economy that has diminishing rewards in store even for the middle classes – the poor of course have even fewer prospects, though Agnes is yet to discover this disparity at the novel's beginning. Visiting her parents' idyllic country home, an emblem of bourgeois success, Agnes realizes that 'she quite possibly might never attain for herself the standard of living to which her upbringing had accustomed her', and that '[t]here might come a time, all too soon, when she herself would need to be saved from the perdition of economic failure' (Cusk 1994: 82). Eventually she comes to a different conclusion: 'For ordinary people, such as herself', there might be no 'defining moment', no ultimate failure or success (217), and if someone is going to be saving her from failure, it ought to be herself: 'I suppose I meant that I shouldn't need to be saved from things. It makes me sound so – naïve' (200). The title, *Saving Agnes*, is thus revealed to be just as ironic as Agnes's self-perception at the novel's beginning. Agnes's conviction that she constitutes a 'failure *extraordinaire*', and her subsequent belief that she needs a man to save her from ruin, is what she must overcome before any kind of success – professional, financial, romantic, artistic – is even possible.

If the traditional *Bildungsroman* concludes when the *Bildungsheld* has found his (or, more rarely, her) station in life, contemporary *Bildungsromane* do not take for granted that the hero can or should be finally integrated into society – nor even that such a thing as 'society' even exists, as Michael Patrick Allen has remarked about the 'Thatcherite Bildungsroman' (2020: 2114). Reading *Saving Agnes* in this lineage reveals it to be equally if not more concerned with questioning the integrity of the neoliberal social order than with narrating its protagonist's integration into this order. Even in the first chapter, Agnes's bourgeois narrative of self-development threatens to collapse when she is forced to retreat inside the house after an interaction with a homeless man goes awry. It takes her brother Tom to point out the reason why her gestures of goodwill backfire with such regularity: 'You don't really care about the poor or the homeless. It's your fear of failure that's behind it. If nobody wins, you can't lose' (Cusk 1994: 83). The lessons Agnes eventually learns are more moderate than Tom's comment suggests, however. Through repeated encounters with others, whose misfortunes far outweigh her own, Agnes realizes that her problems are laughably minor. In other words, more than empathy or genuine solidarity, witnessing suffering teaches Agnes perspective. The emblems of this accumulating perspective in the novel are the mazes – both literal, like the hedge maze Agnes visits with her boyfriend before he dumps her and figurative, like the London Underground and bus network, the main interfaces through which Agnes encounters people outside her social class – in which Agnes gets lost, wanders and eventually finds her way to the centre of the maze, only to discover that '[t]here was nothing there. It was a hoax, an illusion of significance' (117). This cynicism eventually gives way to a more balanced outlook, when Agnes realizes that the world doesn't owe her anything, least of all 'compensation for daily disappointments and injustices' (191), and that if she can just stop expecting that it will, many of her problems will be solved. Not all misfortunes are imaginary, however, and not every problem can be fixed by a change of attitude, as Cusk indicates by tracing Agnes's individualistic narrative of self-development side-by-side with characters facing very real injustices, including Greta, Agnes's friend, colleague and foil, whose cheery optimism fails after she is raped by an acquaintance, and Annie, an elderly homeless woman whom Agnes is powerless to help.

A more profound meditation on failure is evident in how Agnes struggles to distance herself from the neoliberal ideology that causes people like her brother to see the world as consisting of just 'winners' and 'losers'. 'What do you call winning?' Agnes challenges her financial consultant brother, 'What about people who actually do care about things, who reject a system they didn't choose in the first place? Are they losers just because they refuse to play the game?' (Cusk 1994: 83). Tellingly, these questions are never properly answered in the novel. What would it mean for Agnes, or anyone, to reject a system they didn't choose? Is it possible for Agnes to reject not only her parents' middle-class lifestyle, which is moving beyond her reach, but also their bourgeois ideals, which cause Agnes and her brother to equate success with status and material wealth? Is Agnes automatically a failure if she rejects marriage, homeownership, and nuclear family – the emblems of middle-class success? Even though Agnes struggles with such questions, in the end, she neither rejects nor fully embraces the bourgeois values of her parents, but rather finds an uneasy compromise between her desire for autonomy and self-determination and her need for security and social acceptance. She starts pulling her weight at work, which leads to a promotion, which allows her to apply for a mortgage to buy the house she has been renting with friends, which leads to a reconciliation, though one tinged with self-irony, with her parents and their idea of what it means to succeed: 'Agnes's parents had been delighted by this news. It was, they assured her, the right time in her life to be making such a move' (212). By portraying Agnes as she struggles with middle-class ideals and eventually yields to (some of) them, Cusk implies that it is one thing to learn to notice that the way one perceives and evaluates oneself and others is not objective but determined by a variety of factors – including cultural and ideological surroundings, upbringing and personal experience – and another thing entirely to reject this deeply ingrained worldview, *Weltanschauung*, by adopting a different set of values and a different perspective on life.

Even though Agnes ultimately fails to denounce these ideological trappings, her development does not simply culminate in becoming a homeowner or the chief editor of a magazine. Namely, the development that truly matters in *Saving Agnes* takes place largely inside Agnes's mind, having to do with her self-perception, and is therefore much harder to measure than outward signs of success, even by Agnes herself: 'She had changed, she knew, but she didn't quite know how or when' (Cusk 1994: 160). In its very final chapter, *Saving Agnes* takes a turn from the *Bildungsroman* toward the *Künstlerroman*, the artist's novel, by implying that the very last stage of Agnes's internal development might be authorship: 'Her history welled up in her: things burned, frozen, buried alive, a whole disordered catalogue of stories told or hidden. She alone could make sense of them. She alone could tell it as it was, for who else would remember?' (194). Instead of Agnes sitting down to write the novel readers have just finished reading – a common device in the *Bildungsroman* (Slaughter 2010: 4) – the final emphasis on *telling* implies that a literary career might in some distant future be within Agnes's reach. This literary career will centre on realistic depictions of ordinary life – mundane, daily experiences told as they are – but from a perspective that renders some of its opaqueness translucent, imposing order on its chaos. This, at least, is how Cusk seems to imagine authorship at the end of her debut novel, which finally allows even its confused protagonist a newfound perspective, a vantage point, from which life could potentially begin to make sense:

> It was just a question of not looking too closely at things. Close up, the mad weave was bizarre and imageless, but from a distance a pattern could perhaps be discerned and somewhere within it all that she knew: [...] She supposed one only found out how one compared by looking at the picture. It was the final result and she would wait for it, as those around her were now waiting.
>
> Cusk 1994: 217

The equanimity of this conclusion is a far cry from the anguish that has characterized the novel, implying, perhaps, that the perspective which Agnes lacked as a character could be remedied by becoming an author. In contrast, then, to the conclusion of the traditional *Bildungsroman*, which according to Joseph Slaughter 'serves to demonstrate, at least to the protagonist (the *Bildungsheld*), that life is meaningful and that apparently random plot events are actually linked and indispensable for becoming a well-rounded, productive, member of society' (2010: 2), Agnes seems perched to discover that the apparently random events are not but *can be* linked and that this active process of plotting her life can counteract the disillusionment and despair that she has been feeling. Authorship, *Saving Agnes* implies, marks the ultimate success, the ultimate victory, over life itself. Revealing a 'pattern' from 'the mad weave' of existence, writing is what allows recognizable forms to emerge out of the formless mass of experience. All that Agnes needs is to have a little patience – time will take care of the rest, and eventually the 'picture' is revealed. Published twenty-eight years and thirteen books after *Saving Agnes*, *Second Place* comes to the opposite conclusion.

Second Sex: Failure and the Female Artist in *Second Place*

While the theme of authorship is present in a latent form already in *Saving Agnes*, it only becomes a central concern in Cusk's work after the ambivalent and frequently hostile reception of her memoirs, *A Life's Work* (2001) and *Aftermath* (2012). In these memoirs, Cusk experimented with using her own life – her own 'failures' as a mother, as a wife, and perhaps as a woman (see Garrett 2021: 95) – as the raw material that could be rendered in literary form, thus placing herself in a lineage of failing female characters that had begun with Agnes, and continued with *The Temporary*'s (1995) Francine, *The Country Life*'s (1997) Stella, and the disappointed and dispirited women of *Arlington Park* (2006). According to Cusk's admission, the virulent attacks against her person that followed the memoirs with autobiographical writing were what motivated her to begin the formal experimentation that eventually produced *Outline* (2014), her most celebrated novel to date, and a result of her being failed by the memoir as a form of art (see Kellaway 2014). *Kudos* (2018), the final part of the *Outline* trilogy that secured Cusk's reputation as an international literary sensation, fixes a ruthlessly analytical eye to success and failure in the field of literature. In *Second Place*, this criticism becomes self-reflexive, even self-devouring: in it, the artist whose aesthetic merit is being judged harshly is Cusk herself.

Cusk had promised in an interview that *Kudos* would be reaching 'toward termination and vanishing' (Julavits 2015), but the image she leaves readers with is not of a woman about to vanish, let alone be vanquished. Lulling in a darkened ocean while holding eye contact with a man who is urinating belligerently in her direction, the narrator refuses to look away from the scene of her humiliation: 'I looked into his cruel, merry eyes, and I waited for him to stop' (Cusk 2018: 232). *Kudos*'s final sentence doubles as an announcement of the masochistic theme that preoccupies *Second Place*, where the promised journey to 'termination and vanishing' comes into focus. In this novel, we find a middle-aged woman author, identified only as M, who is trapped by her own, hypercritical intellect. Despite suspecting that her judgement may be governed by a sexist double standard, M struggles to overcome this bias on her own, and, ironically, decides to enlist the help of a man, a painter identified only as L, to help her in bringing this final liberation about.

Second Place begins when M invites L to join her and her husband Tony at the annex called 'the second place' that they have renovated on Tony's land. The true reason for the invitation is M's hope that the famous artist's presence will act as a catalyst for the liberating, creative transformation that she yearns for but cannot articulate – though M's letters to L fail to mention this. It is only retrospectively, in the letters that M writes to a mysterious Jeffers after the whole ordeal is over, which constitute the novel's text, that she is able to reflect on her desires and actions. Learning at one point through an intermediary that L has vowed to 'destroy' her (Cusk 2021: 123), M surprises everyone by welcoming the prospect: 'The thing was, Jeffers, part of me wanted to be destroyed, even as I feared that a whole reality would collapse along with it' (ibid.). While M's confessional narration and the novel's pronounced symbolism combine to make *Second Place* an ideal candidate for psychoanalytic interpretation, such a reading risks missing the radical aesthetic critique embedded in the novel's form. Describing this form requires some effort, however, because like much experimental and avant-garde fiction, Cusk's latest novel evades exact definition. Even though M shares some of Cusk's biographical details – both are white, middle-aged, female authors of a vaguely middle-class background who have left the country of their birth and are mothers to at least one child – *Second Place* is not a work of autofiction. Rather, it seems to offer another possible answer to the formal problem that has occupied Cusk since *Outline*, which Ella Ophir has described as an experiment in 'what the novel, the extended, imaginative prose narrative of social experience, brought to the edge of its unmaking, can still genuinely and profitably do' (2022: 2). The solution *Second Place* offers to this formal problem is a complex one. In an endnote, Cusk mentions that her novel owes a 'debt' to another work, which she briefly identifies as *Lorenzo in Taos*. This title belongs to a 1923 memoir by Mable Dodge Luhan (M), an American patron of the arts, who describes through a series of letters that she addressed to her friend, the poet Robinson Jeffers (Jeffers), the events that took place after D. H. Lawrence (L) accepted her invitation to join herself and her Native American husband Tony (Tony) on the ranch that they owned in the Taos Pueblo in New Mexico. In a manner that recalls Joyce's transposition of 'the action of *Odyssey* to twentieth-century Dublin' in *Ulysses* (Genette 1997: 5–6), Cusk has transposed the events that were recorded in Luhan's memoir from a century earlier to the present-day United Kingdom. It would be equally misleading to think of *Second Place* as a work of 'biofiction', because it is not only the characters and the main line of action but all the major elements – characters, plot, theme, epistolary structure, and even style, including the exclamation points that punctuate M's letters to Jeffers – originate in Luhan's memoir. In this sense, Cusk has gone even further than Joyce in her act of literary reappropriation. Instead of 'disqualifying' *Second Place* as a novel, this reappropriation recalls a famous definition of the novel as having a 'cannibal capacity to ingest a wide range of literary genres, modes, and forms' (Cooppan 2018: 23). Crucially, in *Second Place* the reappropriated, 'ingested' material has been rearranged to form a work of art that exists in a derivative relation, 'second place', to another work that came before it.

Even though the formal premise of *Second Place* is more convoluted than *Saving Agnes*'s, in comparison a relatively traditional coming-of-age novel, M does resemble Agnes in that she also thinks of herself as a failure. But whereas Agnes eventually learned to view herself in a different, more forgiving light, M realizes that her self-perception is skewed – and also that there is little she can do about it:

> I said to him that 'second place' pretty much summed up how I felt about myself and my life – that it had been a near miss, requiring just as much effort as victory but with that victory always and forever somehow denied me, by a force that I could only describe as the force of pre-eminence. I could never win, and the reason I couldn't seemed to lie within certain infallible laws of destiny that I was powerless – as the woman I was – to overcome.
>
> Cusk 2021: 145

Where Agnes thought that it was her name that destined her to failure, M's belief clearly has something to do with her gender, though the relationship between failure and femininity is established primarily through the highly ambivalent addition, 'as the woman I was'. This qualifier offers two possible interpretations: It can be taken to mean that to be a woman means to exist in relation to another who must always come first, like Genesis depicts God creating Adam and only fashioning the woman, Eve, as a kind of afterthought to keep him company; or that to be a woman means to be powerless to alter one's destiny whatever that may be. It is in this context, which links femininity with failure, that we can understand M's confession, already noted above, that a 'part of me wanted to be destroyed' (124). Even though M is initially unable to articulate what exactly the 'part' in question would be, it has occurred to her that she needs L's help in getting rid of it; that she 'needed violence, the actual destruction of the ailing part', and something in L's threat to destroy her 'seemed to promise' this (124). A little later, M can give a fuller account of what the 'part' is that she is trying to destroy. 'I don't exist to be seen by you', she now tells L, 'so don't delude yourself on that point, because I'm the one who's trying to free myself how you see me' (132). The 'part' that M wants to have destroyed by L – what she calls the 'the ailing part' – is the 'part' of her that exists to be seen by him and that causes her to see herself as a failure, destined to an eternal 'second place'.

What the phrase 'second place' therefore evokes in the novel is not any real inferiority but the idea – critiqued by Simone de Beauvoir in *Second Sex* ([1949] 1956) – of woman as 'an "imperfect man", an "incidental" being' (1956: 15). Even though *Second Sex* is not explicitly named in Cusk's novel, there are grounds to argue that it functions as the novel's other main subtext – a counterpoint to the rigid ideas about femininity that pervade Luhan's memoir. Throughout the novel, M makes multiple observations that evoke de Beauvoir's theses without directly referring to her. 'Not to have been born in a woman's body was a piece of luck *in the first place*' (Cusk 2021: 65, emphasis mine) is the most obvious link in the string of allusions that evoke the idea of a 'natural' order of the sexes that was critiqued in *Second Sex* while also linking it with Cusk's own title. The cumulative effect of these allusions to women as the 'second sex' is not to strengthen M's disparaging self-estimation, however, but to undermine and subvert it. We can see this subversion enacted by comparing the above statement with M's earlier confession that femininity felt like 'borrowed finery, and sometimes downright impersonation', that she had 'never felt all that womanly *in the first place*', and that there were even parts of her that feel 'male' to her (12, emphasis mine). These two claims about femininity are linked by the figure of speech 'in the first place' that connects them with the titular phrase, 'second place', and with de Beauvoir's title, 'second sex'. The opposition they evoke between (biological) sex and (socially constructed) gender remains unresolved in the novel, however: 'One is not born, but rather becomes, a woman' de Beauvoir famously wrote (1956: 273) – but M is both 'born in a woman's body' *and* becomes a woman through the kind of iterative performance of femininity described by Judith Butler in *Gender Trouble* (1999: 180). What M is trying to free herself from, moreover, is not womanhood per se, but rather, as she tells L, 'from how you see me' and to do so by destroying the 'part' of her in which these ideas and ways of seeing reside (Cusk 2021: 132). The problem is that there is no such 'part' that could simply be 'destroyed' in the human body, male or female. By depicting M's struggle to break free from the culture that made her who she is, the culture that surrounds and sustains her as an author, *Second Place* reveals why, after centuries of feminist campaigning, we have not yet succeeded in abolishing gender inequality. For the novel to succeed in its attempt to portray this profound challenge – one that M is not alone in facing – its protagonist must necessarily fail in her individual liberation. Conversely, were M to succeed in liberating herself from the effects of patriarchal culture, *Second Place* would have failed in representing the radical challenge that feminism still faces today.

The relationship between L and M undergoes a similar destabilization that centres on their artistic abilities. At first, it seems as if the two artists, one male, the other female – who are moreover identified only by initials that reproduce the hierarchy, with *l* coming directly before *m* in the alphabet – confirm the idea of women as a 'second sex'. L is a world-famous painter; M publishes rarely and has a limited readership. Yet no sooner is this opposition evoked than it is revoked, with M increasingly accumulating masculine characteristics through confessions such as the ones cited above, while L becomes increasingly associated with the feminine – to the point that out of the two middle-aged artists, it is the male one who undergoes menopause in the novel. When L attributes his bad mood to what he euphemistically refers to as 'the change', Brett finds the idea ridiculous, but to M 'it seemed [...] like something that might well happen to a creative artist, where a loss or alteration in the sources of potency had occurred' (Cusk 2021: 86). Through the double-meaning word 'potency', the change that L is undergoing becomes linked with a web of ideas that connect creativity with the male sex (-organ). What L is experiencing, moreover, is not limited to a change in his relative position in the symbolic order because of his ageing.

Rather, the symbolic order itself seems to be undergoing a restructuring. Formerly a heavyweight in the art world, L has recently discovered that other artists have eclipsed his reputation: 'Some of them happen to be younger than him', Brett explains to M, 'and a different colour, and a couple of them are actually women' (86–7) – a comment that exposes M's feminism as the de Beauvoirian, second-wave brand that is today sometimes disparagingly called *white* feminism. Whatever cultural change this restructuration promises comes too late for M, however, who is fixed in her conviction that compared to L, she is inferior as an artist:

> This is the difference, I suppose, between an artist and an ordinary person: the artist can create outside himself the perfect replica of his intentions. The rest of us just create a mess, or something hopelessly wooden, no matter how brilliantly we imagined it.
>
> Cusk 2021: 32–3

The phrase 'ordinary person' echoes *Saving Agnes*'s conviction that even with nothing outwardly wrong with her, she is an 'extraordinary' failure. Now, the tables have turned, as M is trapped by a field of vision in which true artists are extraordinary – but *she* can never be that.

The reason M believes that L is an artist while she is something else – a 'writer', perhaps – is determined by what, in M's opinion, constitutes art: 'True art means seeking to capture the unreal', she writes in one of her letters (Cusk 2021: 180). By contrast, M believes that she only possesses the 'more common ability to read the surface of life' (54). This ability sounds very much like the skill that Agnes was just starting to develop at the end of *Saving Agnes*, but in *Second Place* the exact same ability signifies failure instead of success. Being able 'to read the surface of life' may still yield a victory over the sheer chaos of living, but it is not enough to command respect in a world that devalues artists who represent ordinary life, at least according to M. But if M is wrong about herself, as Agnes was, perhaps she is also wrong about what constitutes 'true art'? After all, L first became a sensation when he painted a series of gruesomely realistic works representing animal carcasses – an autobiographical theme for a painter whose childhood home adjoined the slaughterhouse owned by his parents: 'I wonder whether this explains L's failure to ever hit quite the right note with the critics again, since they expected him to go on shocking them, when in fact he had been introspective all along', M muses (53), indicating that she might not be an unreliable critic of *others*' work. If it isn't the 'unreal' that counts, however, then some other criteria must be used to determine whose realities are considered worth representing in a work of art – in L's case, the ultraviolent, hypermasculine, 'shocking' reality of a slaughterhouse, which is a far cry from the suppressed despair of the bourgeois home that *Second Place*, like most of Cusk's novels, depicts. Readers know almost nothing about the books that M writes, by contrast, not even if they are novels or memoirs or poetry, and what little we do know comes from M herself, whose judgement we now know to be influenced by the sexist standards she is futilely trying to free herself from:

> My little books, as he called them, had indeed made hardly any money, partly because they presented themselves to me so infrequently, and only when life had taken an ethical shape by which I had to be thoroughly broken down before I could assume that shape myself in words.
>
> Cusk 2021: 107

Infrequency aside – Cusk herself is a prolific writer, who publishes a book every few years – M's books do somewhat resemble Cusk's both thematically and aesthetically, presenting ruthlessly clinical dissections of ordinary middle-class lives directly after disaster has struck. These books, M believes, are not 'true' works of art, not in the way that L's paintings are – but readers may also choose to question M's judgement, as they are increasingly invited to do while reading. M's other claim – that success when one is still in one's twenties can 'distort the flow of experiences and misshape the personality' (53) – raises the question of whether L might be a truer self-portrait of the author as an ageing artist than M. In neither case is the portrait a flattering one.

Because of the novel's creative reappropriation of Luhan's memoir, however, it is difficult to identify Cusk's own position in this critique of aesthetic double standards, which seems to condemn women artists, particularly those interested in depicting the domestic lives of white middle-class women, to a 'second place'. What these formal evasions show is, perhaps, that Cusk has not quite forgotten the virulent attacks against her person when she dared criticize cultural norms relating to motherhood, femininity, and marriage in her memoirs. M's statement, for instance, that '[t]rue art means seeking to capture the unreal', is originally put forward by Luhan, who insists throughout *Lorenzo in Taos* that, unlike Lawrence, she is not an artist, 'Since I do not know how to invent anything, I could never write about anything except myself and what I saw' (Luhan 1933: 121). In fact, this was the reason that Luhan invited Lawrence to Taos in the first place: 'To take *my* experience, *my* material, *my* Taos, and to formulate it all into a magnificent creation. That was what I wanted him for' (77). Similarly, M originally invited L to stay because she hoped that L would feel moved to paint the marsh landscape that she had spent years contemplating, and that, in doing so, he might finally be able to answer its 'conundrum' (Cusk 2021: 17). But Lawrence never did write a novel about the Taos pueblo, and when L arrives, he begins painting a series of portraits instead of the landscape M had been wishing for. The experience Luhan and M had been hoping Lawrence and L to capture for them is given expression, however, in the letters that they write to another man, the absent 'Jeffers', or, as it might be more accurate to say, in the memoirs that Luhan and M write under the guise of the epistolary device. The real author, Cusk, meanwhile, stays safely tucked away behind the scenes, pulling the strings as M confesses with Luhan's voice, incriminating herself as both the victim and the perpetrator of a hopelessly sexist double standard that fixes her position in an eternal 'second place' relative to L.

Unlike readers of *Saving Agnes*, who perceive Agnes both from within and from without, readers of *Second Place* are trapped inside the perspective whose limitations they are subtly invited to consider. Despite this formal difference, we can no more trust M's insistence that she is doomed to an eternal 'second place' than we could trust Agnes's insistence that she is a 'failure *extraordinaire*'. *Second Place* encourages readers to eventually extend this same judgement to the novel itself – to *Second Place* as a work of art. The main effect of repeated references to the titular phrase, 'second place', within the text is to include the idea of the novel in its textual machinery so that it can become the artwork that is being judged through M's perspective. Because this perspective is faulty – and readers must first learn to recognize it as such, as they did when reading *Saving Agnes* – *Second Place* expects its readers to not only become aware of the double standard but to become aware of it in themselves, in their reading of the novel. The readers who are unable or unwilling to make this move are forced to witness a work of art devour itself alive, subjecting itself to a criticism that is intended to annihilate it. In hindsight, Cusk did issue a warning in *Kudos*: 'The self-destructive novel, like the self-destructive person, was something from which in the end you remained helplessly separated, forced to watch a spectacle – the soul turning on itself – in which you were powerless to intervene' (2018: 182).

Conclusion: The Artist of Failure

Where does this leave Cusk as an artist? What are readers supposed to think about Cusk's creative capabilities relative to Agnes, to M and Luhan, the two 'failed' artists, and even relative to L, the creative success who supposedly embodies the 'true' artist? Is Cusk, too, a failed artist, an *artiste manquée*, because, like Agnes and M, her art consists of 'read[ing] the surface of life' – and not just any life, but the privileged lives of heterosexual, white, middle-class women? On the contrary. In *Second Place*, Cusk is setting herself a challenge that she has no intention of losing. Its dark fantasy world 'capture[s] the unreal,' thus distinguishing Cusk from M and Luhan, the 'mere' writers. Even L, supposedly the 'true' artist, pales in comparison to Cusk: *she is* the author responsible for creating L, whose artistry, like Cusk's own, is proven by his ability to reinvent himself every few years, and whose talent, again like Cusk's, is recognized also by those who dislike or disapprove of his brutalist aesthetic – yet another very Cusk-like characteristic. On the other hand, the question of M's self-perception remains open: is she a failed artist, or is she wrong about herself? Her letters are the only way to judge her talent, but even they are not really *hers*, carrying, as they do, the insignias of Luhan's over-emphatic style – a far cry from Cusk's usual, pared-down, 'austere' minimalism (Vermeulen 2021). In the end, this matters little, because the point of reading *Second Place* is not to decide which one of the characters acts as the author's self-portrait – in one way, they all do – but to become aware of and begin to question the criteria we use to evaluate works of art. How do we judge art if judging it only by aesthetic criteria is impossible? The only way to judge a novel, or any work of art, Cusk seems to be suggesting in *Second Place*, is by asking whether it succeeds or fails in what it is trying to do: whether it manages to adequately represent the thing that it tries to represent, even or especially when it is not immediately clear what this is. In both *Saving Agnes* and *Second Place*, the protagonists' failures are more instructive than their successes: what is at stake in both novels is an attempt to represent the difficulty of liberating oneself from the judgement that society – parents, siblings, friends, lovers, critics and other artists – passes on one. Because capturing this difficulty is only possible if the protagonists fail in their own attempts to break free, their personal failures pave the way for the author's artistic success.

Works Cited

Allen, M. P. (2020), 'The Thatcherite Bildungsroman', *Textual Practice*, 34 (12): 2113–30. Available at: https://doi.org/10.1080/0950236X.2020.1833532

de Beauvoir, S. (1956), *The Second Sex* (trans. H. M. Parshley). London: Jonathan Cape.

Berger, J. ([1965] 1989), *The Success and Failure of Picasso*. New York: Vintage International.

Boileau, N. P. (2013), 'Introduction', *E-rea: Revue électronique d'études sur le monde anglophone*, 10 (2). Available at: http://erea.revues.org/3190 (accessed 30 July 2023).

Bürger, P. (1984), *Theory of the Avant-Garde* (trans. Michael Shaw). Minneapolis: University of Minnesota Press.

Butler, J. ([1990] 1999), *Gender Trouble: Gender and the Subversion of Identity*. London and New York: Routledge.

Cooppan, V. (2018), 'The Novel as Genre', in E. Bulson (ed.), *The Cambridge Companion to the Novel*, 23–42. Cambridge: Cambridge University Press.

Cusk, R. ([1993] 1994), *Saving Agnes*. London: Picador.

Cusk, R. (2018), *Kudos*. London: Faber & Faber.

Cusk, R. (2021), *Second Place*. New York: Farrar, Straus and Giroux.

Faludi, S. (1993), *Backlash: The Undeclared War Against Women*. London: Vintage.

Gablik, S. ([1984] 2004), *Has Modernism Failed?* London: Thames & Hudson.

Garrett, R. (2021), *Writing the Modern Family: Contemporary Literature, Motherhood and Neoliberal Culture*. London: Rowman & Littlefield Publishers.

Genette, G. (1997), *Palimpsest: Literature in the Second Degree* (trans. C. Newman and C. Doubinsky). Lincoln and London: Nebraska University Press.

Harrison, L. (2022), *Late Modernist Styles: Modernist Legacies in Post-Millennial British and Irish Literature*. University of Birmingham. Ph.D. Available at: http://etheses.bham.ac.uk/id/eprint/13130

Halberstam, J. (2011), *The Queer Art of Failure*. Durham and London: Duke University Press.

Howe, S. (1930), *Wilhelm Meister and His English Kinsmen: Apprentices to Life*. New York: Columbia University Press.

Julavits, H. (2015), 'Rachel Cusk's "Outline"', *The New York Times*, 7 January. Available at: www.nytimes.com/2015/01/11/books/review/rachel-cusks-outline.html

Kellaway, K. (2014), 'Rachel Cusk', *The Observer*, 24 August. Available at: www.theguardian.com/books/2014/aug/24/rachel-cusk-interview-aftermath-outline

Luhan, M. D. (1933), *Lorenzo in Taos*. London: Martin Secker.

Moretti, F. (1987), *The Way of the World: The* Bildungsroman *in European Culture*. London: Verso.

Ophir, E. (2022), 'Neomodernism and the Social Novel: Rachel Cusk's *Outline Trilogy*'. *Critique: Studies in Contemporary Fiction*, 64 (2): 353–64. Available at: https://doi.org/10.1080/00111619.2021.2021133

Ross, A. (1986), *The Failure of Modernism: Symptoms of American Poetry*. New York: Columbia University Press.

Sandler, M. (2017), 'Gertrude Stein, Success Manuals, and Failure Studies'. *Twentieth-Century Literature*, 63 (2): 191–212.

Slaughter, J. R. (2010), 'Bildungsroman/Künstlerroman', in P.M. Logan (ed.), *The Encyclopedia of the Novel*. Available at: https://doi.org/10.1002/9781444337815.wbeotnb003

Vermeulen, P. (2021), 'Against Premature Articulation: Empathy, Gender, and Austerity in Rachel Cusk and Katie Kitamura'. *Cultural Critique*, 111 (Spring 2021): 81–103.

5

'Some things are artificial and some are authentic'

Rachel Cusk's Depth Perception

Daniel Lea

'You read, you take the consequences' (Cusk 2017: 243). So warns the diary of one of the narrator's sons in *Transit* (2017), the second novel in Rachel Cusk's *Outline* trilogy. That the act of reading is consequential in Cusk's work barely requires highlighting, but in her recent fiction it has taken a new prominence. There, reading is both a constitutive and transgressive act, one that appropriates the objective world by imposing structure and meaning, but which is always liable to rebound on the subject – one reads, and one is read. That two-way process pins its participants into shapes both real and imagined and Cusk's recent fiction has explored the politics and ethics of this immobilization. *The Bradshaw Variations* (2009) and the *Outline* trilogy (2014–18) focus on identity as the outcome of the reading process, not only in the sense of the self as an articulation of an internal self-understanding, but also as the product of others' reading and over-reading, which makes interpretation a messy and unjust business. This chapter will examine these novels' representation of selfhood through the particular focus of authenticity, a trope Cusk employs to analyse her protagonists' desire for freedom, to contrast against the horizon of bourgeois artificiality in which they are placed, and to critique the neoliberalization of the contemporary literary marketplace.

Authenticity as a philosophical concept has a long history, crystallizing most coherently in two related strands of post-Enlightenment thinking about selfhood: the Romantic cult of the self as inviolable interiority and the Existentialist model of the self as constituted by the individual's choices. Both strands address the self as sovereign, individualized, capable of accessing a sense of personal identity outside the social demands and contexts in which it exists. The authentic self is 'owned' by the subject alone; it is unique and, depending on the tradition, accessible by the individual's inward reflection on its core values and beliefs (Romantic), or constituted by actions that are true to a dynamic and lifelong project of the self (Existentialist). In the twentieth century, the subjective and hermetic qualities of deep interiority, with their promise of a private space beyond and beneath public discourse, were scrutinized critically by poststructuralist and deconstructive thinkers, for whom the notion of authenticity was a relic of humanism. In recent decades, however, a new interpretation has gained ground – largely as a result of the work of the philosopher Charles Taylor – that posits authenticity not as an internalized sovereignty outside the influence of the other or of language, but as foundationally dialogic.[1] The self as monad means very little, Taylor claims, and only takes on substantial form when it sets its eyes on the 'horizon of significance' (Taylor 1991a: 39) that it shares and nurtures with others. The 'horizon of significance' is the collective understanding of ethical value that operates as a point of agreement 'whereby some things are worthwhile and others less so, and still others not at all, quite anterior to choice' (38). Such passive universalism may be enough to make a hard relativist's blood boil, but, for Taylor, to *be someone* is 'to know "where you're coming from"' when it comes to questions of value' (Taylor 1991b: 305), and that can only be established with and through others. Only in dialogue, and with a sense of the collective good, can an individual articulate their particular investment in the 'horizon of significance', one which gives their life meaning and a sense of purpose. Less outwardly directed ideas of the self tend, Taylor argues, to result in entropic subjectivism or ethical relativism. Across all three of these strands, authenticity emerges as an idea of value-conscious, integrated and enduring personhood that, for all its appeal, is difficult to identify and even harder to attain. It is at continuous threat of falling into inauthenticity, betraying itself by succumbing to the will of others, or the call of conventionality.

It is this fear of falling into an inauthenticity represented by the construction of self shaped by the conventionalized desires of others that characterizes Cusk's protagonists in these novels. She portrays her characters *in situ*, embedded, and often trapped within domestic relationships that govern the outline of their identity. They are self-determining, but only within the parameters of their immediate environs and associates, parameters that are rigidly delineated by the institutions of the middle-class life with which Cusk's writing concerns itself. Like Claudia, the frustrated artist of *The Bradshaw Variations*, they find that

---

[1] Taylor's dialogic authenticity has been picked up contemporary philosophers of ethics such as Guignon (2004) and Varga (2012).

responsibility 'sets its pins and screws into your nature, that warps and gnarls you and makes you ugly to yourself' (Cusk 2009: 153). Marriage, family life, career and social respectability are the coordinates by which her characters negotiate their lives and through which they construct a sense of domesticated identity. Like ill-fitting clothes, this identity frequently rubs in the wrong places, restricting a sense of movement and comfort, and, because it is kept in place by an unspoken alliance of stability and conformity, it gives rise to deeply ambivalent emotions.

In an interview with Sheila Heti for the *Paris Review*, Cusk describes her own sense of internal conflict in binary terms, as a tension between the real and the artificial. 'I could almost divide my life on either side of this line,' she states, 'between the things that are real and the things that are imitating reality and are synthetic or inauthentic, and the awful pain of being in the synthetic life or the synthetic relationship, the one that is a bit like the thing you want but is not it' (Heti 2020). This struggle is captured in her writing as a problem of form, that is, as an intense discomfort with the inherited structures of expectation, action and speech through which her protagonists read themselves and others. Form is a 'search for conformity, a search for agreement' (Schwartz 2018), but it is also the antithesis of authenticity, understood by her as something unconstructed and intuitive. Form translates the real into the synthetic bringing often violent and chaotic passions into manageable and interpretable shape. The expectations of respectable bourgeois life, as much as the character-driven conventions of the novel, point to the ways in which the spirit of the authentic is constrained by order and what *The Bradshaw Variations* and the *Outline* trilogy explore is the creative and destructive interplay that those constraints allow.

Harmonic Exercises: *The Bradshaw Variations*

Inauthenticity dogs Cusk's protagonists in *The Bradshaw Variations*, largely because it feels deeply familiar to them. Thomas articulates this in the novel's opening lines: 'Some things are artificial and some are authentic. It is easy to tell when something is artificial. The other is harder' (Cusk 2009: 1). Thomas, his wife, Tonie, and their daughter, Alexa are defined by their ordinary privilege. They live in the better part of a commuter town on the periphery of London, their Georgian house situated on a hill that looks down on and is removed from the 'inalienable and general' (13) life of the town. They are surrounded by liberal professionals – academics, teachers, social workers whose 'capacity for deep, undisclosed suffering and worldly indifference, for extreme feats of virtue or nihilism, for the repression of passions and staunchness in the face of reality, is so violent that it ought to leave some visible mark on their surroundings [...]' (14). All are caught in a desperate moral and aesthetic neutrality where desires are suppressed and social success brings with it a sense of guilt and provisionality. Houses lack 'both luxuries and necessities', characterized by 'rooms empty of furniture or ornament, stained walls with no pictures on them, cardboard boxes that have never been unpacked, desolate shelves' (14). They are trapped in a world of hyper-self-consciousness, too alert to their own artificiality to embrace the choice to change that privilege has put at their disposal. Cusk presents Tonie as the critical perspective in the novel, the eye that perceives the suppressed desires of others, but much of her narrative revolves around her difficulties with her own desires for freedom, authority and authentic self-expression.

Tonie is presented in a form of nether-time 'between childbearing and visible decay'; about to turn forty, she is 'taut with expectation' as if 'the real life of her body is about to begin' (19), and yet she fears that the deep purpose of her body won't reveal itself. Her narrative involves her attempt to trace the authentic purpose into which she feels she should be growing. In this, she butts against the authority and desires of others, particularly men, whose own freedom is expressed through their organization and co-option of her time and body. She accepts the role of Head of the Department of English at her local university with an ambivalence that stems from her sense of her unformed identity, shaped by the years that she has spent caring for her daughter and husband. Her boss is a careerist bureaucrat who tries to erase his reliance on her by the imposition of an authoritarian formalism designed to keep in check the barely suppressed violence of his civility. The reactions to her from other men are either predatory or condescending: they dominate conversations, stare past her when she speaks, or make unappealing sexual passes out of a false sense of entitlement. Frustrated by the sense of her own conventionality and yet unsure of how to break with it, she is beset by doubt about whether she has a functioning identity beyond the home: 'Her own body, the unit of herself, so sealed and single: it is all she is, and yet she lives in it so little. Away from home, she is only this unit of flesh' (67). Her attempt to be herself leads her only to the uncomfortable conclusion that this self either does not exist or is a fantasy of escape. The sexual attraction she feels to fellow academic, Dieter, lies in the fact that he sees her as distinct from him, not entangled in a relationship of dependence or ownership. The possession that's involved in his gaze is one that 'leaves no part of her out' (218). He makes no assumptions about her ability to have control over her decisions and in their brief relationship she experiences an authentic coalescence as a form of existential revelation, one in which 'Her love and her terror lie beyond her scope, at cell-level. They existed before she herself knew what existence was' (221). Her freedom to experience herself as a separate actor is short-lived, however, as matriarchal duty reasserts itself when her daughter falls ill with meningitis, driving her back to family life with all its ambivalence.

Thomas escapes into an idealized bohemianism in which he seeks to outmanoeuvre his spiritual ennui through dedication to learning the piano. Undergoing a comparable mid-life crisis to Tonie, he fetishizes the authentic as a crystalline spirit of originality that can transcend the everyday mundane grind of existence. His sabbatical from working life is the counterbalance to Tonie's assumption of breadwinning duties but is a largely insincere performance of the 'artist life' consisting mainly of idleness and disorderliness rather than stringent self-examination. Where Tonie is presented as confused, Thomas is naïve. His desire to be able to master one thing in his life is ill-considered and indicates his lack of imagination; he is a caricature of a creative drop-out rather than an *artist manqué*. Conquering the piano becomes the master narrative that replaces the youthful illusions burned off by experience. Life, he muses in his opening reflection, squeezes one into shape through centripetal forces creating either a coherent self (which he understands as authentic), or a disintegrating mess of inchoate parts (inauthentic). Art is his force for transformation, the catalyst of coherence.

That desire for escape into something that pulls the parts of the self into a coherent shape so that one can see oneself and be seen by others as whole is as strong for Thomas as it is for Tonie. His will is projected onto the piano and the desire to perform one piece flawlessly, as if his sense of artificiality can be overcome by a single act of artistic transcendence. Attending his lesson, he has a consummatory moment of technical mastery, but the epiphany turns bathetic when he learns from his teacher that success is the consequence of treating music like a mechanical operation: '"It's like a clock," Benjamin says. "Imagine you are inside a clock. The music is the mechanism"' (89). Once Thomas begins to treat the music this way by framing it as an exercise in timing rather than as intuition, he finds that he can no longer believe in its, or his own authenticity.

Keeping time seems a disappointingly utilitarian route to creative expression, but the novel highlights the potential for art in routine both through the 'variations' of the title and in the epigraphs that point to the originality that can be found in repetition: Cusk cites Sartre's view that J. S. Bach 'taught us how to find originality within an established discipline'. It is a sentiment that Thomas recognizes. Music 'could be anything' he muses, 'and at the same time cannot be other than it is' (41). The structure, formality, tension and release, and temporal arc of music are framed by the internal rules that it sets itself, and yet allow for seemingly endless variation and the possibility of transcendence. Tonie, craving definitions of a self not predicated on the routines of domestic duty or the will of other men, comes to a similar conclusion: the urge to own and respond to her body as a self-defining marker of her uniqueness gives way to a recognition that 'She wanted her own duality. She did not want to grow and grow, a branching tree of femininity: she wanted her own conflict of female and male, her own synthesis' (214). For both, self-mastery, the desire for deep, authentic integrity, has to be accommodated with the shapes and routines into which they have been moulded.

The novel ends, unsurprisingly, on an ambivalent note. The restitution of bourgeois conventionality, with Thomas resuming work and Tonie the domestic sphere, returns us to the suppressed agonism of shared life and their relationship is an effort to manage the guilt that their respective flirtations with freedom have induced. On one level, they have resumed attritional conflict 'ratified by a treaty of silence' (249), but on another, the relentless mechanics of time and body represent a familiar constraint that promises creative, as well as destructive, variation. The ability to find new shapes in sameness and art in the familiar is as strong as the likelihood of being crushed by routine and banality. Arriving home from work to his unsatisfactory bourgeois life at the novel's conclusion, Thomas hears 'the trill of a bird joyously piercing [the silence], trilling and trilling, garlanding the still air with a ribbon of song' (249).

Groundworks: The *Outline* Trilogy

In the *Outline* trilogy, Cusk's thinking about the authentic manifests in the tension between surface and depth, real and artificial, honesty and pretension, and between idealized past and disillusioned present. There is, of course, an irony in discussing deep interiority in novels where the idea is so formally negated, but there is a clear bridge between the representation of selfhood in the trilogy and in *The Bradshaw Variations*. Taken as a whole, the narrator, Faye's, trajectory takes her from radical disengagement from her interior life, through gradual re-coalescence, to the recognition that she can work with the institutions of domestic and social life. Though self-realization is not the driver for change that it is for Thomas and Tonie, and authenticity is regarded at points as a trap for the self-deluded, the trilogy moves Faye towards a point of reconciliation with her experiences. This is neither a comfortable nor conclusive reconciliation, but the permeability of Faye's boundary with the world of others, her sense of a self she can call her own, does appear to be hardening by the end of *Kudos* (2018). The final scene of the trilogy, in which misogyny is grotesquely embodied in the figure of the man performatively urinating into the sea close to where she is swimming, is endured in patient silence by Faye. The water bears her up protectively against his inarticulate hostility and she simply, but defiantly waits for him to stop.

Furthermore, authenticity remains a useful metaphorical touchstone for Cusk throughout the trilogy with which she can critique the fundamentalism of neoliberal ideology, the commoditization of literary endeavour, and the nostalgic yearning for meaning that inhabits the stories we tell about our lives. Narrative, with its power to mythologize the incompatible elements of reality into coherence is both the necessary substructure of the self's engagement with the world of others and the means of escaping the painful and inconvenient truths that Cusk's protagonists find in that world. Disillusioned and adrift as a result of divorce at the outset of the trilogy, Faye understands that what has been lost is the shared belief in the narratives of marriage and domestic stability that have sustained her family life. Love, she reflects, is a 'belief in something that only the two of you can see' which, under the spotlight of reality, proves 'to be an impermanent basis for living' (Cusk 2015: 81). The stories that she, and many of the speakers that she encounters relate, function as mutually agreed points of connection, allowing them to maintain the illusion that relationships are not foundationally unequal, cruel and competitive. They can only be sustained by self-delusion and its burning-off is the 'transposition from love to factuality' (81); in factuality, the inequalities and injustices that have underpinned the fantasy become apparent. She experiences this viscerally through her sons. Initially characterized by a 'shared trance in which they created whole imaginary worlds' (80), their relationship becomes argumentative and oppositional as they grow older, leading Faye to conclude that 'what was beautiful in their lives was the result of a shared vision of things that strictly speaking could not have been said to exist' (80–1).

For Faye, identity involves the unavoidable setting of the self both within and against the world of others and of objects; subjectivity is positive in the sense that it casts the objective as negative and that requires the rejection of the narratives of unanimity on which it had formerly relied. As much as for her sons, she is required to redefine her relationship with the stories that she has co-created, and, as it is for many of her locutors, the result is an acute sense of vulnerability to the loss of place within the world of social and personal narrative.

Her billionaire neighbour on the plane at the beginning of *Outline* articulates his own crisis of narrative in the terms of authenticity. He has been unable to reframe his life within alternative stories and find new means for rebuilding faith after his succession of divorces and is beset with nostalgia for the authenticity of his first marriage which 'represented for him a home, a place to which he yearned to return' (15), and which he attempts to recreate in his subsequent marriages. The authenticity he idealizes only occurs to him in retrospect after he is forced to recognize (without being able to reconcile himself to) the post-lapsarian knowledge of his own loneliness. In both the case of her sons and the billionaire, authenticity is represented as a state of natural, unquestioning self-presence prior to and outside the demands of the social. There are echoes here of the Rousseau's state-of-nature that is corrupted by the competitiveness and *amour-propre* that living with others produces and, at times, Cusk uses the Romantic idea of pure self undone by the cruelties and iniquities of unequal power relations and social institutions. It would be wrong to suggest that she portrays the individual as foundationally good – in fact, there is profuse evidence to suggest that her view of the state-of-nature is closer to Hobbes than Rousseau – but it is the inherently unjust organization of the social world in which the narratives of marriage, domesticity, security and gendered self are framed that makes the maintenance of shared illusion impossible.

Stripped of her own narrative illusions at the start of the trilogy, Faye is particularly vulnerable to those of others. That is not to suggest that she is without readerly agency or critical judgement for she curates the stories of others with a strong sense of their rhetorical intentions, but her own lack of narrative coordinates, particularly in *Outline*, makes her difficult to parse as a readable self or character.[2] This begins to shift in *Transit*, which, with its focus on the domestic home-space as also a self-space, sees Faye moving towards an initialization of alternative frames for her identity. In an article published in the *New York Times Magazine* in 2016, Cusk describes her own purgative approach to reclaiming a home for herself and her children following her divorce:

> I caused walls to be knocked down and floors to be ripped up and rooms to be gutted; I threw away decades' worth of clutter and keepsakes and old furniture; with what at times seemed like magic and at others sheer violence, I caused the past to be obliterated and put something new, something of my choosing, in its

---

[2] Some reviewers of the trilogy saw Faye's control over the retelling of others' stories as a direct and even self-serving manipulation on her part. See for instance Clanchy (2018) and Rooney (2018).

place. At home, everywhere I looked I now seemed to see a hidden part of myself that was publicly exposed [...]

Cusk 2016

This 'gut-renovation' (Thurman 2017) is an elimination of one set of self-narratives to allow another to seed, a ground-clearing exercise in self-reinvention that Faye must similarly undergo before the reconstitution of herself. Yet this is not an unproblematic reclamation of one's own space, as for Cusk and her protagonist, the home is an ambivalent site, ground zero for the contradictions of imprisonment and freedom in the novels. As Faye tells her cousin Lawrence in the last section of *Transit*, freedom is 'a home you leave once and can never go back to' (Cusk 2017: 210), a sentiment that, again, recalls the idea of a point of origin coloured by nostalgic longing.

At the outset of the novel, Faye is as conflicted as she was in *Outline*, torn between the possibility of freedom and the spectre of fate. The latter is introduced immediately where she recounts the offer of a fortune-telling provided by an online astrologer. Though she is inclined to reject the fatalism of predestination, she shows little in the early sections to suggest that she is ready to strike out and choose her own story. When she meets her former partner, Gerard, she extols the virtues of the city's anonymity, which allows for a simple and pre-digested reading of people and things *en masse*, whereas life in the country had created problems of interpretation: 'so many unfounded assumptions, so many words failed to maintain an integral meaning' (19). When she is deciding upon her flat, she chooses anonymity over originality: 'I would want what everyone else wanted, even if I couldn't attain it' (7). She does this partly to defy the expectations of the estate agent who imagines that as a 'creative' she would want something distinctive, but, as she acknowledges a page later, it 'whatever we might wish to believe about ourselves, we are only the result of how others have treated us' (9). She believes that fate renders one's life textual – one reads one's own experiences from a distance to 'find out what happens next' (198). The danger this creates, she says, is that it casts others as characters in a predetermined story and therefore exempts them from blame for the destruction they do, though, interestingly, she does not see herself as a character and thus guilty for her own cruelty.

Gerard has passed a life characterized by a lack of desire to change. He still lives in the flat he shared with Faye and seeks out the familiar, for 'It felt wrong for the whole of life to be based on choice' (21). He then moves to Toronto, where he meets his wife, he falls into a schedule that 'had the benefit of erasing the element of choice from his daily life' (23). Fate intervenes when the dog that he has been minding for Diana goes missing, but this releases him into a recognition of the underlying power of his own expectation of failure, which, in turn, grants him the freedom to begin a relationship with Diane based on an awareness of each other's vulnerabilities. 'Maybe it's only in our injuries,' he claims, 'that the future can take root' (32). Gerard's story might seem a seductive justification for giving into fate, but his section is strongly associated with the inauthentic. As he and Faye walk, they comment on the gentrification of poor areas of London as part of the property boom, the ersatz theme pubs that have sprung up, and the standardization of commodity culture. Ultimately, Faye rejects his fatalism and conviction that more-of-the-same can produce difference. It is also a rejection of the nostalgia that afflicts so many of those she encounters, but it is not yet a statement of her own self-determining agency – that can only come with the hardening of the ground beneath her feet.

The renovation of the flat is a question of blocking out the world of others, expelling the noise of the world to allow for a space in which Faye can recover; it is a process in which even her children can play no part. The anonymity and silence that she craves are undermined, however, by her aggressive neighbours who offer continuous commentary on her life-choices and moral character and are grotesque manifestations of the difficulty of breaking away from one's factuality; they dwell unhealthily in the bowels of the house just as they lurk in the darker corners of Faye's conscience as examples of the cost of being left out of social narrative. They also operate as the dark Other of the age of bourgeois gentrification – the repressed surplus that cannot be eradicated from the neoliberal reality. It is only when the soundproof flooring is installed in her flat that Faye begins to recover a sense of her own integrity: 'The rooms were silent, and solid underfoot. I walked across the new surface. I went to the back door and opened it and sat on the steps outside. The sky was clear now and bursting with stars. I sat and looked at the points of light surging forward out of the darkness' (207). The sense of cosmic calm here suggests a gradual solidification of Faye's identity but is undercut by the sound of the neighbour scuttling like an animal below and admonishing her as a 'Fucking bitch' (207). The world beyond Faye is no less judgemental or cruel, but she does, at least, have the foundations of a sound-proofed life in place.

By this point, Faye has grown to regard fate as a byword for exploitation, as a means for those with power to elude justice. Far from being the narrative of an omniscient storyteller, fate is the working of others' wills on the individual in such a way as to render them powerless. In the section where she meets the man that we assume she is to marry, she describes how renovating the flat has become a statement of intent, a repudiation of the will of others and of the narratives that disable her. She had 'started to desire power, because what I now realised was that other people had had it all along' (198). The immediate impact of this on her companion is to make him vulnerable – he is 'naked' without his glasses, as if he had 'removed the shield of adulthood' (198). He responds with memories of childhood in which the barely suppressed anger and disgust of his parents were common features and in which the master narrative of religion was deployed to condemn self-assertion as sin. He had grown accustomed to believing that his life 'was virtually preordained, accounted for before it had even occurred' (204). However, he claims that he is drifting away from the moral outlook that had underscored his sense of failure precisely because such preordination did not require agency. He and Faye collide at a moment of common trajectory towards self-realization as is indicated by the moment of recognition in which her name is spoken for the only time in the volume – as he asserts her individuality and identity she begins to move towards a different relationship with the existing patterns of human togetherness: 'A flooding feeling of relief passed violently through me, as if I was the passenger in a car that had finally swerved away from a sharp drop' (206).

Faye is coming to regard her relationships with others in less starkly oppositional terms. Like the Saluki dogs that she learns about, which hunt in tandem with a hawk, she begins to reconcile herself to an idea of the unitary self as containing the duality that Tonie acknowledges wherein the 'ultimate fulfilment of a conscious being lay not in solitude but in a shared state so intricate and cooperative it might almost be said to represent the entwining of two selves' (192). Such an insight could not have been realized, we infer, without her renovated interior and without her openness to another's vulnerability, and it suggests her movement towards the possibility of symbiotic, companionate co-existence with another. The metaphor of the hunt is particularly resonant because it requires the dogs to *read* the hawk, which leads to shared effort at entering narratives that may function in different ways but have the same end. Yet, that purpose is predatory, not romantic – it involves, ultimately, the imposition of the will over others for mutual benefit. Cusk never relinquishes her conviction in the brutality of the world and the cruelty of others, but Faye is reappraising her power within that reality and to the narratives of injustice paraded as fate.

One of the striking things about *Kudos* is that this slight openness towards the possibility of common ground has not become an embedded assumption – *Transit* concludes with a clear step towards re-entering the story of her life, but the narrative available to her is not one by which Faye is fully persuaded. This militates against reading the trilogy for teleological trajectory or resolution. Instead, Faye encounters the same problems of fate, freedom, coercion, delusion, and will but she regards them from a different perspective. There is progression between the texts only in the sense that we know that Faye has remarried and that she has determined to live within the frameworks of companionate life to try to achieve the best outcomes she can. There is, however, little in the way of optimism for this as a collective endeavour, if anything, there is less faith in the potential of transformation. Where the emphasis in *Transit* was on the choice between fate and freedom, in *Kudos*, Cusk plays on the topicality of the Brexit debate by making the decision between leave and remain. Yet, it seems that Faye's choice has been made and she regards the trials of others with more quizzicality than cynicism. The hotel in which she stays during the literary festival is circular in construction and she ponders 'how much of navigation is the belief in progress, and the assumption of fixity in what you left behind' (Cusk 2018: 34). She has 'walked around the entire circumference of the building in search of things I had been right next to in the first place' (34). Whether she has ended up in a better place than before *Outline* is moot – circles, like progress, have no endpoint, after all – but Faye, it seems, has re-entered her own story as a narrator rather than just a reader.

There is no strong sense, however, in which her evolution across the trilogy amounts to a journey of authentic self-realization, but then that is not really the point. Faye gradually comes to an accommodation with the provisionality of selfhood rather than an integrated interiority, recognizing in the process that power and cruelty are ineliminable realities of human relations, barely kept in check by the structures of social and domestic life. She recognizes, too, that fantasies of freedom are often poorly articulated desires for those destructive qualities to be untrammelled – freedom is the realization of passion, and passion in Cusk is closely related to suffering. Her first locutor in *Kudos* relates the story of his loving family dog who, released from his lead, attacked a herd of deer. The actions of Pilot (a fitting name for a metaphor of flight) are incomprehensible to the man only because his own craving for freedom is so restrained – he maintains a spreadsheet labelled 'Freedom' to chart his progress towards financial independence. Pilot's animal authenticity is a rebuke to his timorousness and a reminder that, for Cusk, the authentic represents the dangerous, wild and unconscious Other to the fictions of sociality.

It is the authentic Other of contemporary literary culture too, which Cusk critiques most acerbically in *Kudos*. Art in the age, and at the mercy of neoliberal economics is a recurring theme, picking up the attack on gentrification from *Transit*. The novel is underscored by a sense of the denaturing of art, its chronic domestication in an age of diminishing attention, weakening sales and waning interest in the challenge to reality that art poses. Faye's youthful European publisher contributes to this etiolation with smug glee. Literary quality, he argues, must be subsidized by popular appeal, it cannot stand alone within the economic reality of the publishing industry. The most palatable compromise, he suggests, is for disguised literariness to find its way into the popular fiction through which he makes his money, but to aesthetic value he is entirely indifferent. People hate what literature asks of them, he claims; wrestling with the human experience is too effortful for most but the snob-value attached to art, like that adhering to success in the property market, speaks to growth potential and cultural capital. Faye counters that it is always better to defend the values of moral justice that literature stands for, but the overall tone of the novel is that of literature shelved under irrelevance, and the festival and conference to which Faye goes offer little in the way of defence for the highbrow. Attendees treat them as ego-boosting junkets, opportunities for self-promotion, or attend with simmering resentment. They are examples of what her publisher calls 'combustion' – the exhaustion of all creative energy or imagination in the interests of capital, illustrated by the hotel in which Faye is interviewed which exploits the fact that it was built on the site of a bookshop to theme itself as a literary landmark – unfortunately, its owners forget to order any books to cement the illusion (175). Everything to do with literature 'was governed by a principle of entropy while everything else proliferated and expanded' (176).

The 'small rock of authentic literature' (105) feels increasingly isolated and embattled according to Gerta, one of the organizers of the festival. Its sublime danger is unpalatable in a culture that privileges reassurance over truth and, without its roots in suffering, creativity can produce little in the way of meaningful, universal insight. The novel, comments another character, had once been like 'the Siberian tiger' but, in its struggle for survival, has likewise become 'fragile and defenceless' (176). Obsessed now with the honesty of writers, literary culture – exemplified by the know-it-all reviewer who has read and highlighted sections of all Faye's work but has no interest in hearing from her – has become a circus where writers like Louis (from *Transit*) and his miserable counterpart in *Kudos*, Luís, perform their authenticity but have little else to say about the society in which they live. Inauthenticity reigns because what passes for truth has combusted.

Conclusion

Authenticity takes two principal forms in Cusk's recent fiction. On the one hand it is an imaginary refuge for those who dwell in self-delusion and who romanticize their freedom as an ideal state in which their own innermost fantasies of coherence are projections of their desire to control others. This fuses nostalgia to narcissism – a sense that if it were not for the needs of other people, everything could be as it once was, and as such it perpetuates the cycle of illusion. On the other hand, authenticity is the chaotic, vitalist substratum beneath human togetherness that underpins the creativity and destructiveness inherent in shared life. It is a dangerous, disruptive energy kept in check by the narratives of civilization, culture, love and family life that maintain stability and promote faith in notions such as justice, progress and freedom. Cusk's fictions pivot on moments when that faith is undermined, when the fantasies that sustain it begin to unravel, and when the cruelty of the Other's will reveals itself. In the face of illusionless reality, the protagonists of *The Bradshaw Variations* and the *Outline* trilogy largely reconcile themselves to the narrative identities from which they have striven to break free and, indeed, discover some solace in the familiarity of their compromises.

Works Cited

Clanchy, K. (2018), 'Kudos by Rachel Cusk – a daringly truthful trilogy concludes'. *The Guardian*, 2 May. Available at: https://www.theguardian.com/books/2018/may/04/kudos-rachel-cusk-review (accessed 25 May 2023).
Cusk, R. (2009), *The Bradshaw Variations*. London: Faber & Faber.
Cusk, R. (2015), *Outline*. London: Vintage.
Cusk, R. (2016). 'Making House: Notes on Domesticity'. *New York Times Magazine*, 31 August. Available at: https://www.nytimes.com/2016/09/04/magazine/making-house-notes-on-domesticity.html (accessed 25 May 2023).
Cusk, R. (2017), *Transit*. London: Vintage.
Cusk, R. (2018), *Kudos*. London: Faber & Faber.
Guignon, C. (2004), *On Being Authentic*. London: Routledge.
Heti, S. (2020), 'Rachel Cusk, The Art of Fiction No. 246'. *Paris Review*, 232. Available at: https://archive.ph/eR3yn#selection-1015.0-1017.28 (accessed 25 May 2023).
Rooney, S. (2018), 'Buried in Bourgeois Life'. *Slate* 25 May. Available at: https://slate.com/culture/2018/05/rachel-cusks-kudos-reviewed-by-sally-rooney.html (accessed 25 May 2023).
Schwartz, A. (2018), '"I Don't Think Character Exists Anymore": A Conversation with Rachel Cusk'. *New Yorker*, 18 November 2018. Available at: https://www.newyorker.com/culture/the-new-yorker-interview/i-dont-think-character-exists-anymore-a-conversation-with-rachel-cusk (accessed 25 May 2023).

Taylor, C. (1991a), *The Ethics of Authenticity*. Cambridge, MA and London: Harvard University Press.

Taylor, C. (1991b), 'The Dialogical Self', in J. Bohman, D. Hiley, R. Shusterman (eds), *The Interpretive Turn: Philosophy, Science, Culture*, 304–14. Ithaca: Cornell University Press.

Thurman, J. (2017), 'Rachel Cusk gut-renovates the novel'. *New Yorker*, 93 (23), 31 July. Available at: https://www.newyorker.com/magazine/2017/08/07/rachel-cusk-gut-renovates-the-novel (accessed 25 May 2023).

Varga, S. (2012), *Authenticity as an Ethical Ideal*. London: Routledge.

6

Autofictional Experiments and Serial Aesthetics in Rachel Cusk's *Outline* Trilogy

Melissa Schuh

> This feeling of being negated at the same time as I was exposed, had had a particularly powerful effect on me, I said. It had seemed to encapsulate something that didn't, strictly speaking, exist.
>
> Cusk [2014] 2018: 167

Detailing the experience of suffering a verbal tirade by a dissatisfied creative writing student on one of her courses to an acquaintance, Faye, *Outline*'s narrator, describes a quintessential paradox of autobiographical expression. The attempt to capture one's self and identity in writing, to portray it towards oneself and others, obviously involves self-exposure through the referential ownership of one's story that is usually signalled through the autobiographical use of one's name. Nevertheless, it can also involve a certain degree of self-negation that is often glossed over. To present a stable, coherent autobiographical self, other versions, variations and ambiguities of self and life are abandoned in favour of a readable, representative autobiographical subject. This contradiction and discrepancy between the self on the page and the more complex and unfinished self that is writing it can lead to an alienating effect for the autobiographer. As Faye observes, being 'negated' and 'exposed' simultaneously touches on something that 'strictly speaking' cannot exist. Consequently, a full autobiographical self would appear to be impossible to record, because such a text would have to contain those autobiographical aspects that the shaping of a life into the form of autobiography already forecloses. Yet, autofiction, a combination of fictional modes of representation and autobiographical impulses, offers possibilities of showing that which 'does not exist' in autobiography alone by following Faye's example of trying to represent it anyway, if only by way of highlighting the absence it creates.

Rachel Cusk's *Outline* trilogy, published between 2014 and 2018 and comprising *Outline* (2014), *Transit* (2016) and *Kudos* (2018), has been regarded as an example of contemporary autofiction in both scholarly and journalistic commentary on the work. A *Guardian* article by Alex Clark, for example, titled 'Drawn from life: why have novelists stopped making things up?' groups Cusk with Karl Ove Knausgaard, Sheila Heti, Edward St Aubyn, Olivia Laing, Chris Kraus and Elena Ferrante in an effort to survey the contemporary literary scene of autofiction as a dominantly emerging literary genre:

> Suddenly this kind of 'autofiction' – fictionalised autobiography that does away with traditional elements of the novel such as plot and character development – is everywhere. Thumping on to your desk in the form of the last volume of Karl Ove Knausgaard's epic account of his life, My Struggle; touching more lightly down in the case of *Kudos*, as Rachel Cusk completes her elegant trilogy in which a novelist, 'Faye', journeys around Europe absorbing the stories strangers and acquaintances tell her [...].
>
> Clark 2018

Clark loosely defines autofiction as 'fictionalised autobiography' and distinguishes it from the novel by highlighting a lack of plot and character development. Cusk's *Kudos* is mentioned with its protagonist's name, Faye, in quotation marks, as if to signal that the novelist Faye cannot just straightforwardly be regarded as a fictional character. A sense that 'Faye' may not just be Faye but an autobiographical subject that is related to Cusk is thus indicated and points to the very combination of self and fiction that autofiction is known to describe. Beyond this basic premise of bringing both autobiographical and fictional elements together, which is contained in its etymology, autofiction has been established as a notoriously difficult genre to pin down.

Coined by French novelist Serge Doubrovsky in 1977, autofiction has since continued to elude clear categorization and its advent into Anglophone literary criticism in recent years is also marked by deliberations on its fluid and open generic make-up. As Hywel Dix observes in *Autofiction in English*, the first essay collection on the topic in English: 'There is no single definition of autofiction either in English or in French' (2018: 2). Similarly, in their more recent edited collection, *The Autofictional* (2022), Alexandra Effe and Hannie Lawlor note 'the impossibility of reaching a satisfactory consensus on the definition of autofiction' given 'the proliferation of meanings and practices with which it is associated' (1–2).

As Clark's collection of examples shows, autofiction is used to describe works that differ in degrees to which fictional or non-fictional contexts are invoked. While Karl Ove Knausgaard's *My Struggle* series evokes a strong autobiographical frame which caused a storm of media attention, due to his father's family suing him as a result of its publication (Knausgaard 2016), Elena Ferrante's Neapolitan novels are near impossible to verify as autobiographically informed, due to the author's anonymity.[1] Falling somewhere into this spectrum, Cusk's narrator, Faye, does clearly not share her author's name as an autobiographical link but reflects some significant biographical details with Cusk as a writer living in England and recently divorced mother of two children. As Clark's highlighting of Faye's name in quotation marks signals, it is possible to read Faye not simply as a character of this name. She can also be interpreted as an autobiographical subject or an alter ego for Cusk as an author, given that their overlap in personal experiences is suggestive of this connection. Furthermore, the trilogy's narrator is only named once in each book, mentioned in passing, and quite late in the first volume, *Outline*, on page 211 out of 249.[2] In combination with the first-person narration, this leads to a degree of slippage between a conventional first-person autobiographical perspective and the narrator's explicit labelling as a fictional character.

Such indeterminacy and fluidity being characteristic of autofiction, the term is sometimes viewed with scepticism because its openness can be interpreted to make it near meaningless. Indeed, Cusk herself has distanced herself from the concept, stating that she does not see herself as writing autofiction: 'I don't think that I write "autofiction," though I admire the people who do, and essentially wish that I did. I think it's an evolution beyond what I'm doing. I'm perhaps stuck in the past, trying to work out the past. I don't think I'm in any way as free as the writer of autofiction. I don't think that anything I do is revolutionary in that way' (Cusk in Treisman 2023). She has also explicitly addressed being grouped 'in a new genre of memoir writing, along with Karl Ove Knausgaard et al.': 'I don't think anyone can even remember what authenticity is, now. And in the end, Knausgaard says the same thing: I'm looking in the mirror and there I am' (Cusk in Wade 2015). Despite such deliberations on the degree to which her own foray into combinations of the fictional and the autobiographical is not autofictional enough, Cusk has also argued in reviewing Yiyun Li's work that labelling

---

[1] There has been some discussion about the possible identity behind the pseudonym of Elena Ferrante with the most credible suggestion having been made by journalist Claudio Gatti who used financial and property records to trace the author and then published his findings in the Italian newspaper *Il Sole 24 Ore* in October 2016. Nevertheless, Ferrante's identity remains unconfirmed, which makes autobiographical interpretations of her work largely speculative although her novels have frequently been read in loose autobiographical terms by readers and literary journalists, especially since Ferrante has also published a volume about her life and writing that can be read alongside the novels. See also: Gatti, (2016a, b) and Ferrante (2016).

[2] See also Cusk ([2014] 2018): 211; ([2016] 2018): 206 and (2018): 227.

autofictions as novels is a disservice to a text that 'cannot be understood without its autobiographical basis' (Cusk 2019). Although Cusk is apparently reluctant to label her work autofiction, it can certainly be located in an autofictional spectrum of different degrees of mirroring. As Alison James has observed: 'The trilogy produces what we might call an "autofictional effect," despite the lack of onomastic identity between author and character' (James 2022: 51). This is not just due to Faye's ambiguous role as a possible autobiographical persona, but also relates to the trilogy's form, which we can read as exactly 'revolutionary in that way' (Cusk in Treisman 2023).

Besides a mix of fictional and autobiographical elements and some correspondence between author and protagonist or narrator, autofiction is often associated with a degree of formal and stylistic, or in other words, literary, experimentation: E. H. Jones sees autofiction's broaching of contemporary questions about self and life as 'a source of innovation and experimentation' (2010: 177), Dix explains that autofiction is 'a project of self-exploration and self-experimentation' (2018: 4), and Effe and Lawlor note autofiction's association with 'hybridity and experimentalism' (2022: 2). Instead of expanding on nuances regarding autofiction's definition in light of its characteristic generic indeterminacy and ambiguity, I will focus on this sense of the experimental potential in autofiction with regard to the *Outline* trilogy as a serial autofictional work. The serial has been widely acknowledged in literary journalism for its innovation. As Sheila Heti in *The Paris Review* observes, '[t]he trilogy has been universally praised for doing something thrillingly new with the novel form' (2020).

Meanwhile, literary critics, too, have noted the *Outline* trilogy's creative exploration of self, life and art as well as remarking on the trilogy's form and style as autofiction.[3] For instance, Karen Valihora comments on the trilogy's autofiction as 'a forum that considers how, to what degree, and to what end, readers may share in the experiences of others', highlighting its unusual use of free indirect discourse and arguing that Cusk 'stages the act of reflection even as she contrives the effect of incidental, ordinary conversation' (2019: 19–20, 25). Meanwhile, this chapter will explore the *Outline* trilogy as autofiction that challenges traditional conventions of autobiographical development, coherence and unity. Specifically, I analyse the trilogy as serial autofiction that uses serial aesthetics of repetition and variation to advance an understanding of life and

---

[3] For further discussions of the *Outline* trilogy as autofiction, see also James (2022), Yanbing Er (2018) and Meg Jensen (2018).

self as contingent, unfinished and multi-faceted – as occupying the alienating space of exposure and negation that Faye conjures by explaining that 'strictly speaking', it does not exist.

Of course, serial publication and aesthetics are, as such, not immediately experimental or innovative. Indeed, assessments of a genre's innovation contain associations of literary prestige and achievement that may be considered problematic due to the implied value judgement: how do we decide which works we should pay attention to as particularly innovative? Experimentalism carries similar connotations but can be perhaps usefully related to the idea of deviating from established formal and genre expectations in ways that seem 'new' or otherwise unusual. Autofictional work is usually seen to do this already simply by virtue of entangling autobiographical and fictional frames of reference; serial autofiction, I argue, can achieve this by deviating from expectations set by popular serial narration and by using serial aesthetics in uncommon ways and contexts. The *Outline* trilogy specifically, as this chapter will show, offers autofictional experiments with conceptions of self and life in relation to art and world that are crafted through serial narrative techniques, themes, and motifs.

Serial Autofiction

Chatting with her hair stylist Dale, Faye learns about a friend of his who is a plumber and creates metal sculptures while high on crystal meth. Since he cannot remember anything about how he made them after the fact, he describes these sculptures as manifestations about himself that are otherwise inaccessible. The experience is 'like seeing a part of yourself that's invisible' (Cusk [2016] 2018: 68). The *Outline* trilogy's serial and autofictional strategies explore the development of a life across several volumes and as suspended between fictionalization and documentation, thus foregrounding these invisible parts of an autobiographical self by exposing the very process that the plumber cannot remember. The trilogy's interpretation and categorization as an autofictional work – although its volumes are labelled as novels by the publisher – is also related to their position within Cusk's oeuvre. Apart from her fiction, the trilogy was preceded by three explicitly autobiographical works: *A Life's Work: On Becoming a Mother* (2001), *The Last Supper: A Summer in Italy* (2009), and *Aftermath: On Marriage and Separation* (2012). These texts entered into a more straightforward autobiographical pact of more unambiguously recounting Cusk's perspective, rather than fictionalizing it, and more frankly addressed her experiences with motherhood, marriage and divorce (Lejeune 1989). *The Last Supper* led to a lawsuit by someone described in the book who objected to being recognisable in the text (Kellaway 2014). These autobiographical books were also criticized for their openness about the author's personal experiences, citing concerns for her children's and her husband's privacy (Clark 2018). As critics later observed, this reproach had a very gendered dimension of weaponizing privacy concerns against a woman writer to 'thwart female creativity' (ibid.). Ethical concerns with writing about oneself in relation to others are not uncommon with autobiographical and autofictional work in general. Nevertheless, male authors are often lauded for honesty and commitment to 'truth' in their autobiographical writing. Knausgaard's *My Struggle*, for instance, has been praised as 'a work of genius' for its addictive 'reality TV' quality (Lerner 2014). By contrast, life writing by women and other marginalized groups has been overlooked and derided in the past as passive and less authentic, literary or introspective than the exemplary lives of 'great men' which make up the traditional canon of autobiography.[4] Cusk has commented on the effects of *Aftermath*'s reception as 'creative death', which left her unable to write for three years before she turned to *Outline* (Kellaway 2014). The *Outline* trilogy's generic ambiguity with regard to fiction or autobiography, the autobiographical similarities between its narrator and author, and its formal experimentation can also be read as autofictional in the context of these earlier works. They also provide a context of serial autobiographical self-representation (as discussed in Ricarda Menn's chapter in this volume in the context of serial revision and metaphors that are revisited in the trilogy), which is continued through the trilogy.

Although the *Outline* trilogy has been frequently discussed as a recent example of contemporary autofiction, little scholarly attention has been paid to its serial aesthetics as a trilogy, and to seriality in life writing and autofiction in general. Nicole Stamant discusses twentieth-century serial memoirs by American authors as enabling a textual space for self-archivization (2014), and Menn explores seriality in John Burnside's autofictions (2018). Menn and myself have recently considered Cusk's trilogy as an example of the autofictional in serial, literary works alongside Dorothy Richardson's and Doris Lessing's work, assessing the *Outline* trilogy as a serial consisting of thematically and conceptually interwoven texts. In this context, we describe serial, literary autofictions 'as an experimental form of life narrative', portraying an autofictional 'sense of self that is unfinished, contingent, and subject to revision' (Menn and Schuh 2022: 103–4). Drawing on these theoretical observations, the question of serial aesthetics

[4] See Julie Rak (2004), Helen M. Buss (2002), Nancy K. Miller (1994) and Mary G. Mason (1980).

and autofictional experimentation in Cusk's *Outline* trilogy warrants further exploration. I will now turn to serial repetition and variation as a narrative pattern and theme to analyse the different ways in which seriality contributes to the trilogy's autofictional experimentation to create a sense of self and life as multi-dimensional and in a constant, ongoing and changing relationship with itself and others.

The trilogy was published as a serial in three separate volumes, and it follows the three aforementioned autobiographical books within Cusk's oeuvre. This serial mode of publication and the division into different instalments already entails a comment about the autobiographical self and life: a sense of self and identity that extends beyond a single coherent story, that is fluid, and open to continuation and revision. Cusk herself has commented on her motivation to continue after *Outline* was published:

> I realized at a certain point in *Outline* that it was all very well to say these things about passivity and disappearance, but the fact was that this person had to actually live. And so, unless she was going to throw herself off the boat on the way home, she had to actually turn up somewhere and exist, and parent her children. I felt I needed to finish it. So that's what caused two more books.
> Cusk in Schwartz 2018

This explanation suggests that Cusk perceived a single volume as insufficient to capture Faye's experience fully, a continuation of her life that showed different facets and angles of her life – her as a parent and with a daily life outside of her travels – was needed 'to finish it'. With its basic serial premise of splitting Faye's story into several parts, the *Outline* trilogy offers related but also separate mediations on self and life, implying a process of self-reflection that is ongoing, unfinished and open to reinterpretation and continuation. Faye argues as much about her own life while in conversation with a journalist in *Kudos*, whose earlier description of her life had struck her because it seemed so conclusive: 'The reason, I thought, was that this description had a finality to it that I couldn't imagine ever attaining in my own circumstances' (Cusk 2018: 62). None of the three volumes provides a clear sense of closure or climax and while following a loose temporal chronology, they could in theory be read in any order or as single individual episodes. This effect too is something Cusk has commented on as a deliberate and important aspect that she wanted to convey:

> No, I mean, the whole book is set up so that you can walk away from it if you're not interested. Go and do something else. There shouldn't be the feeling of, you've paid for an experience and, if you don't get it, you'll be disappointed. I

wanted to make that incredibly clear. And when I wrote *Outline* I truly did not believe anyone would be able to read it.

Cusk in Schwartz 2018

This sense of offering scenes or episodes that a reader may engage with or disengage from at their own discretion without feeling beholden to an investment indicates a seriality which differs from common conceptions of popular serial narration that TV series, comics and genre fiction are known for. Popular seriality, as described by Frank Kelleter, relies heavily on serial plotting and ongoing story arcs that attract audiences by creating suspense and leaving certain questions open for continuation in a cycle of anticipation and satisfaction. Cliffhangers are a prime example of such serial narrative techniques (Kelleter 2017). Cusk's serial aesthetics do not rely on the tension of continuous plotting and the repeated question of 'what will happen next?' In terms of plot very little actually happens in the books, since Faye's conversations with various people make up the central content: She travels to teach creative writing or to read and speak at literary festivals and events and she lives in London, renovating a dilapidated flat while in conflict about the noise with her new downstairs neighbours. Instead, the serial narrative strategies she uses position the *Outline* trilogy as a series of autofictional experiments with selfhood as repetition, revision and variation, as presence and absence, and as recurrence of both exposure and negation.

Repetition and Variation

Reflecting on his mother's life in relation to his own, writer Luís claims: 'Yet in my own life I have been doomed to repetition as anyone else, even when I didn't know what it was I was repeating' (Cusk 2018: 153). He thus articulates a feeling that the trilogy returns to periodically through a series of repetitions and variations. Apart from serial publication and its implications for autofictional texts, serial aesthetics can be traced in terms of formal narrative strategies and motifs. Following Gilles Deleuze, a common notion of seriality rests on repetition with difference and innovation, process and practice.[5] Repetition and variation are prevalent themes and techniques in the trilogy. Particularly relevant to the

---

[5] See Deleuze (2010) and Umberto Eco (2005): 'Let us now see the case in which (1) something is offered as original and different (according to the requirements of modern aesthetics); (2) we are aware that this something is repeating something else that we already know; and (3) notwithstanding this – better, just because of it – we like it (and we buy it)' (195).

portrayal of lives and selves is the idea that one's life could be repeated or mirrored through another, and several characters explicitly voice a feeling as though their experiences are being repeated through others.

In *Transit*, one of Faye's creative writing students, Jane, expresses that the American painter Marsden Hartley, who is the subject of her work, somehow corresponds to her:

> He's me, she said.
> I asked her what she meant.
> I'm him, she said, then added, slightly impatiently: we're the same. I know it sounds a bit strange, she went on, but there's actually no reason why people can't be repeated.
>
> Cusk [2016] 2018: 134

Faye tries to explain Jane's experience as a process of identification with someone else, like one does with 'characters in a book' but Jane refuses this idea, instead insisting that although 'her life and Marsden Hartley's in fact had nothing in common at all', the thoughts she perceives in his art are somehow 'her own' (135). She argues that '[r]ather than mirroring the literal facts of her own life, Marsden Hartley was doing something much bigger and more significant: he was dramatising them' (137–8). With this description, Jane summarizes an autofictional experience that entails the representation of a self not dominantly according to autobiographical facts, but also through the dramatization and imagination of fictionalization. Indeed, although she is talking about another person's life in relation to her own, Jane expresses quite succinctly Gérard Genette's observation about the paradox he finds apparent in autofictional writing: 'It is I and it is not I' ([1991] 1993: 77). While her statement can be read as a metafictional comment on how the *Outline* trilogy autofictionally dramatizes Cusk's life through Faye's fictional encounters with various interlocutors, it also suggests that certain aspects of a life become discernible through their repetition and variation in other lives, be they fictional or autobiographical. Jane – and also Faye – gain knowledge about themselves by seeing their experiences repeated, revised and deviated from in others' versions of their lives. Since the trilogy is largely made up of conversations in which various characters detail stories from their lives, it comprises a series of encounters and therefore also a series of fragments and snippets from different characters' experiences that can be compared to one another and to Faye's responses about her own life.

While Jane sees something essential about herself repeated through Marsden Hartley, Faye is also shown to be the source of such recognition through repetition. Oliver, the partner of an author she reads alongside with at a literary event, shares how emotionally affected and moved he was by seeing himself echoed in the story she read:

> 'I don't know how long ago you wrote the story you read tonight,' he said, 'or whether you still feel those same things now, but –' and to my astonishment he began to weep openly, there at the table – 'but it was me you were describing, that woman was me, her pain was my pain, and I just had to come and tell you in person how much it meant to me.'
>
> Cusk [2016] 2018: 121

Much like Jane, he insists that the character in her story was him, 'her pain was [his] pain'. Jane's and Oliver's experiences of recognizing themselves in another person or character seem to go beyond the process Faye explained to Jane as 'identification'. Their insistence on how identical their thoughts and feelings are to their perceived counterparts suggests not only that the facts of a life may not be the crucial essence of it, but also that such insights into one's life are a continuous and repeated experience. While Oliver hedges when he says that he does not know whether Faye's character's feelings are still felt by her, this kind of recognition may also change, depending on the time and position from which one encounters it. Notably, with Oliver's experience no distinction between fiction and autobiography or history (as Jane's connection to a historical figure alludes to) is made. He readily associates Faye's feelings with those of her character and with his own. In turn, Faye herself also recounts a similar experience in a conversation with a journalist whom she remembered meeting many years prior:

> She had talked, I said, about her husband and two sons and about the simple, regulated life they lived, a life that involved little change and hence little waste, and the fact that in certain details her life had mirrored my own while in no way resembling it had often led me to see my situation in the most unflattering light. I had broken that mirror, I said, without knowing whether I had done so as an act of violence or simply by mistake.
>
> Cusk 2018: 64

Although this comparison and perceived 'mirroring' of lives was discomforting for Faye and prompted her to question aspects of her own married and family life at the time through the contrast, it also describes a revelation of insight that is gained through the resemblance or indeed repetition of lives. In this vein, the trilogy portrays autobiographical and fictional understandings of identity as equally valid sources of self-knowledge and self-representation. Jane, Oliver and

Faye's experiences suggest with the recognition of such processes through repetition and variation that relationships between self and life are a complex, contingent, and unfinished process. The way in which these repetitions recur across the trilogy is far from a circular loop without progression. As Valihora observes in the repetitive behaviours that led to several failed marriages on the part of the 'neighbour' Faye meets on her plane to Greece at the beginning of *Outline*: 'Faye's interest in this man and his story constitutes another form of repetition, yet with a difference; it is in an almost therapeutic form, like a controlled experiment' (2019: 25). The trilogy experiments with repetition alongside difference and variation. The seriality here lies in Faye's series of encounters with characters who provide both repetitions and variations of lives and experiences that resonate with her own (and by extension possibly to Cusk's), and in the resulting impression of presenting serial selves through the various characters she converses with, versions of issues and questions she is also affected by.

The trilogy's volumes are also connected by recurring themes and questions, but each also refers to its title-giving motif in self-referential ways. Storytelling or how to tell and make sense of one's life is a topic that runs through the trilogy, but so are marriage and relationships between men and women, the connections between art, writing and life, and what might make up a person's identity, personality or life. Except for Faye and her children, only one character recurs in more than one volume: Ryan – a fellow writer, who also teaches creative writing in Greece during *Outline* and has become a fitness-obsessed bestselling author in *Kudos*.[6] There is some degree of serial pay-off to re-encountering Ryan in the *Kudos*. He offers a direct cross-volume serial connection running contrary to the more anthological serial structure of the trilogy that largely dispenses with the serial and episodic story arcs and plotting that is common in popular seriality. Nevertheless, Ryan's exception as a recurring character also provides a reflection on the ways in which he is largely unchanged in his arrogance while Faye has quietly absorbed insights through her series of conversations and encounters with others.

Each volume references its title as a thematic concept, offering a loosely episodic structural element: 'Outline' as an idea is picked up towards the end of *Outline* through a conversation that Faye has with Anne, the writer who is next going to stay at the place she was being hosted at in Greece. In a mirroring and repetition of Faye's experiences throughout the book, Anne describes a

---

[6] See Cusk ([2014] 2018: 132) and (2018: 111).

conversation she had on the plane, providing reflections on it that can be read as a metafictional comment on the volume and the serial as a whole:

> He was describing, in other words, what she herself was not: in everything he said about himself, she found in her own nature a corresponding negative. This anti-description, for want of a better way of putting it, had made something clear to her by a reverse kind of exposition: while he talked, she began to see herself as a shape, an outline, with all the detail filled in around it while the shape itself remained blank. Yet this shape, even while its contents remained unknown, gave her for the first time since the incident a sense of who she now was.
>
> Cusk [2014] 2018: 239–49

The trilogy offers an outline of Faye's experience and identity against her many interlocutors with such 'anti-description' that portrays a sense of her self through repetition and variation with the lives and stories of others. Faye's 'blankness' as a narrator who becomes discernible only through her interpretation and responses to other people's life stories and personal reflections and is otherwise noticeably devoid of characterization nevertheless creates a presence through such absence. Overlaps and contrasts between what little we know of her and the lives of those she meets stand out precisely because her lack of direct telling about herself leaves a void. Anne is another and obvious example of this, since the realization she reports on directly ties to Faye's first conversation with her 'neighbour' on the plane at the beginning of the book. 'Outline' therefore serves as a metaphor for the autofictional experiment that is contained in projecting autobiographical presence through its narrative absence. At the same time 'outline' extends this concept to the whole trilogy, conceptually connecting the volumes to form a series of outlines, but it is also an episodic thematic strand for the first book that is followed by different themes and titles for the other two volumes.

'Transit' is referenced in the latter half of *Transit*, also referring back to the beginning of the book, to a spam email by an astrologer that Faye received, offering her guidance through a personal planetary reading, which she then purchased: 'It was the day the astrologer's report had said would be of particular significance in the coming phase of transit' (Cusk [2016] 2018: 176). Much as with 'outline', 'transit' provides a theme for the volume, suggesting connections between Faye's position and its meanings besides the movement of planetary bodies: change or transition, the process of passing through something or travelling from one place to another. Faye is in transit in different ways in this second volume and throughout the serial. She is in the process of moving to London and renovating a very rundown house meant to become a new home for herself and her sons. She is between relationships after her separation from her husband prior to *Outline* and before her marriage to someone else, which is referenced later in *Kudos* (Cusk 2018: 84). And while also travelling frequently in connection to her writing, she is constantly passing by and through the life stories of others as she converses with them.

'Kudos' is addressed in the first half of *Kudos* when Hermann, a guide on a walk from one venue to another that Faye takes with participants of a literary festival, reflects on his college days with reference to an award for the best male and female student:

> To return to the subject of the college's award, he said, the name they had chosen for it was 'Kudos'. As I was probably aware, the Greek word 'kudos' was a singular noun that had become plural by a process of back formation: a kudo on its own had never actually existed, but in modern usage its collective meaning had been altered by the confusing presence of a plural suffix, so that 'kudos' therefore meant, literally, 'prizes', but in its original form it connoted the broader concept of recognition or acclaim , as well as being suggestive of something which might be falsely claimed by someone else.
>
> Cusk 2018: 97–8

Once again, 'kudos' offers a loose theme for the volume and also relates to the trilogy as a whole. Its supposed meaning of something that is unfairly claimed by someone else might relate to the men who have garnered success by using a woman's work – Ryan's collaboration with a woman writer who stays out of the limelight (118) – or by focusing on subjects usually associated with 'women's writing' – Luís's much-praised writing on domesticity and suburban life (138). Its curious grammatical status as a plural for which no singular noun exists anymore, can also be connected to the *Outline* trilogy more broadly, since the autobiographical outline that Faye's conversations delineate only become discernible through the plurality and multitudes of encounters we observe. This cursory analysis of the title-giving themes for each volume shows that the trilogy contains some episodic elements alongside its serial structures, but once again uses them to highlight the contingency and multifacetedness of the autofictional self, thus differing from uses of episodic and serial techniques in popular seriality that aim to generate a tension between satisfaction and anticipation. Instead, the trilogy's serial aesthetics refract and resonate across the trilogy by creating both serial and episodic connections and contrasts that link recurring themes and questions about self and life without offering closure or linear progression.

The trilogy's use of repetition and variation, episodic and serial structures extends to themes of autofictional experimentation that directly question more traditional conventions of autobiographical coherence and unity. A common topic of autobiography, that is memory and its 'truth' status, is addressed as unreliable through its closeness to fiction and imagination. For instance, Gaby in *Transit* describes to Faye how memory, life, and fiction intermingle for her:

> She would start to get this surreal feeling, as if she was looking back on something while it was actually occurring, but for some reason she never blamed it on the book: she always thought the sense of déjà vu was to do with her own life. Also, at other times, she remembered things as if they'd happened to her personally when in fact they were things she'd read. She could swear on her life that this or that scene existed in her own memory, and actually it was nothing to do with her at all.
>
> Cusk [2016] 2018: 245

Gaby suggests that lived memories and fictional stories appear interchangeable to her. This idea counters established autobiographical expectations of memory as truth and goes even further than the concept of 'subjective truth' in autobiography that takes individual perspective into account (Woods 2010: 5). Recollection and imagination are shown as parallel processes, as acts of storytelling. This foregrounding of lives as series of stories that are fragmented, shaped and reshaped is achieved through an autofictional broaching of different narrative modes. Faye's multi-layered function as a fictional narrator and possible autobiographical alter ego creates autofictional uncertainty about life, self and story in concert with reflections, such as Gaby's. Like many of Faye's interlocutors, she displays a degree of narrative insight and literary eloquence that creates slippage between herself, Faye, and the other characters as articulations of an autofictional impulse to represent life and self as inseparable from fiction and storytelling.

The trilogy conceives of lives and relationships as stories that are unreliable, changing and in flux to the extent that Faye voices doubt in *Outline* about the very existence of a stable and unified self: 'I thought the whole idea of a "real" self might be illusory: you might feel, in other words, as though there were some separate, autonomous self within you, but perhaps that self didn't actually exist' (Cusk [2014] 2018: 105). In *Transit*, she expands on an analogous point in conversation with her ex-partner Gerard, posing that 'marriages worked in the same way that stories are said to do, through the suspension of disbelief', suggesting that certain elements 'had been denied or wilfully forgotten in the service of [a] narrative' (Cusk [2016] 2018: 29–30). In doing so, Faye highlights self and life as a construction in relation to others. Nevertheless, she poses elsewhere in the same volume that she considers fellow author Julian as interchangeable with his book – 'As far as I was concerned, I said, they were the same thing' (123) – although she also reflects later on in *Kudos* on suitable techniques to shape painful experiences for profitable retelling: 'The skill, I saw, lay in skirting close enough to what appeared to be the truth without allowing what you actually felt about it to regain its power over you' (2018: 10). Thus, Faye offers differing notions on processes of self-representation in relation to her various conversation partners. However, these shifts also indicate the relationality and contingency of conceptions about life and self across the trilogy's time and relationships. The trilogy overall ultimately undermines straightforward autobiographical truths by practising a form of autobiographical expression that sustains multiple viewpoints and tensions through serial structures and autofictional reflection.

Serial Selves and Experiments

In her first conversation of the *Outline* trilogy, the fellow traveller sitting next to Faye on the plane to Greece whom she calls her neighbour describes the fatal problems of his second marriage, which he locates in his futile race to sustain the wealthy lifestyle his wife expected from him due to the impression she got from his owning a yacht when they first met: 'He was, in effect, manufacturing an illusion: no matter what he did, the gap between illusion and reality could never be closed. Gradually, he said, this gap, this distance between how things were and how I wanted them to be, began to undermine me' (Cusk [2014] 2018: 22). Autofictional writing can occupy this 'gap between illusion and reality' by making use of both autobiographical reflection and fictional imagination. The trilogy's experimental transgression lies in making this gap explicit in its premise, narrative and structure, and in its serial format. Faye is both a character and Cusk's autobiographical subject. Her absence as a conventionally active protagonist ensures her presence as an outline, as a gap, that is filled through the lives and stories of illusion and reality she encounters. The other characters she converses with represent a multitude of variations in life experiences but they also function as repetitions, versions and mirrors of Faye and of each other. The trilogy gives no life story in its entirety, instead it draws scenes, fragments and versions of many lives together as pieces of a puzzle that make the gap, the impossibility of conclusive coherence for a life, explicitly visible. By offering a clearly styled and fictionalized 'illusion', Cusk renders the 'real' inconsistency, unreliability and changeability of self, life, and identity 'readable'.

Thus, the *Outline* trilogy experiments on multiple fronts with autobiography, fiction and seriality: its autofictional preoccupation with the boundaries between life and imagination, fact and fiction, as well as with questioning established autobiographical tropes of 'truth', unity, coherence and closure advances an understanding of self and life that is characterized by ongoing reflection and affirmation of complexity and contradiction. 'Faye' is not quite interchangeable with 'Rachel Cusk', but Cusk is still inseparable from Faye. Although she reveals little about herself directly, she is indirectly autobiographically characterized through every encounter we witness, highlighting aspects in others that mirror her concerns. While the trilogy's narrative follows in no way the common structure of an autobiographical life recounted from cradle to grave, it contains fragments, parts and instalments of life stories that seemingly follow or strain against such expectations of lives as products of progress or success. The trilogy seems stripped of the novel's usual elements of plot and character development. In a 2014 interview about the trilogy, Cusk posed: 'I'm certain autobiography is increasingly the only form in all the arts. Description, character – these are dead or dying in reality as well as in art' (Cusk in Kellaway 2014). However, the *Outline* trilogy is still highly stylized and artfully composed and written. As Valihora notes: 'Cusk's storytellers are wildly, implausibly articulate; they defy every reader's experience of the people it is possible to meet on planes' (2019: 21). While creating the illusion of every-day conversations with strangers and acquaintances, Faye's interlocutors are impossibly eloquent, introspective, and self-aware. The trilogy employs a serial continuity and form but its serial aesthetics follow alternative structures in comparison to the techniques of popular serial narration that engages audiences through patterns of anticipation and satisfaction, episodic familiarity and serially plotted suspense. The work's seriality offers repetitions and variations of themes, questions, selves and relationships that resonate across the volumes, self-referentially and self-consciously drawing connections and contrasts between the multitudes of life stories that refract against Faye's issues and against one another.

Cusk's experimental use of serial and autofictional forms can be read as part of a contemporary literary aesthetic that we might call neo-modernist in its distinct affirmation of contradiction and complexity in the blurred relationship between self and other, world and story-world.[7] The trilogy's serial repetitions and variations of selves constitute an autofictional experiment of constructing

---

[7] See Liam Harrison's chapter and Peter Child's afterword in this volume and Ophir (2023).

an autobiographical subject which emerges from a space of autofictional self-reflection and imagination that is readable only at the limits of both life writing and the literary. Thus, Cusk's development of an unmistakably unconventional form for both novel and autobiography is reminiscent of high modernist interests in capturing the challenging experience of a changing world. The trilogy's exceptional degree of metafictional self-consciousness and its radical focus on self-reflection through serially repeated processes of relational insight through continuous variations of telling and listening are suggestive of both modernist and postmodernist narrative techniques and patterns. Irrespective of its aesthetic inheritances and legacies, the trilogy's contemporary experiment can be located in opening up spaces that 'strictly speaking' do not exist without Faye's sketching around elusive absences, gaps, and invisibilities.

Acknowledgements

I would like to express sincere thanks to Lena Kreft, my research assistant, for surveying literature and offering insightful comments on topics and questions that are explored in this chapter.

Works Cited

Buss, H. M. (2002), *Repossessing the World: Reading Memoirs by Contemporary Women*, Waterloo, Ont.: Wilfrid Laurier University Press.
Clark, A. (2018), 'Drawn from life: why have novelists stopped making things up?' *The Guardian*, 23 June. Available at: https://www.theguardian.com/books/2018/jun/23/drawn-from-life-why-have-novelists-stopped-making-things-up (accessed 3 April 2023).
Cusk, R. ([2014] 2018), *Outline*. London: Faber & Faber.
Cusk, R. ([2016] 2018), *Transit*. London: Faber & Faber.
Cusk, R. (2018), *Kudos*. London: Faber & Faber.
Cusk, R. (2019), 'The Case of Yiyun Li'. *The New York Review of Books*, 18 July. Available at: https://www.nybooks.com/articles/2019/07/18/case-of-yiyun-li/ (accessed 13 March 2023).
Deleuze, G. (2010), *Difference and Repetition*. London: Continuum.
Dix, H. (2018), 'Introduction: Autofiction in English: The Story So Far', in Hywel Dix (ed.), *Autofiction in English*, 1–23. Cham: Palgrave Macmillan.
Eco, U. (2005), 'Innovation & Repetition: Between Modern & Postmodern Aesthetics'. *Daedalus*, 134 (4): 191–207.

Effe, A. and H. Lawlor, 'Introduction: From Autofiction to the Autofictional', in Alexandra Effe and Hannie Lawlor (eds), *The Autofictional: Approaches, Affordances, Forms*, 1–18. Cham: Palgrave Macmillan.

Er, Y. (2018), 'Contemporary Women's Autofiction as Critique of Postfeminist Discourse'. *Australian Feminist Studies*, 33 (97): 316–30.

Ferrante, E. (2016), *Frantumaglia: A Writer's Journey*. New York: Europa Editions.

Gatti, C. (2016a), 'Elena Ferrante: An Answer?' *The New York Review of Books*, 2 October 2016. Available at: http://www.nybooks.com/daily/2016/10/02/elena-ferrante-an-answer/ (accessed 28 March 2017).

Gatti, C. (2016b), 'The Story Behind a Name'. *The New York Review of Books*, 2 October 2016. Available at: http://www.nybooks.com/daily/2016/10/02/story-behind-a-name-elena-ferrante/ (accessed 28 March 2017).

Genette, G. ([1991] 1993), *Fiction and Diction*, trans. Catherine Porter. Ithaca: Cornell University Press.

Heti, S. (2020), 'Rachel Cusk, The Art of Fiction No. 246'. *The Paris Review*, 232 (Spring). Available at: https://www.theparisreview.org/interviews/7535/the-art-of-fiction-no-246-rachel-cusk (accessed 3 April 2023).

James, A. (2022), 'The Fictional in Autofiction', in Alexandra Effe and Hannie Lawlor (eds), *The Autofictional: Approaches, Affordances, Forms*, 41–60. Cham: Palgrave Macmillan.

Jensen, M. (2018), 'How Art Constitutes the Human: Aesthetics, Empathy and the Interesting in Autofiction', in Hywel Dix (ed), *Autofiction in English*, 65–83. Cham: Palgrave Macmillan.

Jones, E. H. (2010), 'Autofiction: A Brief History of a Neologism', in Richard Bradford (ed.), *Life Writing: Essays on Autobiography, Biography and Literature*, 174–84. Basingstoke: Palgrave Macmillan.

Kellaway, K. (2014), 'Interview: Rachel Cusk: "Aftermath was creative death. I was heading into total silence"'. *The Guardian*, 24 August 2014. Available at: https://www.theguardian.com/books/2014/aug/24/rachel-cusk-interview-aftermath-outline (accessed 3 April 2023).

Kelleter, F. (2017), 'Five Ways of Looking at Popular Seriality', in Frank Kelleter (ed.), *Media of Serial Narrative*, 7–34. Columbus: Ohio State University Press.

Knausgaard, K. O. (2016), 'The shame of writing about myself'. *The Guardian*, 26 February 2016. Available at: https://www.theguardian.com/books/2016/feb/26/karl-ove-knausgaard-the-shame-of-writing-about-myself (accessed 3 April 2023).

Lejeune, P. (1989), *On Autobiography*, ed. Paul Eakin. Minneapolis: University of Minnesota Press.

Lerner, B. (2014), 'Each Cornflake'. *The London Review of Books*, 36 (10), 22 May. Available at: https://www.lrb.co.uk/the-paper/v36/n10/ben-lerner/each-cornflake (accessed 3 April 2023).

Mason, M. G. (1980), 'The Other Voice: Autobiographies of Women Writers', in James Olney (ed.), *Autobiography: Essays Theoretical and Critical*, 207–35. Princeton: Princeton University Press.

Menn, R. (2018), 'Unpicked and Remade: Creative Imperatives in John Burnside's Autofictions', in Hywel Dix (ed.), *Autofiction in English*, 163–78. Cham: Palgrave Macmillan.

Menn, R. and M. Schuh (2022), 'The Autofictional in Serial, Literary Works', in Alexandra Effe and Hannie Lawlor (eds), *The Autofictional: Approaches, Affordances, Forms*, 103–4. Cham: Palgrave Macmillan.

Miller, N. K. (1994), 'Representing Others: Genders and Subjects of Autobiography'. *differences: A Journal of Feminist Cultural Studies*, 6 (4): 1–25.

Ophir, E. (2023), 'Neomodernism and the Social Novel: Rachel Cusk's *Outline Trilogy*'. *Critique: Studies in Contemporary Fiction*, 64 (2): 353–64.

Rak, J. (2004), 'Are Memoirs Autobiography? A Consideration of Genre and Public Identity'. *Genre*, 37 (3–4): 305–26.

Schwartz, A. (2018), '"I don't think character exists anymore": A Conversation with Rachel Cusk'. *The New Yorker*, 18 November 2018. Available at: https://www.newyorker.com/culture/the-new-yorker-interview/i-dont-think-character-exists-anymore-a-conversation-with-rachel-cusk (accessed 14 May 2023).

Stamant, N. (2014), *Serial Memoir: Archiving American Lives*. Basingstoke: Palgrave Macmillan.

Treisman, D. (2023), 'Rachel Cusk on the Self in Visual Art', *The New Yorker*, 17 April 2023. Available at: https://www.newyorker.com/books/this-week-in-fiction/rachel-cusk-04-24-23 (accessed 22 May 2023).

Valihora, K. (2019), 'She Got Up and Went Away: Rachel Cusk on Making an Exit'. *ESC: English Studies in Canada*, 45 (1–2): 19–35.

Wade, F. (2015), 'Interview with Rachel Cusk'. *The White Review*, July 2015. Available at: https://www.thewhitereview.org/feature/interview-rachel-cusk/ (accessed 22 May 2023).

Woods, R. (2010), 'Introduction: The Purposes and Problems of German Life Writing in the Twentieth Century', in Birgit Dahlke, Dennis Tate and Roger Woods (eds), *German Life Writing in the Twentieth Century*, 1–24. Rochester, New York: Camden House.

Being Sent to Coventry

Silence, Cruelty and Rachel Cusk's Discrepant Style

Liam Harrison

'Cusk has glimpsed the central truth of modern life', Patricia Lockwood writes in her review of Rachel Cusk's *Outline* trilogy, 'that sometimes it is as sublime as Homer, a sail full of wind with the sun overhead, and sometimes it is like an Ikea where all the couples are fighting' (2018). This blending of the sublime and banal can be seen across Cusk's fiction and non-fiction: a trip to a suburban shopping mall in *Arlington Park* (2006) becomes an arduous, capitalist pilgrimage; at the conclusion of *Kudos* (2018c) a man stares pointedly at the protagonist Faye with 'cruel, merry eyes' while urinating in the sea (232); silent couples in the essay 'Coventry' (2019) flock to the picturesque tourist village in East Anglia where Cusk had made her home:

> They sit like monuments, like commemorations of some opaque history: in their silence and their stillness time seems almost to come to a halt. They are like effigies of the dead standing among the living, mute and motionless amid the helter-skelter families, and the noise and bustle of the pub.
>
> 2019a: 32

Cusk's style of social observation often brings a sense of the sublime to the quotidian and vice versa.[1] She inflects a shopping trip with the same significance as a Greek epic, describes a tacky tourist pub as a catacomb, or segues from airport bickering

---

[1] Roberta Garrett has also noted this mixture in Cusk's work, linking it to a particular modernist legacy in *Aftermath*: 'In a manner that echoes James Joyce's semi-comic juxtaposing of the banal and everyday with the central mythologies of Western culture, she [Cusk] draws on modernist allusionism and defamiliarization to address her fear of marginalization and social stigma' (2021: 90).

and rudeness to profound moral and theological questions, sometimes blending the two: 'In the Bible, Satan is not rude – he is usually rather charming [...] Jesus, on the other hand, often comes across as somewhat terse' (Cusk 2019a: 53–4).

Underpinning these switches between the banal and the profound is Cusk's distinctive narrative style, a style that, I contend, is animated by the particular qualities of silence, absence, and cruelty. These qualities are especially pronounced across the *Outline* trilogy. Or it might be more accurate to say that Cusk's style is animated by the *possibilities* of these qualities, while often deftly subverting them. For example, the trilogy's narrator Faye assumes a guise of withdrawal, a pretence of absconding from the narrative, which allows her to assume a covertly active mode of observation and implicit judgement. In this vein, Sally Rooney argues that the trilogy proffers a 'document of passivity', while at the same time 'the very existence of these highly stylized and innovative books makes nonsense of that idea' of passivity (2018). Similarly, David James has noted how a 'sense of discrepancy' operates in the *Outline* trilogy through the way that Cusk 'assembles distinctly personal disclosures in a suspenseful yet depersonalized register' (James 2021: 142). Cusk's writing style has shifted over the years, from the social realism and satire of earlier novels like *Saving Agnes* (1993) and *Arlington Park*, to the depersonalized, formal opacity of the *Outline* trilogy and epistolary melodrama of *Second Place* (2021).[2] This chapter considers Cusk's style across her most recent fiction and non-fiction, examining it as a site of discrepant tensions, torn between silence and expression, passivity and participation, objectivity and subjectivity, or as Cusk puts it, with characteristic gravitas in *Aftermath* (2012), 'between the story and the truth' (2019b: 2). A character in *Outline* (2014) makes a remark that succinctly captures these tensions, when commenting on an expired relationship, while also providing a crystallization of Cusk's late(st) style: 'What was striking was the sheer negative capability of their former intimacy' (2018a: 81). If, since writing her divorce memoir *Aftermath*, Cusk's major themes have been former intimacies, absence and silence, then the style of her recent texts and their emotional intensity wrestles a kind of presence

---

[2] Writing about this shift in style, Judith Thurman argues: 'The chaste prose of her current trilogy seems almost like a reproach to the self-conscious virtuosity that preceded it. Before she wrote "Outline," Cusk was a wickedly clever stylist, who fired off aphorisms like a French court diarist and made up the sort of metaphors – "cauliflower-haired old ladies"; the "floury haze" of a dry summer – that you flag in the margin' (Thurman 2017). However, Cusk has pushed back against this narrative, and argued that her work should be read as more of a continuous artistic project rather than one of rupture: '[w]henever people talk about these books [the Outline trilogy], they always say, "Oh, the other ones she wrote were very conventional." I think that's not quite true. [...] I think it's pretty much a continuum' (Schwartz 2018).

from these absences.³ As noted throughout this collection, Cusk described experiencing a kind of 'creative death' after writing *Aftermath*: 'That was the end,' Cusk claimed, 'I was heading into total silence – an interesting place to find yourself when you are quite developed as an artist' (Kellaway 2014).

The trilogy is the key fictional text here; it does not simply depict impasses, silences and expired narratives, but stylistically stages them. The stories that Faye is told tend to centre on the breakdown of relationships or the recollection of something lost that eludes the grasp of the teller (for example, an idyllic marriage that disintegrates, the loss of a beloved pet in tragic circumstances, a bitter feud between parents and children etc.). Cusk's artistic focus on silence, absence and the performance of passivity, in turn, animates what I am terming her 'discrepant style'.⁴ I contend that Cusk's discrepant style secretes emotional and affective ambiguity across her work, in the sense that style's covert expressive qualities often stand in contradiction to the façades of absence, silence and withdrawal, which she painstakingly assembles. Cusk has commented on the *Outline* trilogy's distinctive formal structure, stating that it contains 'a new kind of reality which is only surface [...] there's no prior knowledge, there's no assumption', and this allows for a 'migration into completely wild and experimental ways of being, acting in an unconditioned, unfettered way' (Wade 2015). Another discrepancy emerges here, between the 'wild and experimental ways of being' facilitated by Cusk's innovations of subjectivity and authorship – the freedom granted by the absent narrator's act of migration – and the cold precision of her 'depersonalized' style, which is animated, I suggest, by more conditioned, fettered qualities of silence, absence and cruelty.

Cusk's work encapsulates '[t]he contemporary problem of style', proposed by Richard Robinson and Barry Sheils, which they define as 'a problem of sorting and identifying difference, of generational, technological and institutional transmission, of aesthetic judgement and affective response, of the interpretative tension between suspicion and pleasure' (2022: 474). Cusk's style appears to self-reflexively court judgement and affective responses in terms of the interpretative

---

³ The exception in Cusk's work since *Aftermath* is *Second Place*, which subverts the subdued emotional intensity of the trilogy and stages a self-conscious melodrama, that is nonetheless still animated by qualities of absence, silence and cruelty.
⁴ David James's *Discrepant Solace* explores a very different corpus of work and affective vocabulary, but nonetheless resonates with my approach in terms of its focus on style and the discrepancies contained therein. Indeed, like solace, silences can 'manifest [...] linguistically, in the torsion of sentences that contend with, at times tonally counterpoint, the very experience of loss, shame, or fear that they so vividly communicate' (2018: 6).

tensions and temptations it raises. For example, in the *Outline* trilogy Faye both rarely speaks and is the constant mediator of *all* speech throughout these novels, thereby destabilizing expectations of narrative subjectivity, and complicating a perennial question asked of fiction – who is speaking? Alexandra Schwartz gives one possible answer, suggesting that by 'cutting out her own tongue, Cusk's narrator manages to express herself by speaking through everyone else' (2015).[5] These contradictions in Cusk's work create a discord between style and expression; there is a discrepancy between the subjective absence of the narrator and a new kind of presence that emerges through outlines, reversals and negative capabilities. Cusk touches on this discord in an essay on Chekhov, noting his artistic fixation on 'profound silence', and that 'it interests him not as an absence but as a presence', in a sense that reverberates in her own work (2019a: 171). While all writers' styles contain a tension between intention and interpretation, representation and (in)expression, I suggest that Cusk's self-avowed objective to 'break her own style' speaks to the contemporary problems of style noted above, and her writing is therefore particularly suited to an analysis of style's expressive and affective capacities (Schwartz 2018).[6]

This chapter will examine how styles of silence and absence are articulated in Cusk's essay 'Coventry', unpacking how Cusk's non-fiction relates to her recent novels, especially the autofictional *Outline* trilogy, and the quasi-biographical novel *Second Place*. Cusk's novels have drawn critical attention for their formal innovations, particularly their generic hybridity, such as the biographical origins of the *Outline* trilogy, or the use of Mabel Dodge Luhan's memoir in *Second Place*. This chapter addresses how Cusk's non-fiction possesses a pertinent relationship with her autofictional and biographical fiction, and likewise demands close stylistic and formal scrutiny. As Alexandra Kingston-Reese notes of contemporary essays, like Cusk's 'Coventry', they often contain 'a discourse about the novel's aesthetic and epistemological inadequacies' (2022). The essay 'is not just a form that allows novelists to escape form', Kingston-Reese suggests, 'it offers a site to stake a claim on form; to dip their toes into the debate; to contribute to their own culture of reading' (2022). More than simply a cipher for reading her novels, I suggest that Cusk's essays can be analysed for the broader

---

[5] Cusk takes this idea in another direction in her short story, 'The Stuntman', where a character known only as D's wife, responds to her husband's upside down paintings by declaring: 'I want to write upside down' (2023).
[6] In an interview in *The New Yorker*, Cusk states 'You enter these structures, you exist in these structures, they collapse or you leave them [...] that was how I really broke my own style' (Schwartz 2018).

questions they raise about reading, and for their own kind of discrepant style – often anticipating, mirroring, conversing with, or disrupting Cusk's widely celebrated fictional innovations. There are also gendered expectations of what essays and novels should be doing, that Cusk's writing often confounds. Merve Emre, considering Cusk's work, has reflected that 'a woman's confession of her experience is often lauded for its bravery, its honesty, but is rarely scrutinized for its forms of expression' (2018). In turn, this chapter takes on Emre's proposition to consider how 'style can serve as a source of power' (2018), examining how silences and cruelty are articulated in Cusk's recent work, and to what ends.

'Like coldness the silence advances'

In her essay 'Coventry', Cusk excavates the affective and narratological possibilities of silence, in a way that I suggest is deeply entangled with her broader corpus, and specifically, with the development of her own discrepant style. The essay was first published in the literary journal *Granta* in 2016, between the first two novels of the *Outline* trilogy, and later in the essay collection *Coventry* in 2019. In the essay Cusk describes the experience of 'being sent to Coventry', not literally, as she confesses that she has never been to the city, but as an idiomatic metaphor for being given the silent treatment by her parents:

> Every so often, for offences actual or hypothetical, my mother and father stop speaking to me. There's a funny phrase for this phenomenon in England: it's called being sent to Coventry. I don't know what the origins of the expression are, though I suppose I could easily find out. Coventry suffered badly in the war: it once had a beautiful cathedral that in 1940 was bombed into non-existence. Now it's an ordinary town in the Midlands, and if it hasn't made sense of its losses, it has at least survived them.
>
> 2019a: 23

This passage, with its latent and loaded vocabulary, is emblematic of Cusk's style, as she switches between the curios of 'funny phrase[s]' to stark historical reflections on warfare ('bombed into non-existence') and modes of survival. Her style of essay writing, or essayism in Brian Dillon's term, encompasses these deft switches between discrepant subject matters, as quotidian and profound themes speak to each other while never fully cohering. There is a calculated refusal ('I suppose I could easily find out') that suggests forms of not knowing might be preferable to breaking these silences with more conventional essayistic concerns about origins and etymology. As the paragraph closes, Cusk makes a characteristic claim that can be considered in relation to her own artistic practice – there is an emphasis on survival above and beyond fully making sense of past losses.

The focus on survival in 'Coventry' is a narrative tactic deployed throughout Cusk's work. Since she was a child, Cusk writes, 'I have been terrified of Coventry, of its vastness and bleakness and loneliness, and of what it represents, which is ejection from the story,' using terms that resonate with both *Aftermath* and the *Outline* trilogy, which also depict forms of cultural exclusion (2019a: 38). Cusk details the granular and emotional state of being banished to this social hinterland:

> Like coldness the silence advances, making itself known not by presence but by absence, by disturbances of expectation so small that they are registered only half-consciously and instead mount up, so that one only becomes truly aware of it once its progress is complete.
>
> 2019a: 23

Silence and coldness are captured by Cusk's slowly accretive sentences, which similarly 'mount up', as in the passage above (and across the entire *Outline* trilogy), in a form of reverse exposition that becomes increasingly expressive despite, or indeed *because* of the intensity of these absences. As Susan Sontag writes in 'On Style', 'the most potent elements in a work of art are, often, its silence' (2009: 36). 'Coventry' explores a hermeneutics of silence, where the absence of a relationship encourages Cusk, and us as readers, to search for meaning. Cusk's style in 'Coventry' echoes what James terms the 'grippingly impersonal textures' that personify the *Outline* trilogy, as the essay describes the dramatic breakdown of a relationship in a strikingly undramatic or 'depersonalized' manner (2021: 141).[7] Silence in the metaphorical Coventry, rather than signifying negation or the end of the story, becomes a means to examine conflicting theories of narrative (and social) power. In one sense, Cusk links silence to a failure to wield power or to control the narrative, as she also does in *Aftermath*: 'My husband believed that I had treated him monstrously. This belief of his couldn't be shaken: his whole world depended on it. It was his story, and lately I have come to hate stories' (Cusk 2019b: 2). The silence and 'ejection from the story' that Coventry represents might therefore become a

---

[7] These 'grippingly impersonal' aspects of Cusk's writing also relates, as James notes, to how 'style itself – its grammatical fibers, palpable solicitations, and disarming refractions – implicates readers' (2021: 131).

means of survival or creative possibility after disenchantment with certain social and cultural narrative structures – such as marriage or the novel form – a disenchantment that is affectively articulated in Cusk's discrepant style.[8]

'Coventry', like the *Outline* trilogy, gives us only one side of a story or conversation, while the other (Faye in the trilogy, and Cusk's parents in 'Coventry') remains largely silent, thereby complicating ideas about who is holding power in these interactions: 'It is the attempt to recover power through withdrawal, rather as the powerless child indignantly imagines his own death as a punishment to others. Then they'll be sorry!' (2019a: 24). Cusk positions her parents in the role of the powerless child in her essay, in their attempt to 'control the story [...] to control me' (ibid.). The essay raises questions of social decorum, punishment and cruelty, asking us to consider whether Cusk's parents' silent treatment grants them the power of a jailor, or if her newfound sense of exile grants her power to revel in silence beyond certain social, gendered, and artistic expectations. Cusk ruminates:

> They appear to be wielding power, but I've come to understand that their silence is the opposite of power. It is in fact failure, their failure to control the story, their failure to control me. It is a failure so profound that all they have left to throw at it is the value of their own selves, like desperate people taking the last of their possessions to the pawnshop.
>
> 2019a: 24

The essay proceeds by changing tack throughout its meandering contemplations, never fully settling on whether silence is a form of power or powerlessness. As with many of Cusk's essays, the central idea, of 'being sent to Coventry' and the sense of exile it encompasses, allows her to reflect on the conditions of writing, socializing and living more generally, as well as family structures and relationships between parents and their children. Cusk has stated that 'writing and living are the same thing, or they ought to be. It is only by paying great attention to ordinary living that I actually learn anything about writing' (Kellaway 2014). In this self-reflexive vein, 'Coventry' unpacks the relationship between writing and living through its contradictory qualities of silence, in ways that inflect and inform Cusk's broader artistic ideals: 'The thing about Coventry is that it has no words: nothing is explained to you there, nothing made clear. It is entirely representational. And what I've never felt about it, I realise, is

---

[8] Kingston-Reese touches on a similar sentiment, in terms of writers turning to the essay form, as she notes 'the essay is seen as a way out, as a way to make the novel wild again' (2022).

indifference' (2019a: 26). Despite the silence of 'Coventry', Cusk stresses that it produces an emotional response, even if this response, like the conditions from which it is born, contains no words and possesses no explanation – she does not elaborate on this lack of indifference, and we are left to gloss the outline or 'sheer negative capability' of her emotional reaction.

Negative Affects

Cusk's writing has an affinity with works of creative silence, that nonetheless manage to express through negated forms of representation, such as the *Outline* trilogy's absences, the painterly fixations of *Second Place* and the focus on the visual arts in 'The Stuntman' (2023) and *Parade* (2024). Visual art appeals to Cusk because of its silence – like Coventry 'it has no words [...] it is entirely representational' – and it provides a correlative for her own style, which is deeply entangled with the limitations of language. Cusk's essay, 'Marble in Metamorphosis' (2022), describes statues in a manner that her own art reaches towards: 'Silent though they are, they appear to speak. Yet their message is too cryptic: perhaps it is the case that, their meaning having been fundamentally lost to us, we read into them what we want to read' (24).[9] Cusk's work is caught up in these questions of legibility, language and storytelling, and the meditations of her non-fiction acutely emerge in her novels. In *Second Place*, L, Cusk's D. H. Lawrence stand-in, explores a physical manifestation of a place that has echoes of the metaphorical Coventry, the Norfolk marshes: 'I was trying to find the edge', L says, 'but there is no edge [...] it just sort of dissolves, doesn't it? There are no lines here at all' (2021, 144–5). The marshes appear in 'Coventry' too, as another kind of strange dystopia, in the sense of a negated place rather than a malevolent one: 'The marsh has many moods, [...] It is an involuted landscape whose creeks form intestinal patterns amid the springy furze. [...] If you try to walk out across it to the sea, you quickly find yourself unable to progress' (Cusk 2019a: 33–4). The 'involuted' qualities of these landscapes confront us via the style of

---

[9] 'Marble in Metamorphosis' also captures the narrative possibilities in visual art that Cusk is drawn towards: 'The survival of marble, like the survival of certain memories while others vanish, is likewise a kind of subjectivity. A story is made out of what survives. [...] To an extent a story is made out of the juncture between the immaterial and the material. In marble the distance between the two – between fleetingness and survival, between expressiveness and dumbness – is immense' (2022: 17).

description in *Second Place* and 'Coventry', as we encounter details of narrative impasses and the stalled progress, which 'just sort of dissolves' into silence.

Cusk's latest works of fiction and their characters, Faye in the trilogy, M in *Second Place* and the narrator of 'The Stuntman', explore what might be defined as negative affects – such as cruelty, impersonality, withdrawal, silence, loss and absence – all of which are symptomatic of being 'sent to Coventry'. These affects correspond to the negative aesthetics detailed in Lauren Berlant's 'Structures of Unfeeling', in which they define a kind of negative artistic capability that manages to unsettle the senses through 'underperformed emotion' (2015: 191). Berlant links these latent emotions to an emerging 'cultural style that appears as a reticent action, a spatialized suspension of relational clarity that signifies a subtracted response to the urgencies of the moment' (ibid.). These inverted and negative affects often emerge in Cusk's work through the silence or withdrawal of the narrator, a withdrawal that runs in counterflow to the development of plot or character, as actions and responses take place in tonal registers that feel underperformed, emotionally off-kilter and difficult to interpret. For example, in *Transit* ([2016] 2018b), a man named Lawrence fatalistically reflects on developing feelings for a woman outside his marriage, Eloise, he has (or had) yet to meet:

> By the time he actually met Eloise, Lawrence had come to understand a great deal about Susie and about himself; they had already spoken about a trial separation and were seeing a marriage counsellor. [...] He had learned more about Eloise, he believed, from her absences than her presence would have taught him; what he had loved first about her, and still loved, were those very absences, whose mystery and intangibility had caused him to examine the reality of his own life.
>
> Cusk 2018b: 257

Lawrence imagines a fantasy of Eloise that manifests before he has actually met her, and his image of her is created through imaginative absences rather than the realities of her presence. Cusk's accretive narratives and her discrepant style often follow this pattern and allude to kinds of knowledge acquired through negative measures, such as absences, silences and outlines, which then gradually take on their own emotional and affective presence – their own versions of the 'story or the truth'. As Cusk writes in 'Coventry', 'It takes patience to send someone to Coventry: it's not a game for those who require instant satisfaction' (2019a: 23). The intangibility of silence therefore prompts a self-reflexive consideration that may or may not lead to some form of epiphany ('I have come to hate stories'). In this sense, both the fear of banishment and its creative possibilities, the metaphorical heart of Cusk's 'Coventry', plays a central role across her works of fiction.[10]

While Cusk's recent writing is predicated on forms of absence and intangibility, the style of her work is contradictorily generative, containing emotional states and alternative narratives that allows Cusk's characters, narrators, and herself, like Lawrence in *Transit*, to reflect upon the reality of their own lives. However, these reflections emerge in 'underperformed ways', in Berlant's terms, and they occur in narratives and analogies that are hard to understand or parse, emphasizing the difficulty of social interaction within these narratives, and as readers encountering them – the lives described are only glimpsed through a glass darkly. Cusk writes about this hermeneutic struggle in 'Coventry', detailing not just a breakdown in the relationship with her parents, but also a failure to read and recognize that relationship's expiry:

> It takes me a while to notice that my parents have sent me to Coventry. It's not unlike when a central-heating boiler breaks down: there's no explosion, no dramatic sight or sound, merely a growing feeling of discomfort that comes from the gradual drop in temperature that one might be surprisingly slow – depending on one's instinct for habituation – to attribute to an actual cause.
>
> 2019a: 23

We can again trace Cusk's discrepant style, as the absence and negation described underpins something stylistically present. Indeed, Robinson and Sheils note the kind of discrepancy that can occur between style and form, even when a style appears to be particularly passive or absent: 'Style is bound up with volition whereas form can be inert: even the style which says "I am not here", which proclaims itself as impersonal, as art-object, is not reducible to an ideal of form, because it bears a "way of doing"' (2022: 487). Cusk's style appears to loudly proclaim 'I am not here', while always discretely enacting the opposite, and emitting her own kind of 'way of doing' things. Her fiction and non-fiction alike are characterized by an absence of explosions, a lack of dramatic sights and sounds, and instead work with a 'growing feeling of discomfort' and a 'gradual

---

[10] Cusk has spoken about this form of banishment and exile in relation to Faye's passivity in *Outline*, and the possibilities it holds for the narrative: 'Why is she so passive? Well, if there is a narrative opportunity in the book, that is it. And it's the experience of loss of identity that means that in a sense she's a beggar in the street and that's all you really know, that her life in pretty conventional ways – divorce, et cetera – has collapsed. That idea of being out on the street, which is very much an idea from Greek tragedy and the classical world, of war and exiting your home, meaning that there's trouble – and so that's her' (Schwartz, 2018).

drop in temperature', that comes to characterize the social relations depicted, the portrayal of decentred subjectivity and increasing uncertainty around established modes of narration.

'Coventry', with its gradual drops in emotional temperature and slowly accumulating silences, like the *Outline* trilogy, explores the appearance of dramatic inaction, while the performance of withdrawal contains many countermeasures that accumulate to form Cusk's discrepant style. Cusk claims to have never felt 'indifference' at her banishment to the silent realm of Coventry, without articulating what it is that she does feel, in a style that once again 'secretes discrepancies between subject matter and expression' (James 2021: 141). The *Outline* trilogy performs a similar trick, concealing the emotional reactions of Faye, allowing them to covertly accumulate in the intricacies of the narrative style. 'I was beginning to see my own fears and desires manifested outside myself,' Faye confesses, '[I] was beginning to see in other people's lives a commentary on my own' (Cusk 2018a: 75). Underneath the surface appearance of passivity, Faye 'commandeers reality', as Emre writes, 'bending colors, sounds, incidents, and people to her subjective truth' (2015). Silence, once again, becomes a site of discrepant tensions, between absconding from narrative truths and controlling them. The *Outline* trilogy thus escalates the silence of 'Coventry' a step further, and performs a kind of inverted interiority, where all of Faye's interior judgements are refracted through her exterior environment, made legible through the expressions of other people. By disrupting novelistic conventions such as character and plot, as well as the conventions of autobiography, where we would usually expect a clear sense of self, Cusk crafts what she has called an 'annihilated perspective' in the *Outline* trilogy, inverting the silence of Coventry's banishment to turn a mirror on those who have enforced this cultural and social exile (Kellaway 2014).

Cruelty and Self-criticism

'Coventry' captures the kind of formal opacity and absences that we see in Cusk's recent fiction, as she confesses to 'feel safer in Coventry, safer in the silence [...] Coventry is a place where the worst has already happened' (2019a: 39). She also begins to seek 'whatever truth might be found amid the smoking ruins of the story' (ibid.). The essay emphasizes Cusk's resistance to established structures of family, society and storytelling, in a manner that underscores her relationship with modern life – from Homer to Ikea, as Lockwood puts it. Cusk sketches a kind of narrative *Ruinenlust*, preferring to remain in the 'smoking ruins' of old stories rather than creating new ones. 'Freedom meant living in Coventry for ever and making the best of it,' Cusk writes, 'living amid the waste and shattered buildings, the desecrated past' (2019a: 38–9). One risk of stepping out of the ruins and beginning again lies in the possibility of narrative missteps, as M states in *Second Place*, 'I am determined not to falsify anything, even for the sake of a narrative' (Cusk 2021: 130), emphasizing a faith in silence above the fallacies and falsities that narratives are prone to harbour (and perhaps also prioritizing previous forms, such as Luhan's diaries, rather than creating entirely new ones). The trilogy also engages with this conflicting pull between negation and new narrative compulsions, especially the impulse to keep finding new forms of writing, despite frequently disavowing this impulse. In *Kudos*, Faye meets a pompous journalist who manages to both re-affirm and contradict the *Outline* trilogy's own negative capabilities, by stating that '[a] work of art could not, ultimately, be negative: its material existence, its status as an object, could not help but be positive, a gain, an addition to the sum of what was' (Cusk 2018c: 181–2). Like the withdrawal of the narrator, whose act of withdrawal becomes contradictorily expressive, the negative artwork described here contains a discrepancy through its 'material existence' and 'status as an object' that pushes back against the silence.

These self-excoriating tendencies recur throughout Cusk's fiction and non-fiction, as she deploys characters and counternarratives which dismantle the very viewpoints and artistic objects she appears to be assembling. Cusk is frequently the first to criticize herself and her own writing, often within the writing itself, thereby unsettling any potential future criticism. For example, *Aftermath* concludes with an ethically fraught scene of cruelty that illustrates how Cusk's formal concerns with withdrawal, with 'watching, assessing, staying hidden' (2019b: 73), comes into conflict with the expressive capacities of her self-critical style. The memoir ends with a section called 'Trains', as the narrative perspective suddenly switches from Cusk to Sonia, a Lithuanian au pair who works in Cusk's family home before the breakdown of Cusk's marriage. In this section Cusk only refers to herself obliquely as 'the woman', and she anticipates the subjective withdrawal of her narrators and the absence of names in the *Outline* trilogy and *Second Place*, as well as the creative silence of 'Coventry'. Cusk claims to be 'an exile from my own history', by dramatically narrating herself as an exile from her own memoir (2019b: 91). In 'Trains' Cusk portrays herself as an assertive and bullying employer, telling Sonia to do an array of housework, 'I want you to cook dinner. I want you to do the laundry. I want you to tidy up around here' (137), before threatening: 'You need to do these things [...] or you're going to have to go home' (138).

We soon discover that Sonia was raped when she was sixteen years old, blamed for it by her mother, and that she is now recovering from a suicide attempt. As the narrative progresses, Sonia becomes more adept and acclimatized to her new working conditions, taking on a greater role in the household and building a rapport with the children, while 'the woman', Cusk, becomes ill and begins to appear like a ghost in her own home:

> After a while the woman appears in the doorway. She is wearing a crumpled nightdress. Her hair stands up in a shock. Her lips are a bluish colour. She is very white, and much thinner than she was before. She puts her hand against the doorway for support. She looks at them all sitting there. She tries to smile.
>
> 2019b: 144

There is a cruel bluntness in the syntax, in the short, staccato sentences, each beginning with an accusatory 'She' or 'Her', as Cusk's style reemphasizes her anonymity and fading identity. The 'tries' that qualifies the attempt to smile only amplifies its strained superficiality, as if authentic emotions are beyond the reach of a narrator now relegated to being described in the second person. Cusk thus portrays the disintegration of her marriage from an austere and cruel narratological perspective, and she voyeuristically appropriates the perspective of another woman, who Cusk explicitly shows herself to have 'treated monstrously' (the accusation levelled at Cusk by her husband at the beginning of *Aftermath*). While Roberta Garrett has argued that 'Cusk's lacerating view of her own childcare arrangements [...] shows an unusual willingness to acknowledge the exploitation of poorer women by richer ones' (2021: 93), I suggest that this cruel, self-lacerating perspective neither condemns nor excuses Cusk's actions but leaves them in an uneasy state of moral queasiness, where charges of Cusk's cruelty are always met with a pre-empted acknowledgement of meticulous self-awareness. 'That was a truly bleak bit of counterpoint,' Cusk has said of this switch of perspective in *Aftermath*, 'that was me using that method to shoot myself in the head' (Wade 2015).

Cusk pre-empts critical condemnation by anticipating and interposing such criticism into her self-reflexive prose, in her discrepant style, while simultaneously reaching for modes of resistance or survival from criticism through silences or innovations of subjectivity, such as the absent narrator of the trilogy, or the biographical ventriloquism of Luhan and Lawrence in *Second Place*. The discordant relationships at the centre of her fiction and non-fiction are essentially what makes Cusk's work both formally innovative and ethically fraught, in terms of the relationships and social dynamics she sketches. These tensions are animated by what Cusk calls the 'dissonance between interior life and exterior appearance', a 'desire to externalise yourself, and put yourself into space', and which she describes as a 'kind of negative equity' (Wade 2015). These discrepancies, between interiority and exteriority, reality and appearances, 'stories and the truth', take shape through a series of social breakdowns: 'a marriage is a system of belief, a story', Cusk writes at the beginning of *Outline*, anticipating the themes explored in 'Coventry' and echoing *Aftermath*, 'and though it manifests itself in things that are real enough, the impulse that drives it is ultimately mysterious' (2018a: 12). While Cusk's portrayals of social relationships tend to linger in a state of uncertainty, the expressive qualities of her style pushes back against this state of aporia, to convey a pointed and emotionally charged dissatisfaction with subjectivity, existing social structures, and the narrative materials available to her.

Cusk's other essays in *Coventry* are often in dialogue with her fiction's themes of justice, freedom and responsibility. The essay 'Driving as Metaphor' posits that 'the true danger of driving might lie in its capacity for subjectivity, and in the weapons it puts at subjectivity's disposal' (Cusk 2019a: 21). The trilogy similarly puts the ambiguity of subjectivity centre stage, and, like Cusk's essay on driving, circles around the question: 'How can one know when the moment has arrived at which you are no longer capable of being objective?' (21). 'Driving as Metaphor' describes driving as a kind of psychodrama, one that is not 'a shared reality but a kind of fiction'. And yet, the narrative response to these quandaries appears to be steeped in ambivalence, caught in an extended ruminative moment, where stories are only met with counter-stories but never the harmony of resolution. Objectivity, across Cusk's fiction and non-fiction, is held as both a paragon of truth and also constantly undermined by the inherent artifice of and scepticism towards narrative in Cusk's world – her distrust of stories. After listening to a man complain about his ex-wife and family in *Outline*, Faye declares 'I remained dissatisfied by the story of his second marriage. It had lacked objectivity; it relied too heavily on extremes, and the moral properties it ascribed to those extremes were often incorrect' (Cusk 2018a: 29). While the man apparently lacks objectivity and exaggerates to flatter his own character, Faye (and by extension, Cusk) seems to grant herself the exceptional objective certitude to ascertain 'moral properties', and their degree of correctness. Clair Wills notes this quality in *Coventry*, positing that 'what is unusual is not Cusk's distrust of stories but her faith in truth' (2019). Cusk has confessed: 'I'm perhaps stuck in the past, trying to work out the past. [...] I have a moral agenda, a willingness to commit myself to morality, that feels extracted at great cost from the "novel," as we define it currently' (Treisman 2023).

The other central themes in *Coventry* are rudeness and cruelty. 'The last time my parents spoke to me,' Cusk writes in 'On Rudeness', 'my father said something rude. He said I was full of shit,' baiting the reader to take a side in the Coventry standoff in the previous essay (2019a: 66).[11] Rudeness becomes a cipher for all kinds of social relations, from theological considerations of Jesus's manners, to acts of rudeness from airport security that synecdochally provide a comment upon Brexit, racism, and wider cultural rituals. Rudeness also allows Cusk to turn the tables, to fling insults at herself, or at her stand-in Faye, that act as a form of inoculation. In *Transit*, for example, the downstairs neighbour Paula is one of the few characters in the trilogy to explicitly comment upon Faye's appearance and lifestyle. 'People like you make me sick [...] The way people like you carry on' (Cusk 2018b: 158). Paula overhears a man in Faye's flat one evening and accusatorily deduces that Faye is 'dancing around in your high heels and throwing yourself at men' (ibid.). 'Disgusting,' she declares, before delivering a cruel flourish that ends a later chapter, 'Fucking bitch' (207). Paula reverses the stakes of Faye's annihilated perspective, returning the gaze and articulating her own judgement values, that once again, like *Aftermath*, sees Cusk ventriloquize her detractors through a fraught style that contains a latent sense of self-awareness and self-criticism which is difficult to gauge, and remains in a state of discrepant tension.

Throughout *Coventry*, Cusk often uses the terms 'truth' and 'honesty', however, as Wills notes, they are not the same thing; 'truth' makes 'a claim to universality' while honesty relates to 'personal accountability' (2019). Wills takes issue with this moral position: 'Cusk knows that she has no more purchase on universal truth than the rest of us and maybe that is why she courts opprobrium in the way she does. She keeps claiming a right to the role of seer to which she knows she is not entitled' (2019). Wills critiques the essentialism and universalism that Cusk's essays often lay claim to: 'Categories such as "reality," "truth," and "woman" are loaded with a freight they cannot bear' (2019). Honesty in Cusk's essays tends

---

[11] In her review of *Coventry*, Clair Wills considers that Cusk's parents might be justified in inflicting the silent treatment upon their daughter (and perhaps implicitly suggests that Cusk is 'full of shit'): 'Cusk's essay depends on a distinction between story and truth, but it failed to get me on its side because I kept finding myself thinking about alternatives to Cusk's version of the story [...] As a reader I stayed resolutely on the side of "story," and, in effect, therefore, on the side of the parents' (2019).

to refer to faith in certain structures – familial, social, cultural, etc. When faith in these structures is eroded or breaks, their edifice as a manufactured narrative becomes, almost suddenly, apparent: 'It was as if driving was a story I had suddenly stopped believing in and without that belief I was being overwhelmed by the horror of reality' (Cusk 2019a: 21). In *Essayism*, Brian Dillon identifies this as:

> [a] conflict inside the essay as form: it aspires to express the quintessence or crux of its matter, thus to a sort of polish and integrity, and it wants at the same time to insist that its purview is partial, that being incomplete is a value in itself, for it better reflects the brave and curious but faltering nature of the writing mind.
>
> 2017: 4

Such a standpoint seems to capture not just the conflict in Cusk's essays, but also the annihilated perspective of her recent fiction, and her essays can therefore be understood in relation to her dissatisfaction with available forms of fiction and non-fiction. Cusk's essayism is built upon unstable narrative foundations, stories which come under fire and have their strengths and weaknesses probed, especially her claims on 'truth' and 'honesty', in ways that thematically reverberate throughout the volatile and expressive silences and absences of her fictional work.

Conclusion: Embarrassing Fiction

Cusk concludes 'Coventry' by turning to the literal Coventry, and she details the construction of the city's modernist cathedral designed by Basil Spence in the aftermath of the Second World War, which suggests a way of emerging from the ruins:

> People were suspicious, apparently, of the cathedral's modernist design: when what you're used to is irretrievably gone, it's hard to believe in something new. But they suspended their disbelief. The new things came to be, became reality. What needed to change was changed, just as the old things were destroyed – not by time, but by force of human will.
>
> 2019a: 44–5

In terms of Cusk's style, then, we can trace a discrepancy between destruction and reinvention, as well as an attitude towards literary form, perspective, character and autobiography that is similarly predicated on a belief that 'what needed to change was changed', or will change, through a suspension of certain beliefs, such as the notion of 'having a self', even when these suspensions themselves begin to collapse. Coventry contains the possibility of another kind of creative destruction, as well as the opportunity to start again – an impulse that finds a correlative in the new cathedral built upon the ruins of the old one.

Cusk has routinely disparaged the forms of fiction available to her as a writer, while nonetheless continuing to write fiction. In the aftermath of *Aftermath*, Cusk claimed the prospect of writing novels felt 'fake and embarrassing', and she proposed that 'once you have suffered sufficiently, the idea of making up John and Jane and having them do things together seems utterly ridiculous' (Kellaway 2014).[12] Cusk also confessed that 'my mode of autobiography had come to an end. I could not do it without being misunderstood and making people angry' (ibid.). In 2018 she told the *New Yorker*: 'I'm not interested in character because I don't think character exists anymore' (Schwartz). In 2023, after writing a short story for *The New Yorker*, 'The Stuntman' (which does indeed contain characters), Cusk touches upon a familiar sense of an ending:

> I always think and feel that I'm coming to the end of writing as a useful occupation, which is maybe a suicidal impulse given to female creators. I want to break through, yet I don't want to destroy, which I suppose is one version of that impulse.
>
> Treisman 2023

There is a tension in Cusk's style, caught between creativity and termination, between silence and expression. As with the often-heralded death of the novel, there is something cyclical in this death of old styles or arrival of the new, that never manages to fully materialize. The sense of an ending in Cusk's work thus becomes a hallmark of her style, found in the marrow of her sentences and the absences that pervade her work.

'Coventry' speaks to the 'suicidal' creative impulses that Cusk has returned to over the years, and it reflects upon the ethical stakes of narrating the truth, as Cusk writes, 'silence represents the problem of reconnecting to reality once the story has ended' (2019a: 33). The potent silences in the metaphorical wastelands of 'Coventry' resembles Cusk's powerlessness in *Aftermath* and the struggle to challenge her husband's story, as well as recalling the 'creative death' she experienced after the very public criticism of the memoir's publication. And

---

[12] It bears noting that after the 'creative death' of publishing *Aftermath*, which itself was developed from an essay first published in *Granta*, Cusk republished the original essay in *Coventry*, granting *Aftermath* a third outing; the aftermath of *Aftermath* has contained many versions of *Aftermath*.

yet, as with the trilogy, there is a kind of narrative power wielded through silence, and 'Coventry' explores the possibilities of remaining in the shadows, as an outsider or part of an avant-garde, or as a self-appointed exile. Just as Rooney remarks how the stylization of passivity in the trilogy creates something paradoxically expressive and judgemental, the silence in 'Coventry' begins to cohere into a latent form of expression. At the end of 'Coventry', her parents seek a reconciliation, but Cusk rejects a return to previous relations and narratives: 'I don't want to leave Coventry. I've decided to stay' (2019a: 43). Silence and stories, then, emblematize two conflicting approaches towards narrative power, which Cusk deploys throughout her recent fiction and non-fiction, even as both tactics prove insufficient in their aspirations towards complete narrative control, caught somewhere between the impulse to 'break through' without quite breaking her style:

> There's always something, some new development, some incident or issue, some theme that needs attending to: the story still insists on telling itself, despite our best efforts to block our ears. If it does happen, one place we'll have to go is Coventry.
>
> 2019a: 44

Works Cited

Berlant, L. (2015), 'Structures of Unfeeling: "Mysterious Skin"'. *International Journal of Politics, Culture, and Society*, 28 (3): 191–213.
Cusk, R. (2018a), *Outline*. London: Faber & Faber.
Cusk, R. (2018b), *Transit*. London: Faber & Faber.
Cusk, R. (2018c), *Kudos*. London: Faber & Faber.
Cusk, R. (2019a), *Coventry*. London: Faber & Faber.
Cusk, R. (2019b), *Aftermath*. London: Faber & Faber.
Cusk, R. (2021), *Second Place*. London: Faber & Faber.
Cusk, R. (2022), 'Marble in Metamorphosis'. Collingwood: Molongo.
Cusk, R. (2023), 'The Stuntman', *The New Yorker*, 17 April. Available at: https://www.newyorker.com/magazine/2023/04/24/the-stuntman-fiction-rachel-cusk (accessed 20 July 2023).
Dillon, B. (2017), *Essayism*. London: Fitzcarraldo Editions.
Emre, M. (2018), 'Of Note'. *Harper's Magazine*. 1 June. Available at: https://harpers.org/archive/2018/06/of-note/ (accessed 20 July 2023).
Garrett, R. (2021), *Writing the Modern Family: Contemporary Literature, Motherhood and Neoliberal Culture*. London: Rowman & Littlefield.

James, D. (2021), 'Affect's Vocabularies: Literature and Feeling after 1890', in D. Mao (ed.), *The New Modernist Studies*. Cambridge: Cambridge University Press.

Kellaway, K. (2014), 'Rachel Cusk: "Aftermath Was Creative Death. I Was Heading into Total Silence"'. *The Observer*, 24 August. Available at: https://www.theguardian.com/books/2014/aug/24/rachel-cusk-interview-aftermath-outline (accessed 20 July 2023).

Kingston-Reese, A. (2022), 'Novel Nausea'. *ASAP/J*. Available at: https://asapjournal.com/the-contemporary-essay-novel-nausea-alexandra-kingston-reese/ (accessed 20 July 2023).

Lockwood, P. (2018), 'On Rachel Cusk "Why Do I Have to Know What McDonald's Is?"'. *London Review of Books*, 10 May. Available at: https://www.lrb.co.uk/the-paper/v40/n09/patricia-lockwood/why-do-i-have-to-know-what-mcdonald-s-is (accessed 20 July 2023)

Robinson, R. and B. Sheils (2022), 'The Contemporary Problem of Style'. *Textual Practice*, 36 (4): 473–500.

Rooney, S. (2018), 'Buried in Bourgeois Life'. *Slate*, 25 May. Available at: https://slate.com/culture/2018/05/rachel-cusks-kudos-reviewed-by-sally-rooney.html (accessed 20 July 2023).

Schwartz, A. (2015), 'The Passivity Project'. *The Nation*, 2 July. Available at: https://www.thenation.com/article/archive/the-passivity-project/ (accessed 20 July 2023).

Schwartz, A. (2018), '"I Don't Think Character Exists Anymore": A Conversation with Rachel Cusk'. *The New Yorker*, 18 November. Available at: https://www.newyorker.com/culture/the-new-yorker-interview/i-dont-think-character-exists-anymore-a-conversation-with-rachel-cusk (accessed 20 July 2023).

Sontag, S. (2009), 'On Style', in *Against Interpretation*. London: Penguin Books.

Thurman, J. (2017), 'Rachel Cusk Gut-Renovates the Novel'. *The New Yorker*, 7 August. Available at: https://www.newyorker.com/magazine/2017/08/07/rachel-cusk-gut-renovates-the-novel (accessed 20 July 2023).

Treisman, D. (2023), 'Rachel Cusk on the Self in Visual Art'. *The New Yorker*, 17 April. Available at: https://www.newyorker.com/books/this-week-in-fiction/rachel-cusk-04-24-23 (accessed 20 July 2023).

Wade, F. (2015), 'Interview with Rachel Cusk'. *The White Review*, 14 July. Available at: https://www.thewhitereview.org/feature/interview-rachel-cusk/ (accessed 20 July 2023).

Wills, C. (2019), 'The Truth Alone'. *The New York Review of Books*, 26 September. Available at: https://www.nybooks.com/articles/2019/09/26/rachel-cusk-coventry-truth-alone/ (accessed 20 July 2023).

Afterword

Second Text: Biography, Intertextuality, and Art in *Second Place*

Peter Childs

Building on the study of self and gender in her *Outline* trilogy, Cusk's novel *Second Place* (2021) takes its starting point from Mabel Dodge Luhan's *Lorenzo in Taos*, a 1932 conversational memoir by the patron who invited D. H. Lawrence to America. After leaving New York, Luhan had set up an arts colony in Taos, New Mexico, and persuaded the Lawrences to make an extended stay on their 'savage pilgrimage' of the 1920s. A long-term admirer of Lawrence's writing, Cusk reinvents Luhan's narrative for the twenty-first century, creating a nuanced first-person portrait of shrouded intentions, confused motives, and personal power behind a façade of good and ill manners. The emotional as much as social drama that ensues, and enwraps Cusk's narrator M in a struggle between the claims of art and life, is given depth by the contrasting presences of her second husband Tony, her rebellious daughter Justine, and the privileged heiress Brett. However, it centres on the implications of the complex recognition of herself that M detected years ago in the work of the artist L.

An author who has long picked away at the many intersections of life and art, Rachel Cusk has frequently shown her interest in the example and legacy of modernist writers, as several chapters in this collection note. To select one example, Cusk's 2006 novel *Arlington Park* is a book brimming with passages reminiscent of early twentieth-century writers, such that the overall narrative, with its single-day timeframe and its set pieces in a park and at a party, has clear echoes of Virginia Woolf's *Mrs Dalloway*, while its opening gambit, focalizing the narrative voice through a weather pattern, thematically and formally echoes the ending of James Joyce's 'The Dead'. *Second Place*, in turn, explicitly derives from a memoir whose principal object, if not subject, is a refracted version of D. H. Lawrence. This gives us reason to recall points of connection between these two influential writers that might resonate with Cusk. For example, both pursued independence, as outlined by Woolf in *A Room of One's Own* and lived out by Lawrence on his 'savage pilgrimage'. Both were preoccupied by quotidian domesticity, and both were childless (though Frieda Lawrence was not). Woolf and Lawrence were artists free from parental responsibility, whereas Cusk has written of the personal sacrifice that motherhood demands of the artist and commented in an article written in 2005, that she is 'fascinated by where you go as a woman once you are a mother, and if you ever come back' ('Saving Rachel Cusk' 2005). Again, Cusk is aware that Woolf and Lawrence were both writers interested in freeing the body as much as the mind. For instance, in her Introduction to *The Rainbow* (2010), reprinted in the non-fiction collection *Coventry*, Cusk states that Lawrence will always be treated with suspicion 'as long as the formation of the human personality is based around the denial or misrepresentation of the body's wants' (2019: 208).

With *Second Place*, Cusk's curiosity about the legacy of these authors and their writing is framed in a re-imagining of another text whose form and narration provide her with a further precedent for her own writing: Mabel Dodge Luhan's 1932 memoir *Lorenzo in Taos*, published two years after Lawrence's death. Luhan moved to Taos in 1921 and established a literature and arts colony there that attracted writers and artists, including Georgia O'Keefe, Aldous Huxley and Willa Cather. In 1922, at Luhan's repeated invitation, the Lawrences first arrived. Cusk says her 'version' is a tribute to the spirit of the memoirist, whose voice she inhabits in the novel. Indeed, it is Luhan who becomes the writer supplying the greatest inspiration for Cusk throughout the book. Luhan's position as a parent, unlike Woolf or Lawrence, also features as a way into the narrative's exploration of identity and familial relations. To begin with, in *Second Place* motherhood is presented as a ceding of priority through displacement: 'I could never reconcile myself to the fact that just as you've recovered from your own childhood, [...] you have to give up your place in the sun to a baby who you're determined won't suffer the way you did' (Cusk 2021: 27). It is also Luhan, and not Lawrence, whose insights underscore Cusk's experiences as an artist. Gender differentiates degrees of freedom for the writer, and so does parenthood, their intersection in motherhood providing a springboard for the novel's consideration of primacy and relative positioning in a book primarily about location. Thus, in her essay 'Making House: Notes on Domesticity', Cusk describes remodelling her flat in London: 'It always felt to me like if I wanted to live as a writer, I had to almost create, as a woman, the conditions for me as a writer to be able to exist' (2016).

Luhan wrote several memoirs that have a similar philosophical, reflective tone to Cusk's later novels and deploy a central figure who recounts the stories of others around her more than her own. *Second Place* emerges as a kind of meditative reflection on this secondary positioning, its effects and implications. In Cusk's novel, Luhan's Lorenzo is now a painter called L, not a writer, and at around sixty years of age, an older man than Lawrence was ever to be. The setting has shifted from New Mexico in 1922 to unspecified marsh country similar to the salt marshes of the Norfolk area of Stiffkey where Cusk was living at the time of writing *Second Place*. The time is the present (there is an allusion to the Coronavirus pandemic) but there are few contemporary reference points. For her novel, Cusk does retain the name of the nearby annex Luhan and her husband Tony lent to the Lawrences – the 'Second Place' – and it is this decision, combined with its use as the title for the novel, that I want to explore. As a narrative that in one simple sense accords first place to Luhan's memoir, Cusk's novel interrogates the abiding question of precedence and what, or who, is displaced into a second 'place', understood as location, role or status.

As a painter, the character of L picks up on another novel by Cusk that has a woman indebted to Woolf's portrayal of Lily Briscoe in *To the Lighthouse*. In *The Bradshaw Variations*, using words that anticipate Faye's reflections on her own position in the *Outline* trilogy, a character thinks of when she used to paint, and how that part of herself seems 'to stand poised between existence and annihilation, just as she in that moment felt herself to hover, a dissolving image, at the very brink of identity' (Cusk 2009: 239). *Second Place* also touches on the Woolfian notion of the 'moment of being' (Cusk 2021: 16) to denote both experience and importance in life. Late in the novel, M expands this in a way that resonates with the Nietzschean idea of eternal recurrence: 'If we treated each moment as though it were a permanent condition, a place where we might find ourselves compelled to remain forever, how differently most of us would choose the things that moment contains!' (176); Luhan was inspired by Nietzsche and M accordingly mentions him later in her narrative (204).

There are several reasons why Cusk makes the significant shift to a visual medium for L, but Lawrence was himself a noted painter, whose work was censored and confiscated by Scotland Yard after it was exhibited on 14 June 1929 at the Dorothy Warren Gallery in London. Art historian, Andrew Graham-Dixon observes that 'Most of the paintings showed nude men and women embracing or otherwise communing with themselves and one another in Arcadian landscapes of an abstract character' (2003). This suggests that the images L paints in Cusk's novel are in keeping with those of his literary forebear, which were 'set in a naturist idyll where men and women are free to wander naked in groves of shameless bliss' (Graham-Dixon 2003). Here, it can also be remarked that Cusk also found a connection with an artist L, the French-American sculptor, painter, and printmaker Louise Bourgeois, who like Cusk explored themes in her work of the body and sexuality, domesticity and the family, childhood and parenthood. In her essay on Bourgeois, Cusk notes a crucial aspect to the artist's project that reflects too on the portrayal of M in *Second Place*: 'The artist-mother has to maintain her own links to childhood and to the sense of freedom and irresponsibility that is the condition of her creativity' (2019: 141). In replicating the relationship of herself as a writer-mother alongside an artist L, Cusk notes that in *Second Place* the use of a visual art, without the limitations of language, left her 'better able to express my ideas about femininity and perception as ideas about painting' (Booker 2021).

If we again consider the example of the trilogy that precedes *Second Place*, Cusk situates the writer as storyteller more than protagonist, despite Faye being herself the narrator. Many critics have noted that Faye is a cipher at the heart of her own memoirs, dislodged into second place by the accounts she gives of others' lives. In *Second Place*, this is continued with Cusk's portrayal of another writer, M: 'I ceased to be immersed in the story of my own life and became distinct from it' (2021: 13). However, in the case of M, this is a writer who wishes to express herself above all else. M appears as a first-person narrator struggling for recognition in the narrative of her life. Her drives and anxieties focus on her seemingly conflicted feelings around control and visibility. M wishes to both be in control and to lose control; hence she is drawn to the act of summoning the wilful artist whose paintings spoke to her fifteen years ago in Paris. L is invited as an experiment in art and identity for M, who seeks the tension between contradictions and wishes for recognition from L of the kind she saw in his paintings. That L will not conform to the wants of others is immediately apparent on his arrival since he brings with him a young companion called Brett (named after the painter Dorothy Brett, who accompanied the Lawrences on their return visit to Taos and contributed to the tumultuous relationship between Luhan and Lawrence; Brett, the daughter of a viscount, had responded to Lawrence's request for volunteers to start a new society in New Mexico). Brett adds to the sense of threat towards M's equanimity as the guests are installed in the 'Second Place' across the way. M's account of L's sojourn with her was envisaged by Cusk as a spoken address to a friend (Booker 2021). It thus emerges as a kind of talking cure, as an attempt by M to gain understanding or insight through an exploration in words of her expressive feelings about her relationship with paintings as well as people.

The new perception that L's arrival is hoped to bring centres on art and freedom: the liberty that L has as a male artist but M does not, and which consequently appears only available to her vicariously. As wife, mother, hostess, as well as writer and woman, M's interaction with others is an enactment of the constraints around her, none of which apply to L. As in Cusk's other novels, M wishes to be free from the gendered narrative that has dictated her life: 'Not to have been born in a woman's body was a piece of luck *in the first place*', M says at one point (2021: 72 emphasis mine).

The principal characters of Cusk's novel, which is largely set in the one location aside from its framing scenes in Paris, can be easily listed. *Second Place* is addressed by M to someone called Jeffers, in imitation of Luhan's memoir written to poet Robinson Jeffers. 'Jeffers' is therefore a device retained by Cusk as an addressee for M's writing to create an almost epistolary tone, but otherwise his significance is obscure, beyond an allusion to the presence in M's life of a confidante. M is married to second husband Tony, who is not an artist and in his practical labouring appears emblematic of a life devoted to nature rather than culture. Almost as a contrast to Tony, M invites the celebrated painter L, who works mainly out of New York, to stay in the annexe of her marshland residence; she considers the cottage 'a home for the things that weren't already here – the higher things' (Cusk 2021: 19). However, while Tony installs irrigation for the garden, M is put out by the unexpected appearance alongside L of thirty-two-year-old Brett, a free-spirited, multi-talented heiress who seems effortlessly able to influence M's otherwise implacable twenty-one-year-old daughter, Justine. Justine herself is accompanied by her boyfriend Kurt.

The catalyst for the story occurs fifteen years earlier when M recognizes herself in the paintings by L that she sees in an art gallery in Paris. A subsequent encounter on the train leaving Paris with a diabolical figure, indeed understood by M to be 'the devil', has tempted her to seek freedom over the ties of married, parental domesticity. Reference to the devil raises the spectre of hell, the 'other place' in Christianity, which prefigures the use L makes of the home M lends him. The culmination of this allusive thread occurs when L finally asks to paint M herself towards the end of the novel. Having prepared for a sitting, M leaves her house in her wedding dress one evening, to find L and Brett painting the walls of the Second Place, centred on a mural of a snake wrapped around a tree. They seem to be creating a perverse paradise: 'It was a Garden of Eden, Jeffers, but a hellish one!' (Cusk 2021: 161) As M watches from outside through the windows, the half-naked pair then paint a grotesque figure of M as a middle-aged Eve, mocking her with a pot belly and a moustache 'to show she's in charge' (161).

Up to this point, M has repeatedly voiced an anxiety over her sense that she's not seen, recognized or wanted. 'My individuality,' she says, 'had tormented me my whole life with its demand to be recognised' (Cusk 2021: 114). Her insecurity appears to both drive her and undermine her as a need to control is simultaneously fulfilled and unsatisfied: 'Everything I determined to happen happened but not as I wanted it' (28). Yet failure appears an inevitable concomitant of her 'compartmentalised nature': 'whatever my object-value as a woman, the powerful feelings of ugliness or repulsiveness that beset me were coming not from some outward scrutiny or reality but from inside my own self' (64).

This externalization appears repeatedly in the novel as a struggle of wills over primacy. L is assigned the Second Place but is not contained by it; not least because of the freedom accorded each gender by society, but fundamentally because of the intersection of gender and art. As Cusk writes elsewhere: 'In *A Room of One's Own* Woolf asserts two things: first, that the world – and hence its representations in art – is demonstrably male; and second, that a woman cannot create art out of a male reality' (2019: 167). The quest for a female reality, one that is not in a second place, is a question inherited from Woolf by Cusk. It is also a basis for the exploration of freedom and art by using the model of Luhan's memoir; as Cusk says about *Second Place*, 'in the case of this novel I was thinking quite specifically about a lack of literary influences in terms of the female voice' (Booker 2021).

The idea of a 'Second' Place in relation to gender inevitably echoes Simone De Beauvoir's *The Second Sex*, in which she argued that Lawrence demanded feminine devotion as a duty. Discussing *The Second Sex* in her essay 'Shakespeare's Daughters', Cusk writes about the persistent relegation of aspects of female reality:

> in my own experience as a writer, it is in the places where honesty is most required – because it is here that compromise and false consciousness and 'mystification' continue to endanger the integrity of a woman's life – that it is most vehemently rejected. I am talking, of course, about the book of repetition, about fiction that concerns itself with what is eternal and unvarying, with domesticity and motherhood and family life. The sheer intolerance, in 2009, for these subjects is the unarguable proof that woman is on the verge of surrendering important aspects of her modern identity.
>
> Cusk 2019: 176

Cusk also seems in this essay to anticipate a lineage between Woolf, Mabel Dodge Luhan and her character of M: '*Mrs Dalloway* might be read as a novel about its author's fear of her own ordinariness and triviality, her dread sexual ancestry with its silence and compromise and mediocrity, the awful frailty of her expressive gift, without which, as she wrote in her diary, she believed she would be nothing at all' (2019: 174). M in *Second Place* is drawn to L's paintings because of their suggestion of an escape from such feelings, but only at second hand: 'the aura of absolute freedom his paintings emanate, a freedom elementally and unrepentingly male down to the last brushstroke' (Cusk 2021: 11). M connects with this male representation of the world, positioning it as something with which she wishes to identify, 'a case of borrowed finery, and sometimes downright impersonation' (11). She also feels that a potential for androgyny applies more to her because she does not feel especially 'womanly', perhaps in the way that she thinks Brett or Justine do: 'in the first place, I feel the habit of impersonation goes deeper in me than most, to the extent that some aspects of me do seem in fact to be male' (11–12). To recapture the feeling inspired by the paintings in Paris, M invites L to the Second Place. What ensues is a battle of wills and egos, as M seeks recognition and acknowledgement from L, in person and in painting, but finds only opposition: 'to lose my will would be to lose my hold on life – to go mad – and I was in no doubt that it could break one day of its own accord, I said to L, but it was my suspicion that a woman's madness represents the final refuge of the male secret, the place where he would destroy her rather than be revealed' (153).

Another struggle for primacy occurs between writing and painting, words and pictures, together with their larger context of the relationship between art and life. As Cusk explains:

> The big project for me with *Second Place* was thinking about location, something needing to have a location [...] and that's a question about painting versus writing, and something I've been increasingly interested in is the location in itself of a visual work, and how almost location-less a written work is, and I guess that also in my head connected with femininity as a location or as something that is lacking a location.
>
> Booker 2021

The novel itself makes this point: unlike words, M thinks that paintings 'give you a location, a place to be, when the rest of the time the space has been taken up because the criticism got there first' (Cusk 2021: 13). When she sees the hideous Garden of Eden mural that L and Brett paint in the Second Place, she then wonders whether art is itself a serpent, whispering of higher realities within us while undermining belief in the tangible things of the world, those M associates with Tony, who does not subscribe to the cult of art and has been throughout the novel instead cultivating the real garden on their property. Burdened by his own demons, L is only released from identity and memory when he suffers a stroke, which brings about a freeing from illusions for both he and M, leading soon to his death in Paris and her realization that 'nothing exists except what one creates for oneself' (204). M relinquishes her dreams and starts to accept her life: 'So I gave up L, gave him up in my heart, and filled in the secret place inside myself that I had kept free for him all along' (204–5).

One final posthumous letter appears from L stating both that 'I miss your place' and where he is now, the hotel room in which he will die, 'is a bad place' (Cusk 2021: 207). The reality of the marshes and M's domestic existence is finally accorded recognition and acknowledgement, while the Paris where M met L's paintings and then the devil, is now distanced as unreal: M says 'I have come to see something of what L saw at the end, and recorded in the night paintings. The truth lies not in any claim to reality, but in the place where what is real moves beyond our interpretation of it' (207). This is as close as Cusk's fiction approaches to a conclusion. The novel explores the escape to another place that art provides, together with its illusions, which can displace life as much as illuminate it. Similarly, the vicarious taste of freedom experienced through her encounters with other people provides an escape from responsibility for M, but one that is primarily imaginative: 'it is not Tony's business to change places with me, nor I with him. We are separate people and we each have our separate part to play, and no matter how much I yearned on occasion for that law to be broken, I have always known that the very basis of my life rested on it' (57). Here, lessons of freedom are learned: that identity and life cannot be experienced vicariously, that they are more likely found not through the inspiration of 'art' but through 'the book of repetition' in the patient, iterative practice of craft, and that despite the restrictions of society, freedom is the necessary source of creativity personal to the individual. *Second Place* establishes itself importantly as not a retelling of a memoir whose subject is a revered artist, whether L or Lawrence, but as a book written in recognition of the voice and precedent of the memoirist 'M' Luhan.

Works Cited

Booker Q&A with Cusk (2021), available at: https://thebookerprizes.com/the-booker-library/features/rachel-cusk-qa (accessed 1 August 2022).

Cusk, R. (2006), *Arlington Park*. London: Faber & Faber.
Cusk, R. (2009), *The Bradshaw Variations*. London: Faber & Faber.
Cusk, R. (2016), 'Making House: Notes on Domesticity'. *The New York Times Magazine*, August. Available at: https://www.nytimes.com/2016/09/04/magazine/making-house-notes-on-domesticity.html (accessed 1 August 2022).
Cusk, R. (2019), *Coventry*. London: Faber & Faber.
Cusk, R. (2021), *Second Place*. London: Faber & Faber.
Graham-Dixon, A. (2003), 'Rude Awakening' *The Telegraph*, 5 November. Available at: https://www.telegraph.co.uk/culture/art/3605916/Rude-awakening.html (accessed 1 August 2022).
Luhan, M. D. ([1932] 2007), *Lorenzo in Taos*. Santa Fe: Sunstone Press.
'Saving Rachel Cusk' (2005), *Daily Mail,* 3 November. Available at: https://www.dailymail.co.uk/home/books/article-367512/Saving-Rachel-Cusk.html. (accessed 1 August 2022).

An Interview with Rachel Cusk

Merve Emre

Rachel Cusk is the most unsettling and philosophically astute English novelist at work today. The author of fifteen books, she is best known for her memoirs, *A Life's Work* (2001) and *Aftermath: On Marriage and Separation* (2012), and the novels that comprise the *Outline* trilogy (2014–18). The narrator of the trilogy is a divorced writer named Faye who participates in writer's workshops and literary festivals across Europe. She is self-effacing, passive and unusually receptive to other people's stories, which she listens to without any explicit commentary. Yet Faye's narration of these stories is rigorous, controlled and judgemental – at moments, shockingly so – shifting from tenderness to cruelty in its descriptions of her interlocutors' faces, figures and confessions. The result is a tense, dramatic experiment in novelistic ethics, a struggle between self and other that led Cusk to declare, in a 2018 interview with Alexandra Schwartz, 'I don't think character exists anymore.'

Cusk's 2021 novel, *Second Place*, returns to many of her preoccupations, among them fate and freedom, the burdens of femininity, the ethics of parenthood, and the moral status of art works. The narrator is a woman, M, who is thrown into an inchoate state of longing and self-doubt by L the painter whom she invites to stay in her guest house, a cottage for artists that M refers to as the 'second place'. Although *Second Place* is set at a time much like the pandemic, in a place much like Norfolk, England, where Cusk used to live, the novel is more mythic than realist in tone and structure. The marsh on which M lives teems with symbols of nature's innocence and its corruptions. M and L are both references to historic individuals – the novel is inspired by Mabel Dodge Luhan's *Lorenzo in Taos*, about D. H. Lawrence – and to archetypes of male and female creators. What is at stake in their relationship feels like nothing less than a battle between cosmic elements: desire and dread, good and evil, life and death, or, as Lawrence put it, 'being and non-being'.

Cusk and I discussed *Second Place* at the Southbank Centre, London on 8 December 2022. Our conversation has been edited for clarity and length.

Merve Emre

Merve Emre: *Second Place* is narrated by a writer, M, who invites a famous painter, L, to live and work in the guest house on the marsh where M and her husband Tony, live, along with Justine, M's daughter, who has relocated there with her boyfriend Kurt. But before the novel takes us to the marsh, it shows us M leaving Paris on a train, where she is pursued by the devil, 'horrible in appearance, yellow and bloated with bloodshot bile-coloured eyes, and when he laughed, he showed dirty teeth with one entirely black tooth right in the middle'. It is a memorable opening, because the devil is, on the one hand, disgusting, lascivious, and abject, and, on the other hand, tempting. What does the devil portend in *Second Place*?

Rachel Cusk: I was thinking a little bit of *Death in Venice* and the feeling of fate – of reality taking fateful shapes in a psychodrama of the self. I think I thought: 'Okay, you can just say it. You can have the devil in your book.' I wanted to introduce the concept of evil in a very melodramatic way that would make it a presence in the book that didn't have to be too philosophically thought out. It could be a feeling of great vulnerability on the part of the person who's speaking, something that could replace a moral sense or a religious sense of vulnerability. That kind of drama or melodrama was very much how I wanted the book to be.

ME: The presence of evil and the possibility that art may offer us a moral vision to either channel or counter that evil is an important idea in many of your books. But evil is not usually presented as dramatically as it is here, with the devil chasing someone up and down the train car. Why did you want to personify it this time?

RC: What felt important to me in the book was to sever certain links with reality and to try to sort of destabilize the book from its narrative or linear foundations and to suggest some unreality, some kind of other realm. At the point I was writing the book, the question of time in a novel and the length of a novel in its dealings with time and linearity felt unbelievably oppressive. I had gone quite a long way in *Outline* and the other two books in that trilogy in reformulating how to deal with that. But I had a great feeling of not wanting to go back, of not wanting to do all that again. I wanted this book to be free of those constraints and yet not to feel fanciful, made up. I felt there was a space, in literary form, for a fable or a tale with links to reality, but that wasn't constrained by a reality that people would be able to recognize. And part of that is the book being spoken to another person, which immediately interferes with how it has to justify itself.

ME: That other person is addressed as Jeffers. Is that an epistolary address? Or is it a scene of face-to-face speech?

RC: The Jeffers character is a sort of strange, leftover bit from the book that *Second Place* is taken from, which is *Lorenzo in Taos*, Mabel Dodge Luhan's memoir about D. H. Lawrence coming to stay with her. And that book, indeed, is spoken to Jeffers. When I read that book, I had no idea who Jeffers was. I didn't realize he was Robinson Jeffers, a poet and friend of Mabel Dodge Luhan who was famous in his time and is possibly still famous somewhere. But I didn't know who Jeffers was until the very last page of *Lorenzo in Taos* where there's a photo of him. And I thought, I've read this whole book not knowing who Jeffers is. And yet, what Jeffers had come to be for me, how I imagined him or her, had such an extraordinary effect on me. I thought, that's the one thing I'll keep as a little relic or antique, a remnant of that original book.

ME: I want to go back to your observation about time and the linear form of the novel. One effect of beginning with a melodramatic, mythic or fabular structure is to reinforce the sense of fatedness that you mentioned, as if these events merely had to be set in motion as opposed to resulting from the exercise of free will. How do you think about the relationship between fate and freedom – another concept that seems important for you throughout the novel and in your other writing?

RC: The way I think about that slightly fabular construction is very confused by the pandemic. I thought, what would be the best conditions in which to try to grasp the condition of a sort of post-being – a female future that comes after many, many roles and forms of femininity that you half choose, half live, half don't choose, or don't want, and at a certain point, walk out of. It seemed to me that that condition was quite a difficult thing to describe. And it was particularly difficult to describe if everything else remained stably located in space and in time. How could you summon up this directionless non-state of non-being, this difficult-to-grasp phase of femininity? It would have to be in a world in which nothing worked, everything had stopped, no one could go anywhere. That then became the environment in which I wrote at least the second half of the book.

ME: This feminine non-state of non-being exists in a world in which one has very few social relations through which to define the self. There's a small cast of characters in this novel compared to the trilogy.

RC: Character is a very difficult thing to believe in or to assert the existence of in anything other than a very static set of circumstances, where character can confirm itself all the time. But now I think slightly differently, certainly, about the question of time. I wonder why I have never used my ability to slow down time and why, actually, in the Anglophone novel, it's really a rare thing for anyone to do – to make time go very, very, very slowly in a book. I've moved to France, I'm reading French novels in French all day, every day, and this is the thing that I'm most struck by: they go much more slowly. Time pauses. The book's location in time is completely different.

ME: M has a strong sense that there are certain forms of freedom, and certain ways of 'being and becoming', to quote Lawrence, that are unique to men. There is an aesthetic and moral freedom, or a freedom from morality, that certain creative people enjoy. M is ultimately quite ambivalent about this freedom. What are the moral ramifications of how freedom allows you to impose your will onto others?

RC: I think that question is the conundrum of the book and something that I haven't gotten to the end of thinking about. The question is very, very bound to the whole idea of the female voice and what that is – what it really is. Is the female voice a set of values that have to remain unlived or undisclosed? Does its value derive from its non-existence or its existence in silence, in not being free, in not having things, and the kind of knowledge comes out of that? Or is it actually a distinct existence and a distinct spirituality in itself? *Second Place* very much arrives at the question, what is it that I have? I have something: I've been alive. I've lived in time. What I have doesn't feel like freedom, it doesn't feel like anything. And yet it might be defined by others and by the fulfilment of their identity or autonomy or desire. Somehow death or exhaustion or not being defined attains a weird adverse value.

That's easily summed up by saying, 'Okay, I have a child. I have a home. I have these things that I do for people, that I am for people. And I haven't expressed myself, but maybe that means I haven't spent myself.' The thing that's easy enough to see in the book is how those values just disappear. They're invisible in the light of L, who is unrelentingly free and selfish. It almost seems that you can measure every sort of moment of female non-being by that, by the being of this other person.

ME: The novel is preoccupied with people's competing perceptions of one another. It can be tempting to see yourself through another person's eyes, and it can be difficult to triumph over another person's perception of you. There's a wonderful moment where you write, 'I believe there is also a more common ability to read the surface of life, and the forms that it takes, that either grows from or becomes an ability to attend to and understand the works of the creators. One can feel, in other words, a strange proximity to the process of creation when one sees the principles of art – or of a particular artist – mirrored in the texture of living.' You go on: 'I'm unsure of the moral status of these half creations, which I can only hazard is akin to the moral status of influence, and therefore a powerful force for both good and evil in human affairs.' What kind of morality can or cannot be communicated by the vision of the artist? Or the non-artist?

RC: It's the fun thing about not being an artist – the fun thing about being, you know, normal. M says, 'I'm had remained a devourer, while yearning to become a creator.' But there is an onerousness to creating and defining and putting things in space all the time. One of the things that I really loved about the voice of Mabel Dodge Luhan was this feeling that she entirely and only existed in this voice and that nobody was listening to it. But if you open the book, there it was, and it's started talking again. And it felt that that sort of immateriality gave a good account of a non-artist, a person who thinks that an artist is not what she is. For whatever reason, Mabel Dodge Luhan had the confidence or the ability to write this down. She wrote several volumes of it. And it all has precisely the same tone of, there's not an artist in charge. There's not an egotistical creator. And that, to me, is a very, very fragile and difficult thing to grasp.

ME: It reminds me of what you said in another interview about character no longer existing or having trouble in believing that character exists. What I took you to be saying there was that it's hard to believe in the singularity of one's ego. What the contemporary Anglophone novel needs to do is try to shatter ego, so that its voice can get at something more elemental, a substratum of being and becoming that is shared between everyone in this room, that doesn't require on people being fully individuated or subjectified. Do you still think that way about character and its disappearance?

RC: I think the problem with character is that it and various other things take the novel – if one cares about the novel or even thinks that the novel still exists – through so many successive stages of kind of cloning of itself. The character in the novel is the result of the writer having read a lot of other novels, and the reader believes the character because they've read a lot of novels too. And so you're actually in some sort of barter system whose links to reality are pretty remote. I think seeing the world like that is much more related to society than to art. The novel takes itself off into a different category by relying on those stratagems. In fact, if we re-examined our relationship to one another, we'd probably find that there are not that many links between literary form or conventional literary form and living. And then when you look at, I don't know, Donald Trump, you say, 'Okay, that's a character.' So maybe character is fanaticism. Maybe that's where it's gone now.

ME: One of the other ways that the novel is interested in character, fanaticism, and will is in its descriptions of parenting, especially parenting older children. M has a daughter, Justine, who is in her early twenties and is starting come into her own into the world. Her dawning independence raises the questions: To what degree is having a child an act of the will? And at what point must one withdraw one's will? How did your thoughts about the relationship between parent and child change from *A Life's Work* to *Second Place*?

RC: One of the features of this featurelessness that I'm trying to give some kind of shape to is the feeling that one's own female history is a footprint in the sand. There's a feeling of moving forward in time with no landmark. But the details of one's female history, the difficulty of commemorating it, or it even remaining tangible, is counterweighted by the continuing existence of things like one's child. The novel is trying to compare that continuing existence to painting – to externalizing your intentions, externalizing something of yourself that can survive without you. You can walk away, and it'll still be there, and it will do what it's meant to do. Is painting in any way similar to reproduction, to having a child? I've written quite a lot about reproduction and what it is and the difference between copying and generating or creating. And I think having a child is probably reproduction – copying, not generating.

ME: What you said about the footprints in the sand makes me think that another question of existence that this novel grapples with is: Where does life go? What happens when you want more of it? And what happens when that feeling of life, that vitality, is tied to suffering? M tells us that she was living in this perfectly beautiful place, in a perfectly content life, and then she went and mucked it all up. Is that what the devil tempts us with? More life, more feeling, more vitality – none of it especially conducive to happiness.

RC: And running counter to that is aging. And that is the other subject in the book: the fact that these ardent desires that seem so much to be the wellsprings of living are connected, in many ways, to creative urge. One of the things that I saw when I was writing it was how funny it is that men and women almost aren't men and women anymore after a certain age. I had this image of cursedness, or a grudging resentment, of these same two figures who have lived through so many narratives – not these specific individuals, but the figure of man and woman that has generated so much content and so much meaning at different phases of life. And perhaps one of the characteristics of this phase of life was that there was no more gender and that in order to re-gender yourself, you would have to become interested in a younger person or in yourself being seen in a different way.

ME: There's a relationship here between desire and freedom. Freedom comes from wanting and being wanted. To want is to feel a kind of possibility is to feel the possibility of a creative freedom. M is surrounded by younger women who are making her own unwantedness palpable in painful ways. There is her daughter, Justine, who is there with her boyfriend, and when L comes to live in her guest house, he brings his attractive young friend, Brett. What happens when you feel like you exist outside of that circulation of erotic and creative desire?

RC: I think in the book and, in general, these things are not what you think they are. People are not as you think they are. And it's only really within your own time that reality obeys your preconceptions of it. And if you try and put those preconceptions on a younger person, you'll find that they don't conform at all to any of the roles you've played. And what is tragic about that is if it means that, at heart, we are linear, and we only realize it at the very moment that we come to the end of these illusions or desires. I think the question in the book is whether – this is, again, a question about character – one's own character exists and in fact, whether what you've done your whole life has served this idea of character, of who you are, of what you want. Because the ebbing away of that entity, of the things that have motivated it and driven it, is a frightening feeling. The unboundedness of art seems deeply preferable. The envy that M has, that possibly I have, of the person creating the image, seems a very real thing to me.

ME: Is your own character linear? Or do you feel it as a series of ruptures?

RC: I think I don't have a character.

ME: In this novel, painting is the locus of knowledge about existence. When M looks at L's painting in Paris, L's painting seems to speak to her: '*I am here*'. But she refuses to articulate what that means because to articulate it would be to destroy it. There's a contest in *Second Place* between painting and writing as mediums that make themselves available to different ideas about representation. A lot of contemporary novelists have been turning to painting as the locus of the ineffable, of non-being. What attracted you to painting?

RC: It's non-language. It could have been something else that was non-language. For me, the exhaustion with the language economy was something I started to feel in parenthood when I first thought, 'Why do I have to do this?' If this baby does *this*, I have to say *this*. Also, there were all sorts of new types of language: languages of reprimand or management or ordering people to do things. It seemed like the pre-formation of language was far more insidious than I had thought it to be. And that really did become a massive preoccupation for me: pre-formation in terms of nationality, in terms of social class, all sorts of other things. I began to wonder how I could read the language of things that I wasn't even aware of – that spoke without saying anything. There's a bit in the book where L expresses the idea that painters are created by their fathers and writers are created by their mothers.

ME: Do you think that's true?

RC: I actually do think it's quite true because I think that the mother is language. The woman controls the language economy. Part of what is kind of going on in *Second Place* is a great frustration with the medium of language. If there is a desire for freedom, it is freedom from language. And that's the next thing I'm going to think about: what potential does the body itself have as a non-language? As an object? And what does it mean for femininity? What is the body's non-language value? I'm sure there's a whole other story that could be written, or has been written, about a woman wanting only to be her body and not a communicative entity at all. I suppose it is a reverse kind of objectification, or an inverting of and a taking control of that objectification.

ME: Are you writing about this?

RC: I have, in fact, just written an essay called 'The Stuntman'. I thought the stuntman was quite a good image for this idea of a divide in feminine identity. Each woman has a stuntman. And the stuntman is the person who lives physical experiences, like childbirth. Or enables character to exist, which is what the stuntman does in a film. The stuntman takes the actual risks so that this character can be a risk-taking character. I thought that that was a kind of interesting idea of a psychology that is possibly a contemporary phenomenon.

ME: The way you described the stuntman is as a sense or a situation of compartmentalization. And what your narrator describes in *Second Place* is also a kind of compartmentalization: someone who feels assaulted by the wills of others, but perhaps doesn't consciously recognize how her will operates. There's a moment when M says to Jeffers, 'Tony sometimes says to me that I underestimate my own power'. To what degree does your narrator possess the self-understanding to assess the moral consequences of her own actions?

RC: That's the impasse. It's the membrane that she's in. The alternative to it is violence. The alternative to it is saying, 'I'll break this table. And I'll then look at the broken table and know that I did that, and therefore that I exist, and that's the effect I've had on the world.'

ME: One notable thing about *Second Place* is how exclamatory and agitated the language is. It seems like a real change from the *Outline* trilogy, which feels much more tightly controlled. But despite its tone, we still only have one narrator, who's showing us everything through her point of view.

RC: To me, *Second Place*'s exclamatory voice is not so different from a voice in the trilogy. It's just that there's only one voice. I felt that the spokenness of *Second Place*, which takes almost a dramatic form, a monologue form, could justify itself in the same way that I used different voices in the trilogy to justify themselves. In the case of *Outline*, the voices exist because the narrator is seeing the characters. And in the case of *Second Place*, that's not so. She is speaking of her own accord. But maybe I won't use exclamation marks.

ME: No, you should. I like them. Lawrence used a lot of exclamation marks too. I think the larger observation was just about how there can be a tendency, I think, among many of us to not see the forms of power that we wield. And that raises all sorts of fascinating moral and ethical questions for what it means to act on, or with, other people, in fiction and in life.

RC: It's a global problem, in a sense. It requires more unravelling. I think my process is I know that I've lived something right if I find I have more power afterward in writing. And that's a very, very difficult sort of index to draw. The process feels almost amoral, actually, in how little it differs – writing things that have really upset people, shocked them, and writing things that no one takes any notice of and then something they like. It seems astonishing to me that it's still the same place.

ME: Or perhaps the way you conceive of writing has a different relationship to morality. Your narrator observes in the beginning of the novel that there is a certain type of person who is always redefining the meanings of good and evil. It's a very Nietzschean sentiment – that within the world of the novel, one creates one's own ideas, or puts into play one's own ideas, of what is good and what is evil and what the point is of these values is in the first place.

RC: But I think it's also that the writer is doing something that, as I say, has no morality in itself. It has to exist without anyone giving it any attention. And its links to attention have to be non-existent. It has to be capable of just waiting. And then someone comes along and thinks something about it. And the thing that the next person thinks about it a few years down the line is different. So there's some feeling of irreducibility to that.

ME: There are certain scenes that you return to over and over again in your fiction. I was thinking about the ending of *Kudos*, where Faye is in the water and there's a man urinating into the water on the shore. It's a moment of perfect, ridiculous cosmic balance between the sexes. Near the end of *Second Place*, you have a scene where M and Justine are in the water, and L is watching them from the shore. According to M, that scene ends up as the subject of L's most important painting. I know that some writers have images that they keep going back to. Is this one particularly important for you?

RC: I think it's more wanting to have some sort of concrete materiality that isn't in language that approaches the image. And also a feeling of locations, experiences, or periods of time, that seem to me to encapsulate what is scarring in femininity and in the biological trajectory that vanishes behind you. I've written about this in different guises before, but it's the feeling of experiences going beyond experience – becoming actually representational so that they're always happening. And that being, again, part of a big footprint in the sand. How can you ever express that? How can you express that experiences have been so indelible?

ME: The novel is, in part, a representation of your experience reading and reading about a particular writer: D. H. Lawrence. How scarring was that for your sense of femininity?

RC: This book was about me chucking D. H. Lawrence, getting him out of my life. I will survive without D. H. Lawrence. I turned against him and got rid of him. That was what happened in this book.

And I think really, the main point of the relationship between this book and the memoir by Mabel Dodge Luhan is that her account of Lawrence resolves the question. He was wrong. And that was extremely difficult for me to admit because he's a writer who has freed a lot of women writers, who has enabled women writers, some of them, to find their voice. And that seemed so unarguable to me. And it didn't matter that he went slightly mad in the end of his life when he wrote *The Plumed Serpent* and said and did some very odd things. He was an extremely unfortunate person who suffered terrible physical pain and illness and who was hurt in the most absolutely horrible ways. I'm sure that that deformed his nature and his character. Of course it did. By the time he gets to Taos, New Mexico, he's fully deformed by that. But for me, the view of him that I found in this book, it was like an opportunity to really reconsider the people who have dominated you, like your parents, or the things that you've sort of gone along with but never really challenged and never really walked away from.

Index

Ahmed, Sarah 54
Antigone xi–xii
austerity 21, 22, 24, 28, 29, 34
autobiography 38, 58–9, 60, 63, 64–5, 66,
    71, 86, 109–11, 111 n.1, 112–13,
    114, 122, 124
autofiction 5, 20–1, 21 n.4, 21 n.5, 22, 33–4,
    69, 70–1, 109–11, 114

Beauvoir, Simone de 84–5, 86, 154
    Second Sex 84–5, 154
Berlant, Lauren 137, 138
Boileau, Nicolas 2, 75
Brexit (UK leaving the European Union)
    1, 13 n.3, 30, 104, 143
Butler, Judith xi, 85

capitalism 20 n.3, 26, 76 n.1, 78, 129
Case Study Houses 31
Chabon, Michael 19–20
Chayka, Kyle 22, 23, 25–6, 27, 28, 31, 32–3
childcare 39–4, 48, 54, 141
Christianity xi, 153
Clarke, Adrian (Cusk's second husband)
    6–7, 60–1, 114, 134, 141, 145
Cold Comfort Farm (Gibbon) 3
Cole, Teju 9, 21 n.5
Cooke, Jennifer 14–15
Coventry, being sent to x, 129, 133–40,
    143, 144, 146
Coventry (city) 133, 139, 144–5
Cusk, Rachel
    absence in writing 10, 11, 62, 88, 109,
        116, 120, 123, 125, 130–2,
        131 n.3, 134, 136–8, 139, 141,
        144, 145
    aesthetics 14, 21 n.5, 22–26, 29, 30, 32,
        62, 63–4, 69, 75–6, 82, 89, 96,
        105, 109–125, 131, 132, 137, 162
    on age and ageing 66–7, 85, 87, 165–6
    ambivalence 5, 8, 47, 49, 63, 64, 65–6,
        84, 95, 96–7, 98, 101, 142, 162

authenticity 6, 8, 15, 93–106,
    94 n.1, 111
authorship 57–9, 67, 69, 70, 80–1, 131
autobiographical writing 3, 5, 8, 9, 10,
    14, 37–8, 54, 58–9, 60–2, 65,
    67–9, 70–1, 81, 109, 113–15,
    144–5
    Aftermath 60–1, 63, 113–4
    A Life's Work 60, 62, 63, 66–7, 113–4
    The Last Supper 63–5, 67, 113–4
    Outline trilogy xii, 10, 58–9, 68–9,
        70, 109, 110–12, 113, 114,
        117–25, 139
    Saving Agnes 77
    Second Place 86
autofictional writing x, 5, 9–10, 10 n.1,
    13, 33, 58–9, 67, 70–1, 82,
    109–25
    Outline trilogy 10, 22, 57–59, 69, 70,
        109–125, 112 n.3, 132
    Saving Agnes 77

biographical details 1–2, 68

on character xiii, 1, 8, 11, 12, 13, 30, 58,
    95, 100, 101, 110, 111–12,
    117–18, 123–4, 137, 139, 144–5,
    159, 162, 163–6, 167, 170
on class 2, 3, 5–6, 9, 13–14, 25–7, 27 n.6,
    28, 37, 43, 44–7, 52, 58, 76–80,
    82, 87, 89, 94, 166
on conventionality 2, 8, 13, 14, 28,
    43, 49, 94 96–8, 133–4,
    138 n.10, 164
'creative death' 3, 9, 13, 70, 114, 131,
    145, 145 n.12
critical responses xi, 2
    ambivalent 70, 81
    negative 3, 4–5, 7–9, 13–14, 40,
        42–3, 59, 70, 81, 87, 114, 145,
        168
    positive 40, 54, 66, 70, 168

cruelty 8, 43, 49, 51, 54, 82, 99–104, 106, 129–143, 131 n.3, 159

on domesticity 4, 15, 42, 51, 53, 67, 87, 94–5, 98, 99, 100, 121, 140–1, 150, 153, 154, 156

on evil 25, 29, 159, 160, 163, 168
on exclusion 14, 25, 26, 28, 29, 32, 50, 63, 67–8, 134
as experimental writer x, 2, 5, 6, 10, 11–12, 14, 37, 43, 58–59, 71, 81–83, 109–125, 159

Faber editions and branding 11, 57–8, 62
on failure xi, xii, 2–3, 9, 14, 15, 75–89, 76 n.1, 102, 103, 135, 154
on family life x–xii, 3–4, 6, 38–52, 54, 58, 60, 67–8, 69, 79, 95–99, 106, 118–19, 131, 135, 139, 142, 152, 154
on fate 15, 76, 101–2, 103–4, 159, 160, 161–2
on fathers and fatherhood xi, 4, 28, 42, 46–7, 68, 133, 143, 166
on femininity / being female xii, xiv, 2–4, 6, 37, 44, 47, 58, 78, 84–5, 87, 98, 154, 155, 159, 161–3, 164, 167, 169
as 'feminist killjoy' 54
as feminist writer 4, 5, 6, 14, 28, 37–54, 59, 66, 71, 78, 85–6
on fiction / the novel x, xiii, 1–2, 7, 8, 9–10, 10 n.1, 23–4, 43, 58, 61, 70–1, 80, 83, 88–9, 93, 104–5, 112, 118, 122, 124, 125, 132, 135, 137–8, 142–3, 144–6, 154–5, 156, 160–2, 163–5, 169
residence in France 1, 13 n.3, 162
on freedom xiii, 11, 15, 47, 93, 96–8, 101, 103–4, 105–6, 140, 142, 150, 152–5, 156, 159, 161, 162, 165, 167

on gender roles and expectations xii, 2–3, 6–8, 11, 37, 37 n.1, 53, 66, 84–5, 100, 114, 135, 149, 150, 153–5
and ageing 165

and creativity xii, 114, 154
and criticism 8–9, 114
debate on 4
double standards 5, 47
inequalities 40–1, 44
injustice of 6, 44–5
in literary industry 21, 69, 133
and parenting 40, 41, 43, 47, 50–1
reversal of xii, 96–8
on 'good' 49, 100, 159, 163, 168

on home making / ownership / renovation 4, 23, 24, 26, 27–9, 30–1, 33, 40–1, 50, 66–8, 79–80, 95–6, 100–1, 102, 120–1, 150, 153
on honesty 105, 114, 133, 143–4, 154

as innovative writer x, 1, 5, 10, 11, 14, 15, 112–3, 116, 130, 131, 132–3, 141–2

on language 14–15, 65, 136–7, 152, 166–7, 168, 169
on D.H. Lawrence xii, 12, 141, 150, 169–70
literary reappropriation 83, 87, 132
on literary / publishing industry 11, 21, 69, 70, 81–2, 93, 99, 104–5, 116, 118, 121, 159

on male–female relationships xii, 6–7, 21, 41, 43 n.4, 46–7, 49–50, 54, 60, 78, 82, 85, 94, 95–8, 99, 100, 102–3, 104, 119, 121, 123, 130–1, 134, 137, 142, 143, 145, 149, 151–4, 156, 165
on marriage and divorce xi–xii, 4, 6–7, 8, 42, 51, 52, 60–1, 67–9, 70, 79, 87, 95, 99, 100–1, 102, 104, 111, 113–14, 118–19, 121, 122, 123, 130–1, 134–5, 137 140, 141, 142, 145, 153, 156
on masculinity / being male xi, xiii–xiv, 43–4, 46–7, 52, 84–5, 87, 98, 154–5
memoir x, xiii, 13, 58–70, 75, 87, 111
   Aftermath 6–7, 8, 57, 59, 60, 68–9, 81, 130, 140–1, 145, 159

A Life's Work xi, 4–5, 8, 39–40, 57, 59, 60, 65–7, 81, 159
The Last Supper 57, 60, 63–5, 67
Outline trilogy 68–9, 152
Second Place 88, 132, 150, 154, 156
use of metaphor 5, 11, 29, 59–68, 71, 99, 114, 120, 130 n.2, 138
    clothing 61–2
    confinement 63
    (being sent to) Coventry 133–4, 136, 138, 145
    driving 52, 142, 144
    flight 104
    homelessness 23–4
    house 63
    hunting 103
    jigsaw 60
    labyrinths 64
    space 59, 63, 65–7
    travel 71
    vegetation 47
minimalism 8, 14, 22–34, 89
on misogyny 5, 46, 46 n.7, 48, 51–2, 54, 82, 99, 129, 169
motifs 59, 60, 65, 67, 71, 75, 113, 116, 119
motherhood *See* on pregnancy and motherhood

on neoliberalism 3, 45, 53, 78–80, 93, 99, 102, 104–5
(neo-)modernism xiii, 11, 37, 75–76, 124–5, 129 n.1, 144, 149
on nostalgia 100, 102, 106

on painting and visual art 15, 25, 63, 136, 136 n.9, 151–4, 155–6, 159, 160, 164–6, 169
her parents 133, 135, 138, 143, 143 n.11, 146, 170
postmodernism 10, 37, 125
on pregnancy and motherhood xi, 3–5, 14, 37–38, 39–45, 46–52, 54, 60, 62, 63, 65–7, 68–9, 70, 81, 82, 87, 99, 111, 113, 116, 150, 152, 153, 154, 164, 166–7
on privilege 5–6, 9, 14, 22, 27, 43 n.4, 44–47, 50, 51, 53, 76, 89, 95–96, 149

on race 25, 42, 53, 143
role of reader xii, xiv, 5, 14, 33, 45, 46, 47, 93, 112, 116, 133, 143, 143 n.11, 164
on rudeness 130, 143

on selfhood x–xi, 3, 4, 6, 8–9, 11, 12–13, 15, 31–2, 58–9, 61–5, 68, 71, 75–7, 93–101, 103, 104, 106, 109–10, 112–20, 121–5, 139, 145, 149, 151, 159
self-reflexivity xii, 5, 8, 13, 19, 21 n.5, 37, 82, 131–2, 135–6, 137–8, 141
as serial writer 11, 12, 57–9, 62, 67, 69, 70–1, 112–16, 119–20, 121–2, 123–5
on sexism 3, 42, 82, 87, 88, 96
silence in writing 8, 9, 10, 13, 15, 99, 102, 129–37, 131 n.4, 139–41, 144, 145–6, 155, 162
status as writer x, 1, 11, 37, 57, 70, 77, 87, 88–9, 159
storytelling 60–2, 70, 102, 122, 136, 139, 152
style of writing 7, 13–14, 14–5, 23, 25–6, 30, 32, 37, 59, 62, 68, 69, 70, 71, 83, 89, 112, 123, 124, 130, 130 n.2, 131–3, 132 n.6, 133–4, 134 n.7, 136–7, 138–9, 140–6
    'discrepant' style 13, 129–146, 131 n.4
on success 2, 45, 50, 75–6, 78–82, 85–9, 96, 97, 105, 121, 124

tone of writing 2, 3, 51, 62, 105, 137, 151, 153, 159, 168
on travel 60, 63–4, 65, 71, 115, 116, 120–1, 123
on 'truth' xii, xiv, 7, 10, 32, 54, 61, 70, 105, 114, 122–3, 124, 130, 137, 139, 142, 143–4, 143 n.11, 145, 156

on violence xii, 12–13, 15, 65, 84, 87, 96, 100, 118, 167

Whitbread First Novel Award 2, 77

works:

Aftermath: On Marriage and Separation xi, 3, 6–9, 11, 13, 57, 58, 63, 70, 130–1, 131 n.3, 134, 142, 143, 145, 145 n.12
  as autobiography 60–1, 63, 113–4, 145
  'creative death' after writing 3, 9, 13, 70, 114, 131, 145, 145 n.12
  as memoir 6–7, 8, 57, 59, 60, 68–9, 81, 130, 140–1, 145, 159
  metaphors 60, 63, 67–8
  modernism 129 n.1
  reception 5, 7–8, 13, 59, 70, 81, 114
  reference in *Outline* 68–9
  self-criticism 14, 140–1
  Sonia (Cusk's au pair) 14, 140–1
  'Trains' (chapter) 60, 140

A Life's Work: Becoming a Mother 9, 53, 164
  as autobiography 60, 62, 63, 66–7, 113–4
  metaphors 63, 65, 66
  on culture of motherhood 3–5, 38, 39–43, 47, 62
  as memoir xi, 4–5, 8, 39–40, 57, 59, 60, 65–7, 81, 159
  reception 4–5, 7–8, 42–3, 59, 81

Arlington Park 3, 9, 51 n.8, 81, 129
  on class and inequality 5–6
  Juliet (character) 4, 51–2, 54
  literary allusions (Woolf, Kafka, Joyce) 51–4, 149
  on marriage and motherhood 4, 38, 50–54
  as satire 51, 53, 130
  as social realism 5, 130

Bradshaw Variations, The 3, 9
  on identity and self 15, 93, 94–8, 106, 151
  on middle-class life 6, 94–8
  Thomas (character) 95, 97–8
  Tonie (character) 95–8, 103

Country Life, The 2, 3, 81, 99

Coventry (collection) 6, 58, 133, 142, 143 n.11, 145 n.12, 150
  'Coventry' (essay) 129, 132–9, 140, 142, 145, 146
  'Driving as Metaphor' (essay) 142, 144
  themes 142–3
  on 'truth' and 'honesty' 143–4

In the Fold 3

Kudos xii, 9, 21, 28, 81, 88, 103–5, 115, 121, 123, 140
  as autofiction 109–10
  Faye (character/narrator) *see Outline trilogy*
  final scene 82, 99, 129, 169
  'kudos' (theme) 121
  on literary industry and culture 81–2, 104–5
  Luís (character) 105, 116, 121
  Ryan (character) 119, 121

Last Supper: A Summer in Italy, The 3, 9
  as autobiography 63–5, 67, 113–4
  England–Italy dichotomy 63, 64–5
  lawsuit 9, 114
  as memoir 57, 60, 63–5, 67
  spatial metaphors 63–65, 67
  reception 70, 114
  as travel writing 63–65, 67

Lucky Ones, The 3, 38, 53, 54
  Christine (character) 52–3
  'Confinement' (chapter) 44–5
  Daley, Mrs Barbara (character) 48–9
  Jane (character) 44–6, 48
  Josephine (character) 47–9
  Kirsty (character) 44–5, 47, 48, 50
  Martin (character) 46–8
  'Matters of Life and Death' (chapter) 49–50
  Michelle (character) 44, 45
  'Mrs Daley's Daughter' (chapter) 47–9
  on parenting 38, 43–51, 54
  as social comment 5–6, 14, 43–51
  as social realism 5–6

structure 43, 51 n.8
'The Way You Do it' (chapter) 45–7
Vanessa (character) 49–50
Victor (character) 44–5, 49, 50

'Marble in Metamorphosis' (essay) 136, 136 n.9

Outline (novel) 9, 21, 28, 81, 82–3, 100, 101, 104, 109, 111, 114, 115–16, 119–21, 122–3, 130, 130 n.2, 138 n.10, 142, 151, 160
   Anne (character) 119–20
   Faye (character/narrator) *see Outline trilogy*
   on identity and selfhood 99–100, 122–3
   on marriage and divorce xii, 100, 119, 121, 123, 142

Outline (trilogy) xii, 9–13, 14, 15, 21–2, 28–30, 43, 46, 57–9, 68–9, 70–1, 81–82, 93, 95, 98–106, 109–125, 129–135, 130 n.2, 136–7, 139, 140, 149, 159, 160, 168
   articulacy of interlocutors 124
   as autobiographical writing xii, 10, 15, 58–9, 68–9, 70, 109, 110–12, 113, 114, 117–25, 139
   as autofictional writing 10, 11, 22, 57–59, 69, 70–1, 109–125, 112 n.3, 132
   book titles as themes 69, 119–21
   critique of misogyny 46, 46 n.7, 99
   on divorce xii, 68–9, 99–100, 111, 121, 138 n.10, 159
   as experimental writing 10, 43, 58–9, 81, 82–3, 112–3, 114–6, 119–20, 122, 123–4, 159
   Faye (character / narrator) xii, 9–11, 21, 24–5, 26, 28, 29–30, 46, 58, 68–9, 98–105, 109–11, 112, 113, 115–16, 117–25, 129, 130, 131, 132, 135, 137, 139, 140, 142, 143, 152, 159, 169
   as feminist writing 28, 69, 71
   on identity and selfhood 11, 12, 15, 68, 93, 98–100, 104, 106, 112–113, 115, 116–19, 121, 122–3, 151

   on literary industry and culture 21, 69, 81–2, 104–5
   on marriage xii, 100, 118, 119, 121, 123, 131, 142
   as memoir 68–9, 152
   metaphors 71, 120
   repetition 59, 71, 112, 115–20, 116 n.5, 122, 123, 124–5
   Ryan (character) 119, 121
   as serial autofiction 58, 59–60, 62, 67, 69, 70–1, 112–25, 132
   structure 58, 113, 115–16, 117, 121, 125, 131
   style 59, 68, 71, 112, 124, 130, 130 n.2, 131–2

Parade 12, 136

Saving Agnes x, 2–3, 77, 86, 88–89, 130
   Agnes Day (character) 15, 75–81, 83–4, 86, 88–9
   as *Bildungsroman* 15, 77–81
   on class 78–80
   on failure 2–3, 9, 15, 75–81
   on identity x, 2–3
   irony 2, 78, 79–80
   as *Künstlerroman* 80–1
   as satire 76–9, 130
   as social realism 5, 130
   Whitbread first novel award 2, 77

Second Place xii–xiv, 11–12 ,15, 23, 29–32, 33, 75, 81–9, 132, 136–7, 140, 141, 149–156, 159–170
   autobiography and memoir in 12, 86, 88, 132, 150, 154, 156
   as biographical innovation 11, 15, 132, 141
   Brett (character) 85–6, 149, 152, 153–4, 155, 165
   on creativity xiii–xiv, 82, 152, 156
   as epistolary novel 29–30, 83, 88, 130, 153, 161
   on failure 15, 75–6, 83–9
   on gender xiii–xiv, 82, 84–6, 88, 153–5
   Jeffers (absent character) 29–30, 82, 83, 88, 153, 161, 167

Justine (character) 149, 153, 155, 160, 164, 165, 169
L (character) xiii, 12, 30–2, 82–9, 136, 149, 151–6, 159–60, 163, 165–6, 169
  as literary reappropriation 83, 87, 132
  M (character / narrator) xiii–xiv, 12, 15, 75–6, 82–9, 137, 140, 149, 151–6, 159–60, 162–7, 169
  as melodrama 130, 131 n.3, 160, 161
  minimalism 29–32
  painting 31, 32, 86, 87–8, 151–2, 153–4, 155
  Tony (character) 82, 83, 149, 153, 155–6, 160, 167
  unreality in xiii, 15, 86–7, 89, 156, 160
  See also Lawrence, D.H. and Luhan, Mabel Dodge

'Stuntman, The' 12–13, 15, 132 n.5, 136, 145, 167
  on selfhood 10 n.1, 12, 137

Temporary, The 81

Transit 9, 13–14, 21, 23–30, 65, 67, 69, 93, 100, 103–5, 109, 117, 120, 122–3
  fate vs. freedom 104
  Faye (character/narrator) *see Outline trilogy*
  Gaby (character) 122
  Gerard (character) 24, 28, 28 n.7, 101–2, 122
  home making / renovation 23–25, 67, 100
  Jane (character) 30, 117–19
  Lawrence (character) 101, 137, 138
  metaphors 67
  minimalism 24–6, 27, 28
  Oliver (character) 118–19
  portrayal of neighbours 13, 24–6, 27 n.6, 143
  prose style 14, 25

Dango, Michael 22, 26, 31
devil, the / Satan 130, 153, 156, 160, 165

Dillon, Brian 133, 144
Dix, Hywel 70–1, 110, 112
Doloughan, Fiona 58, 70
domesticity 38, 39, 41, 152

Eardley, Joan (painter) xii, xiv
Eden, Garden of 31, 153–4, 155
Effe, Alexandra and Hannie Lawlor 110, 112
Emma's Diary 41–2
England 5, 6, 43, 44, 53, 63, 64–5, 111
Ernaux, Annie 5, 14–15
Eve (and Adam) 84, 154
existentialism 6, 29, 51, 93–4, 96–7

Faber & Faber (publisher) 11, 57, 62
fathers / paternal role 39, 41, 42–3, 111
femininity 85, 154
feminism 5, 39–41, 43, 45, 54, 85
  maternal 37–40, 49, 53–4, 66
Ferrante, Elena 110, 111, 111 n.1
Fried, Michael 33

gender roles and expectations xii, 2–3, 11, 20, 41, 66, 114, 133, 150
Genette, Gérard 69, 117
genre 10, 20, 20 n.2, 21 n.4, 23, 33, 58, 59, 70, 110, 111, 113, 116
Gill, Rosalind 3, 41
Glass House (Johnson) 27–8, 31
Greece xi, 21, 28, 119, 123

Hartley, Marsden 117
Heti, Sheila 5, 9, 21 n.5, 95, 110, 112
homelessness 23–4, 79
Hornby, Gill 42–3, 43 n.3
'hysterical realism' 13, 20–1, 22

Italy 63, 64–5

James, David 28, 130, 131 n.4, 134, 134 n.7
Jeffers, Robinson (poet) 83, 153, 161
Johnson, Philip (architect) 25, 27–8, 31
Joyce, James 83, 129 n.1, 149
Judd, Donald 32–4

Kafka, Franz 37, 51, 54
Knausgaard, Karl Ove 9, 21 n.4, 110–11, 114
  My Struggle 21 n.4, 110–11, 114

Knight, India 42–3
Kushner, Rachel 14

Lawrence, D.H. xii–xiii, 11–12, 12 n.1, 37, 83, 87–8, 136, 141, 149–151, 152, 154, 156, 159, 161, 162, 168, 169–70
Lerner, Ben 21 n.5, 33–34
Lockwood, Patricia 8, 129, 139
London 1, 24, 28, 28 n.7, 51, 68–9, 76, 79, 95, 102, 116, 120, 150, 151, 160
Long, Camilla 5, 7
Luhan, Mabel Dodge xiii, 11–12, 83, 84, 87–9, 132, 140, 141, 149, 150–5, 156, 161, 163, 169
    Lorenzo in Taos xii, 11–12, 83, 87, 149, 150, 159, 161
Lukács, Georg 23–4

Marfa, Texas 33, 34
marshlands 15, 30, 87–8, 136, 151, 153, 156, 159, 160
maximalism 13, 19–20, 20 n.1, 21 n.4–5, 26, 30, 31–2, 34
memoir xiii, 5, 11–12, 38, 39–40, 60, 66, 83, 84, 87–8, 114, 132, 149–50, 151, 153, 154, 156, 161, 169
minimalism 20 n.2, 21 n.4–5, 26, 27–8, 31, 32–4
modernism 31, 64, 76, 76 n.1, 144
motherhood xi, 4–5, 37–54, 37 n.1, 60, 66, 68, 87
music 31, 97–8

neoliberalism 21, 21 n.5, 38–9, 45 n.6
New Labour (UK government 1997–2010) 4, 38
New York 19, 33, 149, 153
Norfolk 1, 15, 129, 136, 151, 159

Ophir, Ella 11, 76, 82, 124 n.7

painting, visual art xii–xiv, 22, 30, 31–2, 63, 82, 85, 86–8, 117, 132 n.5
paratexts 57, 60
parenting 38–40, 42–4, 47–8, 50–1, 164
Paris 1, 152, 153, 155, 156, 160, 166
Paris Review 95, 112
patriarchy 3, 43, 43 n.4, 48, 59, 71, 78, 85
postmodernism 20–1, 38

Quiney, Ruth (aka Cain, Ruth) 66

Richardson, Dorothy 64, 114
Robinson, Richard and Barry Sheils 131, 138
Romanticism 6, 93–4, 100, 105–6
Rooney, Sally 27 n.6, 100 n.2, 130, 146
Rose, Jacqueline 53–4

Sandler, Matthew 76, 76 n.1
Satan *see* devil, the
Schwartz, Alexandra 132, 159
Smith, Sidonie 59, 60, 64, 71
Smith, Zadie 19–20, 19 n.1

Taos, New Mexico xiii, 83, 87–8, 149, 150, 152, 170
Taylor, Charles 6, 94, 94 n.1
travel writing 64

United Kingdom (UK) 1, 5, 24, 38, 41, 83

Valihora, Karen 112, 119, 124
Wills, Clair 142, 143, 143 n.11

Wood, James 20–1, 22

Woolf, Virginia xiii, 6, 37, 53, 149–50, 151, 154–5
    A Room of One's Own 6, 150, 154
    Mrs Dalloway 6, 51, 52–3, 149, 155
    To the Lighthouse 51, 151

www.ingramcontent.com/pod-product-compliance
Lightning Source LLC
Chambersburg PA
CBHW052121300426
44116CB00010B/1764